EVERY DAY WITH

JESUS

Dr. Mary Amore

Our Sunday Visitor
Huntington, Indiana

Nihil Obstat
Msgr. Michael Heintz, Ph.D.
Censor Librorum

Imprimatur
Kevin C. Rhoades
Bishop of Fort Wayne-South Bend
July 18, 2023

Our Sunday Visitor Publishing Division
Our Sunday Visitor, Inc.
200 Noll Plaza
Huntington, IN 46750
www.osv.com
1-800-348-2440

ISBN: 978-1-63966-065-0 (Inventory No. T2808)
1. RELIGION—Christianity—Catholic.
2. RELIGION—Christian Living—Devotional.
3. RELIGION—Christian Rituals & Practice—Sacraments.

eISBN: 978-1-63966-066-7
LCCN: 2023944412

Cover design: Tyler Ottinger
Cover art: AdobeStock
Interior design: Amanda Falk

PRINTED IN THE UNITED STATES OF AMERICA

To my family, to the staff and affiliates of Mayslake Ministries, and to Fr. Edward Foley

Contents

Introduction

Every Day with Jesus is a daily devotional written to help you begin — or deepen — your experience of Jesus in the Eucharist by helping you connect your daily life with the mystery of the Eucharistic Presence of Jesus. There are twelve sections, and each month focuses on a specific spiritual experience that is reflective of our life with Jesus. By prayerfully reflecting on these spiritual experiences day by day, month by month, we can immerse our lives into this greatest mystery of our Faith, as we reawaken our senses to the many ways that our encounter with Jesus in the Eucharist invites us to become the very mystery we receive at the Eucharistic table. As you pray with this book, I encourage you to turn your hearts and minds to Jesus, who is present in tabernacles across the globe, in every parish, in every land. Our Lord is with us always in the Eucharist.

I wrote this book out of my love and reverence for the Eucharistic Presence of Jesus, and my heartfelt desire to help others experience the life-giving presence of Jesus in the Eucharist. It is a profound honor for me to share the countless ways that the Eucharist has touched my life, and, with the help of the Holy Spirit, will touch your life, too.

The daily reflections in this book are relevant for people of all ages and from all walks of life, from young single adults to parents struggling to raise their children in the Faith. From professionals in the workplace to people enjoying the fruits of retirement. From those who are home-bound to those with unusual work schedules, these timely and relevant reflections will inspire you on your spiritual journey to become the very mystery you receive at this Eucharistic table of Our Lord. Today and every day, as you ponder each reflection, I invite you to enter into prayerful reflection on the presence of Jesus in the Eucharist.

— Dr. Mary Amore
Executive Director, Mayslake Ministries

~ FAITH ~

January 1

Ask and it will be given to you; seek and you will find; knock and the door will be opened to you. — Matthew 7:7

Growing up in the 1950s, I learned my Catholic Faith by memorizing the Baltimore Catechism. As I grew into adulthood, and encountered the challenges of life, I soon realized that while I knew my Catholic doctrine, something was missing in my faith life. I felt disconnected to Jesus; so, I began to pray before the Blessed Sacrament. Each time I received the Eucharist, I prayerfully asked the Lord to increase my faith that I may experience his loving Presence. Over time, the Lord answered my prayers. Today, my encounter with Jesus in the Eucharist fills me with love and gratitude for all that Jesus has done for me.

Faith is a supernatural gift by which we choose to cooperate with God in thought and actions. Without faith, belief in the Eucharist is almost impossible, for our human intellect fails to grasp the mystical workings of God. After the consecration, our human eyes still see bread and wine, yet it is our faith in Jesus that helps us to believe his words, "This is my Body. This is my Blood." It is our faith that makes our encounter with the Risen Christ in the Eucharist a life-giving, transformational experience.

Do you struggle with belief in the Real Presence? Ask the Lord to reveal his Divine Presence to you each time you come to the altar.

Lord Jesus, increase my faith that I may come to know and love you in the Eucharist.

January 2

Peter said to him in reply, "Lord, if it is you, command me to come to you
on the water." He said, "Come." Peter got out of the boat and began to
walk on the water toward Jesus. But when he saw how [strong] the wind
was, he became frightened; and, beginning to sink, he cried out, "Lord, save
me!" Immediately Jesus stretched out his hand and caught him, and said to
him, "O you of little faith, why did you doubt?" — Matthew 14:28–31

During times of isolation and hardship, there are many days that I
have felt like Peter, drowning in a sea of uncertainty. It was faith in
Jesus that kept me afloat in those dark days. Faith is essential to our
spiritual well-being.

At the Last Supper, Jesus took bread and wine, said the blessing,
broke the bread and said, "Take and eat; this is my body" (Mt 26:26).
Likewise, he took the cup and said, "Drink from it, all of you, for this
is my blood of the covenant, which will be shed on behalf of many for
the forgiveness of sins" (Mt 26:27–28). Having faith in the words of
Jesus will open our hearts to us experiencing his Real Presence in the
Eucharist, giving us hope in the darkest of times.

Have you ever doubted the presence of Jesus in the Eucharist? Seek
the Lord's help to increase your faith.

Lord Jesus, your Real Presence is a lifeline. Strengthen my faith, that I may
believe and experience your Divine Presence in the Eucharist.

January 3

His mother said to the servers, "Do whatever he tells you." — *John 2:5*

In these words at the Wedding Feast at Cana, Mary demonstrated great faith in her son, which resulted in Jesus performing his first public miracle as he transformed water into wine, in the presence of his mother, disciples, and wedding guests. No one at the wedding feast knew what Jesus had done until the head waiter tasted the miraculous wine.

Faith in Jesus is essential to our spiritual life, for faith gives us the eyes to see Jesus at work in our world and in our own lives. Unfortunately, many people today are experiencing a crisis of faith. They have physical sight, but they lack the eyes of faith to see the Real Presence of Jesus in the Eucharist. When we doubt this mystery of our Catholic Faith, we are like the wedding guests at Cana, who missed the miraculous transformation of water into wine even though it happened before their very eyes. At the consecration of the Mass, we hear the words that Jesus spoke to us at the Last Supper, "This is my Body. This is my Blood." Let us have faith in this gift that Jesus has given us.

In what ways does my heart seek to deepen my faith in the Eucharistic Presence of Jesus?

Jesus, increase my faith, that I may encounter your life-giving Presence each time I come to the Eucharistic table.

January 4

Jesus said to them in reply, "Have faith in God. Amen, I say to you, whoever says to this mountain, 'Be lifted up and thrown into the sea,' and does not doubt in his heart but believes that what he says will happen, it shall be done for him." — Mark 11:22–23

I remember hearing this Scripture passage for the first time as a child, and thinking to myself, "How is it possible for a mountain to be moved into the sea?" I was young and skeptical, and I had no understanding of the power that comes from faith in God. Through the years, my faith has matured, and I have come to believe that with God all things are possible. Miracles occur every day.

Sadly, during seasons when we are struggling in our faith, our eyes fail to see the miracle unfolding before us at the altar of transformation. We see with physical sight, not with the eyes of faith in God. Jesus is present in the Sacrament of the Eucharist; let us believe this mystery of faith with our entire being.

How can I desire a deeper faith in the presence of Jesus in the Eucharist? Imagine you are praying in the presence of a tabernacle. Do you feel his Divine Presence around you?

Lord, increase my faith and strengthen my belief in your Real Presence in the Eucharist.

January 5

*Holy, holy, holy is the Lord God almighty, who was,
and who is, and who is to come. — Revelation 4:8*

The Eucharistic Prayer invites us to enter into the "Holy, Holy, Holy," an ancient song of praise that joins our voices with all of creation in the action of worshipping and praising our Lord God Almighty. This includes our saintly mothers and fathers, husbands and wives, sons and daughters, and family and friends, all those who have gone before us in faith. This is a mystical moment in the Eucharistic liturgy that opens the doorway for spiritual transformation, not only for the bread and wine, but also for the living Body of Christ.

At Mass, the Holy Spirit is the agent of transformation. During the consecration, the priest calls down the Spirit upon the gifts of bread and wine placed on the altar. In a similar fashion, the Spirit is also called down upon the living Body of Christ, who is gathered around the table. Sanctification and transformation are possible for each of us. Let us pray that during the Eucharistic Prayer, our faith in God can sanctify and transform us into the very mystery we receive at the Eucharistic table of Our Lord.

What are the elements in your life that need spiritual transformation?

Lord Jesus, increase my faith, that I may freely offer up all that keeps me from loving and serving you.

January 6

In all your ways be mindful of him,
and he will make straight your paths. — Proverbs 3:6

Is your calendar so overbooked with upcoming meetings, appointments, and engagements that you have no idea how you will fulfill all of these obligations? When I get to a point where I am feeling overwhelmed, I turn everything over to the Lord in prayer, for I trust him to lead and guide me. My faith in the Lord helps me to trust in his wisdom and not mine. I fear that if I relied on my own judgment, I would not accomplish much. Faith in God is essential to our spiritual growth. Without faith and trust in God, we begin to question everything, relying on our own intelligence.

If we relied only on our human senses, it would be difficult for us to believe in the Eucharist, for after the consecration, our human eyes see bread and wine. Yet our faith in the words of Jesus at the Last Supper invite us to experience a deeper spiritual reality, which is the Body and Blood, soul and divinity of Jesus present in the Eucharist. Let us confidently place our trust in the presence of our Savior Jesus Christ, and not rely on our human sight.

Do I desire to see the world with the renewed sight of faith?

Lord God, strengthen me in faith, that I may encounter your Divine Presence in the Eucharist.

January 7

Therefore I tell you, all that you ask for in prayer, believe that you will receive it and it shall be yours. — Mark 11:24

People who struggle with faith will often say, "Seeing is believing." In other words, if I can see it, then it must be true. If life were only that simple. At Mass, after the act of consecration, the bread and wine are transformed into the Body and Blood of Christ through the power of the Holy Spirit, yet to our human eyes, they look no different. Only with the eyes of faith can we fully enter into this greatest mystery of our Catholic Faith.

Encountering Jesus in the Eucharist will give the spiritual sight to see his hand at work in our life and in the lives of those we love. In faith, Jesus invites us to bring our needs to the Eucharistic table, and in faith, invites us to believe that he will hear and answer our prayers as he desires. Jesus came into this world that we may have life abundantly. In faith, let us bring our prayers before Our Lord, whose Real Presence we encounter in the Eucharist.

Faith is a catalyst for transformation. What are some ways your faith in Jesus has changed your life?

Lord Jesus, increase my faith in you, that I may experience the gift of your life-saving Eucharistic bread and wine.

January 8

For this reason I kneel before the Father, from whom every family in heaven
and on earth is named, that he may grant you in accord with the riches
of his glory to be strengthened with power through his Spirit in the inner
self, and that Christ may dwell in your hearts through faith; that you,
rooted and grounded in love, may have strength to comprehend with all
the holy ones what is the breadth and length and height and depth, and
to know the love of Christ that surpasses knowledge, so that you may
be filled with all the fullness of God. — Ephesians 3:14–19

In this Scripture passage, Saint Paul is praying that we might realize that the scope of God's love for us is experienced in Christ Jesus. Saint Paul prays that, through the power of the Spirit, we may have the faith to receive Christ into our hearts. Faith is essential for our spiritual lives, our spiritual growth, and our ability to believe in the Real Presence of Christ in the Eucharist.

With the gift of faith, we can experience Christ's bountiful love that is waiting for us in the Eucharist. Jesus died on the cross for our sins; we cannot even begin to comprehend the Lord's love, for it surpasses all human knowledge. When we faithfully partake of the Body and Blood of Christ, we have an opportunity to experience the depths of God's love for us present in Christ Jesus.

How can your love for Jesus draw you into a deeper belief in his Eucharistic Presence?

Lord Jesus, strengthen me, that I may be filled with the fullness of faith.

January 9

Faith is the realization of what is hoped for and
evidence of things not seen. — Hebrews 11:1

Everyone exercises the gift of faith, even nonbelievers. Think about it. If you drive a car, you have faith that the red traffic light will stop cars at an intersection. If you like to travel, you have faith that a titanium aircraft will take flight and get you to your destination safely; and if you work, you have faith in your employer that your paycheck will be in your account on payday. If human-made things can inspire faith, surely the words of Jesus, "Do this in memory of me," invite us to a more profound depth of belief.

For two thousand years, the Church has enacted this Eucharistic action in the faith of Christ. The Eucharist is the greatest of all sacraments, for here, in the consecrated elements of bread and wine, we experience the Real Presence of Jesus — Body broken, Blood poured out for the many. Our faith in Jesus calls us to believe in his life-giving words and actions at the Eucharistic table.

What is preventing you from believing in the words of Jesus?

Lord Jesus, strengthen me in faith, that I may never doubt you again.

January 10

For we walk by faith, not by sight. — 2 Corinthians 5:7

In those early months of the pandemic, when it seemed like the entire world shut down, and chaos and fear were everywhere, I thought to myself, "Where is God in all of this?" As I began to pray, I heard his reassuring words "*I am with you.*" It is my faith in Jesus alone that keeps me going during difficult times. Faith dispels fear and it offers us the ability to turn obstacles into opportunities for new life. This requires a shift in our perspective on life, for it challenges us to look at the world through the eyes of Jesus, and not through our own physical sight. It requires the grace to walk by faith and not by sight.

Prayer — which is simply a conversation with God — is essential to our spiritual life. Taking time to pray before the Blessed Sacrament offers us a grace-filled opportunity to enjoy a private conversation with Our Lord. Jesus is present in the Blessed Sacrament and is waiting for us to be with him. Take time to pray before the Eucharist, and in faith, to listen for the reassuring words of Jesus, *"I am with you."*

What is an obstacle in your life that, with the help of Jesus, you can turn into an opportunity for new life?

Lord Jesus, you are with us always, most especially in the Blessed Sacrament. Help me to turn to you in faith with all my needs.

January 11

Jesus said to her, "Did I not tell you that if you believe you will
see the glory of God?" So they took away the stone. And Jesus
raised his eyes and said, "Father, I thank you for hearing me.
I know that you always hear me; but because of the crowd here I have said
this, that they may believe that you sent me." And when he had said this,
he cried out in a loud voice, "Lazarus, come out!" — John 11:40–43

Miracles still occur in our modern world, though often, people fail to see them. Our culture attempts to credit science rather than credit God for his divine hand at work. Jesus encountered a similar kind of disbelief from the people of his time. Even after raising Lazarus from the dead, people, including his apostles, wavered in their faith in Jesus.

The Eucharist is the greatest mystery of our Catholic Faith. Celebrated for two thousand years, this mystery of faith occurs before our eyes at every Mass, for at the consecration, through the power of the Holy Spirit, bread and wine are transformed into the sacramental Real Presence of Jesus. Yet we still waver in disbelief. Today, let us ask the Lord to increase our faith, that we might be living witnesses to the miracle of the Eucharist.

How does your faith impact your understanding of Eucharist?

Lord Jesus, strengthen my faith, that I may see the glory of God unfold at every Mass.

January 12

*Although you have not seen him you love him; even though
you do not see him now yet believe in him, you rejoice with an
indescribable and glorious joy, as you attain the goal of [your]
faith, the salvation of your souls.* — 1 Peter 1:8–9

This Scripture passage offers us an incredible insight of the glorious
experience of Jesus that awaits us at the Eucharistic table. As Catholics, even though Jesus lived two thousand years ago, we know and love
him. It is our Catholic Faith that draws us into the truth of the Gospel
and invites us freely to choose to believe because of our faith in Jesus.

Our Catholic Faith affirms that Jesus is fully present in the Eucharist, and although we do not physically see his Body, we believe that he
abides under the appearances of bread and wine. When our faith brings
us to this spiritual awareness that Jesus is indeed present, our joy is indescribable, and this joy has to be shared with others. How can we keep
this glorious experience of the Eucharist to ourselves? In essence, our
belief in the Eucharistic Presence of Jesus will attain the salvation of our
souls, and hopefully, all those the Lord brings into our life.

**What are some ways you can lead others to experience the Eucha-
ristic Presence of Jesus?**

*Lord Jesus, lead me deeper into the mystery of the Eucharist, that I may boldly
proclaim what I have experienced in love.*

January 13

Jesus said to them, "I am the bread of life; whoever comes to me will never hunger, and whoever believes in me will never thirst." — John 6:35

As human beings, we often hunger and thirst for things that will satisfy us only for a brief moment. A friend of mine was struggling to make ends meet. He had a large family and bills to pay, and he hungered for a better position. After an exhaustive job search, he finally received an offer from a national company with excellent pay and benefits. He accepted the role. After a few months, he chose to quit his job because the demands on him were more than he expected. While his salary was excellent, he had little time to spend with his precious family, which was his top priority.

Jesus tells us that he is the bread of life, and if we seek him in faith, we will never hunger or thirst again. Like my friend, we, too, need to establish our priorities, making our faith in Jesus our most important relationship. At the Eucharistic table, Jesus is inviting us to eat and drink of the bread of life and the chalice of salvation, for he will satisfy all our needs. Let us accept his holy invitation.

What do you hunger for? A new job? A vacation? Seek the Lord's help to refocus your priorities that you may hunger for the presence of Jesus in the Eucharist.

Lord Jesus, thank you for satisfying my every need.

January 14

For through faith you are all children of God in Christ Jesus.
For all of you who were baptized into Christ have clothed
yourselves with Christ. — Galatians 3:26–27

Anyone who has ever worked in a parish with the Order of Christian Initiation for Adults (OCIA) or has been a sponsor for someone seeking to become Catholic knows that the unbaptized members in the program are dismissed from the celebration of Mass before the second half of the Mass, known as the Liturgy of the Eucharist, begins. What is the meaning behind this ritual? It is an ancient tradition rooted in the understanding that one needs to be initiated into the Catholic Church before one can enter into the mystery of the Eucharistic celebration. Baptism and Eucharist are intimately linked together.

As baptized members of the Catholic Faith, we have been clothed with Christ. Each time we participate in the Eucharist banquet, we enter into communion with Jesus and with our brothers and sisters who are in union with Christ. Our encounter with Jesus in the Eucharist strengthens us in faith and helps us to live in this world as children of God in Christ Jesus.

How can you thank the Lord today for your Catholic Faith?

Lord Jesus, help me to fully live out my Catholic Faith today and every day of my life.

January 15

If any of you lacks wisdom, he should ask God who gives to all
generously and ungrudgingly, and he will be given it. But he should
ask in faith, not doubting, for the one who doubts is like a wave of the
sea that is driven and tossed about by the wind. — *James 1:5–6*

Have you ever prayed earnestly for a special intention and felt like the Lord was not hearing your prayers? Jesus assures us that God hears and answers all prayers if we have faith to see his hand at work. If we doubt God's ability to answer our petitions, we will experience waves of uncertainty in the turbulent seas of disbelief, and we can begin to falter in our faith.

Spending time before the Blessed Sacrament or the tabernacle in church is a wonderful way for us to increase our faith in Jesus. As you sit quietly before his sacred Presence, ask the Lord to strengthen you amid your doubts. Thank Jesus for the gift of his Presence in the Eucharist, and in silence listen for the Lord to answer you. The Lord gives generously and ungrudgingly to all who ask in faith.

In faith, what intentions will you bring before the Eucharistic Presence of Our Lord this day?

Lord Jesus, you answer all who ask in faith. Hear my prayers and answer them as you know best.

January 16

Consider it all joy, my brothers, when you encounter various trials, for you know that the testing of your faith produces perseverance. And let perseverance be perfect, so that you may be perfect and complete, lacking in nothing. — James 1:2–4

After my mom died, my dad remained by himself in our family home, but he needed a live-in caretaker. We hired someone for the weekdays; and every weekend I would come and stay with my dad. It took a lot of work and perseverance to maintain my dad's rigorous schedule of caretaking, while juggling my own family life. While those times may have tested my good nature, they did not test my faith in God. The more difficult life became, the more I prayed to the Lord, for he was my rock. I drew strength from my encounter with him in the Eucharist. When I went to Mass, I took a pyx (a special container to carry consecrated Hosts to the sick and homebound) so that I could take Communion home to my dad. It was a joy to see his face when I offered him the Eucharist.

We all have various trials in life, and in those difficult moments, it is comforting to know that the Real Presence of Jesus in the Eucharist is here to give us strength to help us persevere in faith. Jesus is with us always. Let us turn to his Eucharistic Presence, that we might lack for nothing in life.

How do you handle difficult situations in your life?

Lord Jesus, in times of trials, increase my faith, that I may persevere.

January 17

Be on your guard, stand firm in the faith, be courageous, be strong. Your every act should be done with love. — *1 Corinthians 16:13–14*

Spiritual growth hinges on our ability to hold fast to our faith no matter what the circumstance. When we stand firm in faith, we allow the Lord to lead and guide us, even in the midst of trials and tribulations, and fear no longer has a hold over us. Standing firm in our faith instills a sense of spiritual courage within, directing us to serve others with love.

Jesus gathered at table with his apostles on the night before his crucifixion. During the supper, in an act of selfless love, Jesus gave us the gift of his Body and Blood in the elements of bread and wine that we might have eternal life. When we eat and drink of the Body and Blood of Christ, his divine love fills us, inviting us to be courageous and strong in our belief in Jesus. May we stand firm in our faith in Christ and serve with love all those the Lord sends our way.

What needs to change in your life, that you may stand firm in your faith in Jesus?

Lord Jesus, may the Eucharist strengthen me in faith, that I may act with love each day.

January 18

So also faith of itself, if it does not have works, is dead. Indeed someone may say, "You have faith and I have works." Demonstrate your faith to me without works, and I will demonstrate my faith to you from my works. — James 2:17–18

When I was a freshman in high school, I joined the FIA club, which stood for Faith in Action. As a young teenager, I had no idea what this slogan meant. Soon afterward, I learned that knowledge about our Catholic religion was not enough. The Lord calls us to put our faith into action: to love and serve our brothers and sisters in Christ. This was eye-opening, and completely changed my cradle-Catholic understanding of my faith. Faith without works is like dropping water onto oil; the water just sits on the top, it does not blend in. Our actions should flow from our faith in Christ. If our conduct does not reflect what we profess and believe in Christ, we need to reexamine our behavior.

The Eucharist will help us live out our faith. Our encounter with Jesus in the Eucharist reawakens our sense of service to others by helping us to see the world through the eyes of Jesus, and gives us the strength to love and care for all those in need. Let us come with hearts seeking the grace to put our faith in action.

Do your daily actions reflect your faith in Christ?

Lord Jesus, help me to live out my faith in loving service to others.

January 19

If you confess with your mouth that Jesus is Lord and believe in your heart that God raised him from the dead, you will be saved. For one believes with the heart and so is justified, and one confesses with the mouth and so is saved. For the scripture says, "No one who believes in him will be put to shame." — Romans 10:9–11

It is easy to have faith in God when things are going our way, when life is good. But is our faith strong when life takes a downward spiral and we cannot find our way out of the darkness? Faith is a gift from God and is given to all who profess that Jesus is Lord. Like any gift, faith needs to be nurtured so that it may grow and flourish. How do we increase our faith?

When we come to Mass, Jesus is present in four ways: in the congregation, in the priest, the Word, and most especially in the Eucharist. Jesus is present in the consecrated elements of bread and wine, and he desires that we turn to him. Ask the Lord to strengthen your faith in him; seek his divine help in deepening your dependence upon his grace. The Lord is waiting to nourish you.

Is your faith strong, even in dark times? Turn to the Lord for assistance.

Lord Jesus, increase my faith, that I may confess that you are Lord and Savior.

January 20

*We ought to thank God always for you, brothers, as is fitting, because
your faith flourishes ever more, and the love of every one of you for
one another grows ever greater. Accordingly, we ourselves boast of you
in the churches of God regarding your endurance and faith in all your
persecutions and the afflictions you endure. — 2 Thessalonians 1:3–4*

When I was in my late thirties, God called me out of the kitchen and
into ministry. I was married and the mother of two young children, so
this call from God turned my household upside down. I had to juggle
the commitments of graduate school while keeping things going at
home. At times, well-meaning friends and family questioned why I was
doing all of this. I persevered, for I believed that my call from God was
genuine. Every day, I prayed that the Lord would help me overcome the
opposition I experienced through others. As time went on, my friends
and family came around and supported me on my journey.

The Body and Blood of Christ that we receive at Mass strengthens
us in faith and gives us the grace to persevere in the face of opposition.
Let us pray that through our encounter with Jesus in the Eucharist our
faith may flourish and grow.

Have you experienced hardships because of your faith?

Lord Jesus, increase my faith, that I may persevere in my love for you.

January 21

Be still and know that I am God!
I am exalted among the nations,
exalted on the earth. — Psalm 46:11

We deal with a lot of "tinsel" noise in our life. Annoying sounds from cell phones and incoming emails bombard our senses, disturbing our peace on a daily basis. God is inviting us to step away and spend quality time in silence, that we might listen as the Lord speaks to us. In the stillness of prayer, we are able to hear the Lord assure us that he is in charge and that he will take care of us. We simply need to be still and know that he is God, and we are not.

One of the most spiritually rewarding ways to grow in faith is to spend prayer time in adoration before Jesus in the Blessed Sacrament. Genuflect when you come into his Presence as a sign of respect. Sit or kneel. Quiet your heart, dismissing all anxiety and distractions from your mind. Gaze lovingly at the Lord's Presence in the Blessed Sacrament and open your heart to receiving his grace. Listen. The Lord may speak to you in the form of a new idea, a feeling of peace, or renewed insight into a situation. Be still and know that Jesus is with you.

Do you pray before the Blessed Sacrament? Enrich your life today by spending time with Jesus.

Lord Jesus, help me to listen as you speak to me in the recesses of my heart.

January 22

*Therefore, since we have been justified by faith, we have peace
with God through our Lord Jesus Christ, through whom we have
gained access [by faith] to this grace in which we stand,
and we boast in hope of the glory of God. — Romans 5:1–2*

Being at odds with a loved one can be quite a heavy emotional burden to carry. Once you talk things through, and clear the air about the disagreement, there is a huge sense of relief which comes over us, for now there is peace. Our life with God is similar. Through original sin, our covenant with God was broken; and we carried the heavy burden of sin with no hope. In an act of immense love, God sent his only Son, Jesus, who suffered and died that our covenant relationship with God could be restored.

Each time we receive the consecrated bread and wine, we encounter the Real Presence of Jesus who gave his life so that we could live in peaceful harmony with God forever. His Blood shed for the many is the Blood of the new and everlasting covenant between God and his people. In faith, we stand in grace and boast in hope of the glory of God.

What does a covenant relationship mean in your faith life?

Lord Jesus, thank you for making peace for us with God our Father in heaven.

January 23

Your heavenly Father knows that you need them all. But seek first the kingdom [of God] and his righteousness, and all these things will be given you besides. Do not worry about tomorrow; tomorrow will take care of itself. — *Matthew 6:32–34*

As we grow in faith, we become increasingly aware that Jesus is with us each day. His Divine Presence invites us to live in the present moment, and not to worry about the unknown path that lies ahead. If we believe that Jesus, the Son of God, walks with us, then we need to trust that he will show us the way, and help us discern which path to follow in life. We are never alone. The Lord knows what we need before we ask.

One of the most fruitful ways to increase our trust and faith in Jesus is to spend time with him in the presence of the Blessed Sacrament. His Divine Presence is here to listen to our worries, to comfort us, and to help dispel our fears and anxieties. Seek the Real Presence of Jesus, and all things will be given to you.

Are you often preoccupied with what will happen tomorrow? Seek the Lord's grace to stay in the present, aware that he is with you always.

Lord Jesus, help me to be aware that you are with me each day, and that I have nothing to fear.

January 24

For I know well the plans I have in mind for you … plans for your welfare and not for woe, so as to give you a future of hope. When you call me, and come and pray to me, I will listen to you. When you look for me, you will find me. Yes, when you seek me with all your heart. — Jeremiah 29:11–13

The Lord knows well the plan he has for our lives, and no matter how difficult things may seem, the Lord will not abandon us; he is in control and will give us a future filled with hope, if we have the courage to believe in him. In an act of pure love for his people, God sent his only Son, Jesus, to restore the covenant relationship between God and his people. Jesus is the visible presence of our invisible God.

When we come to the Eucharistic table, and we partake of the sacramental Real Presence of Jesus, we reaffirm our faith in Christ who, by his death on the cross, restored our covenant relationship with God. In faith, let us eat and drink of the Eucharistic Presence of Jesus, that we might have life eternal.

When life is difficult, do you feel God's Presence with you?

Lord Jesus, help me to receive your Eucharistic Body and Blood in faith, that I may follow you all the days of my life.

January 25

Those who know your name trust in you;
you never forsake those who seek you, LORD. — Psalm 9:11

Years ago, someone I cared about deeply was experiencing a serious medical issue, and I was not sure what the outcome would be. Scared and helpless, I turned to the Lord in prayer, seeking his help day and night for a resolution to the situation. I trusted Jesus to help me; and the Lord answered my prayers with healing and inner strength. My faith in Jesus has helped me through some very difficult times. The Lord will never forsake us in our times of trial; we just need to trust in him, even when we can't always see how he is helping us.

When we encounter the Real Presence of Jesus in the Eucharist, we receive the graces to overcome difficult situations, because our Catholic Faith assures us that Jesus is with us, and we are not alone to carry our crosses. The Eucharistic Presence of Jesus is here to help us even in the darkest of times. In faith, let us turn to him with our needs; for he will never forsake those who seek him.

How do you handle a crisis? Do you try to solve it yourself, or do you turn to the Lord for help?

Lord Jesus, I place all my trust in you. May I always turn to you in times of need, for you are always with me.

January 26

Do not let your hearts be troubled. You have faith in God; have faith also in me. In my Father's house there are many dwelling places. If there were not, would I have told you that I am going to prepare a place for you? And if I go and prepare a place for you, I will come back again and take you to myself, so that where I am you also may be. — *John 14:1–3*

Conversion is a mysterious spiritual concept. What triggers such a major shift in a person's way of believing? While the responses for everyone are vast and varied, one thing is constant. Jesus is at work in each person, and whatever spiritual path one may be on, the Lord can bring him home. We need to have faith in the process; we need to have faith in Jesus.

Our Lord, present in the Blessed Sacrament, is waiting for us to come to him with our deepest longings. Jesus promised that there is a dwelling place for each of us in the Father's house. Let us place our prayers for conversion of souls before the Blessed Sacrament, having faith in the words of Jesus. For he assured us he will come back and take us to himself, so that all may be one in the kingdom of heaven.

Is there someone you know in need of conversion? Pray for them before the Blessed Sacrament.

Lord Jesus, please hear my prayers and lead all souls back to you.

January 27

May the God of hope fill you with all joy and peace in believing, so that you may abound in hope by the power of the holy Spirit. — Romans 15:13

After attending Mass, my dad was crossing the street on a rainy Saturday night and was struck by a hit-and-run driver and left for dead in the middle of the street. He suffered multiple broken bones and was hospitalized in traction. Our family was devastated and wondered why God let this happen, especially coming out of Mass. We struggled to find hope in all of this. While my dad was in the hospital, the doctors discovered a large aneurysm in his heart wall, which could rupture and kill him at any time. The cardiology team performed emergency open-heart surgery and took care of the aneurysm. It was in that moment that I realized that the accident had saved my dad's life. I know now that God is with us always, especially in the darkest moments of life, and we should never lose hope.

Jesus is waiting for us in the Blessed Sacrament to calm our fears and restore hope to our weary souls. Let us bring our needs and place them before the Real Presence of Jesus in the Eucharist, and savor the peace that only Jesus can bring.

Have you experienced an unpleasant event that turned out to be a moment of great grace?

Lord Jesus, may your Presence in the Blessed Sacrament strengthen me in faith and in hope.

January 28

Do not fear, for I have redeemed you;
I have called you by name: you are mine. — Isaiah 43:1

I grew up in a small suburban parish where everyone knew my name, and this instilled in me a sense of belonging. When I got married, my husband and I moved to a different town and to a new parish. It was a traumatic experience for me. I felt lost because no one knew my name, nor even cared to ask. After several months, the pastor finally came up to me and introduced himself. It was a graced moment, for after that I felt like I was back at my home parish. Every time I came to Mass, the pastor greeted me by name.

There is great power in calling someone by name. One of the most powerful names we can say is the name of Jesus. He is our Redeemer, and he has called us by name. When we come to the table of the Eucharist, we encounter the Real Presence of Jesus, who out of love has redeemed us by his Blood. Let us approach the altar with hearts seeking Jesus, for we belong to him. May his Eucharistic Presence dispel our fears and fill us with the peace that only Jesus can bring.

Do you make an effort to call people by name? How does it make you feel when someone addresses you by name?

Lord Jesus, you have called me by name, and I am yours.

January 29

Blessed are those who trust in the LORD;
the LORD will be their trust.
They are like a tree planted beside the waters
that stretches out its roots to the stream:
It does not fear heat when it comes,
its leaves stay green;
In the year of drought it shows no distress,
but still produces fruit. — Jeremiah 17:7–8

When we are close to the Lord, we are like a tree planted by water and we have nothing to fear, because the Lord is our life source of water, and we can never suffer from drought as long as our trust is in the Lord. Even when difficult times come, we show no distress because our faith is in the Lord.

Jesus is our living water, and in him we have life forever. Each time we come to the Eucharistic table, we refresh our soul with the life-giving nutrients of his Body and Blood that will sustain us even in the darkest moments of life. Jesus is waiting at the altar for us; let us come with hearts hungry for the bread of life and the chalice of salvation, that we may produce abundant fruit.

Does your soul feel parched? Trust in the Lord to nourish you.

Lord Jesus, nourish me with your Body and Blood, that I may flourish and bear great fruit for the Kingdom.

January 30

*Trust in the LORD with all your heart,
on your own intelligence do not rely. — Proverbs 3:5*

There have been countless times in my life where I could have taken one pathway, but the Lord redirected my steps to follow another. I am sure the same is true for you. We all have choices. The Lord has given us the gift of free will; but if we rely solely on our own intelligence, without consulting the Lord in prayer, we can run into trouble. Our relationship with Jesus invites us to discern our choices before we act; to trust in the Lord to lead and guide us, and not to rely solely on our own decision-making process.

Building a relationship based on trust takes time. Jesus is present in the Eucharist, and each time we receive his Body and Blood, we have an opportunity to deepen our faith and trust in the Lord. Jesus loves us, and desires only our best interest. If we learn to trust in the Lord with all of our heart, we will be able to discern his movement in our life and follow as he leads and guides us to paths of righteousness. Let us seek his Presence in the Eucharist.

Do you pray before making decisions in life? No situation is insignificant to the Lord. Trust in him.

Lord Jesus, I place all my trust in you. Please help me to seek your wisdom before making decisions.

January 31

Then he questioned his father, "How long has this been happening to him?" He replied, "Since childhood. It has often thrown him into fire and into water to kill him. But if you can do anything, have compassion on us and help us." Jesus said to him, " 'If you can!' Everything is possible to one who has faith." Then the boy's father cried out, "I do believe, help my unbelief!" — Mark 9:21–24

Miracles unfold before our eyes every day; but we can only see them with the eyes of faith. Faith is a key component to our spiritual growth: with faith, we can walk without sight, follow without knowing where the road may lead us, and believe that with God all things are possible. Our faith in Jesus invites us to believe in his Presence in the Eucharist.

The Eucharist is not a holy symbol; it is the Real Presence of Jesus, Body, Blood, soul, and divinity. When we encounter Our Lord in the Eucharist, we have an opportunity to receive healing, transformation, and forgiveness of sin from Jesus, for everything is possible to one who has faith. Let us turn to our Eucharistic Lord, asking him to help our unbelief.

Are you open to seeking the Lord's help to increase your faith and belief in the Eucharist?

Lord Jesus, help me to believe that with God all things are possible.

~ MERCY AND COMPASSION ~

February 1

Jesus was going through a field of grain on the sabbath. His disciples were hungry and began to pick the heads of grain and eat them. When the Pharisees saw this, they said to him, "See, your disciples are doing what is unlawful to do on the sabbath." [Jesus said,] "I say to you, something greater than the temple is here. If you knew what this meant, 'I desire mercy, not sacrifice,' you would not have condemned these innocent men. For the Son of Man is Lord of the sabbath." — Matthew 12:1–2, 6–8

The Pharisees are quick to judge the actions of Jesus and his apostles, citing Jewish rules against working on the Sabbath; but Jesus challenges them to reach beyond their narrow, legalistic viewpoints, and to realize that God desires mercy, not the sacrifices of the old law.

Our Catholic Faith is more than a set of rules and regulations put in place to help us get to heaven. We are followers of Jesus, and as such, we are called to live as people of mercy and compassion — which means we are moved to help those in need. When we partake of the Eucharistic banquet, we encounter the merciful heart of Jesus, who died for our sins. May his loving Presence fill us with the grace to treat others with mercy and compassion.

How can you offer mercy to all those you meet today?

Lord Jesus, you are the Lord of the Sabbath. Help me to live my life with mercy and compassion toward all people.

February 2

Therefore, since we have a great high priest who has passed through the heavens, Jesus, the Son of God, let us hold fast to our confession. For we do not have a high priest who is unable to sympathize with our weaknesses, but one who has similarly been tested in every way, yet without sin. So let us confidently approach the throne of grace to receive mercy and to find grace for timely help. — Hebrews 4:14–16

I love this quote: "A good friend is someone who knows you and still stands by you." I think the same sentiment can be said of Jesus. He knows us and will always stand by us. Fully human and divine, Jesus experienced many of the same struggles we experience every day; and he sees us with the eyes of mercy and compassion because he understands what we are going through.

At every Mass, it is Jesus who invites us to confidently approach the table of Lord, that we may receive the grace and mercy we need to help us live a good and faithful life. Let us not miss the opportunity to encounter his life-giving Presence as we partake of the Eucharist.

Who in your life is in need of your mercy and compassion? Seek the Lord's help, that you may find the grace to be of help.

Lord Jesus, your mercy is without end. Help me to offer compassion to all those in need.

February 3

He heard this and said, "Those who are well do not need a physician, but the sick do. Go and learn the meaning of the words, 'I desire mercy, not sacrifice.' I did not come to call the righteous but sinners." — Matthew 9:12–13

When we are not feeling well, we are not at our best. Fatigue sets in, and we have no energy. Our road to healing often includes taking medicine and following the doctor's orders to rest and drink plenty of fluids. In a similar fashion, when we suffer from spiritual illness, we share many of the same symptoms. Our souls are afflicted with spiritual exhaustion, for they have drifted away from their life source, the Lord; and our souls are vulnerable to the toxins of our culture. We are in need of Jesus, but often we do not even know it.

In Jesus, we have a divine physician who lovingly treats our souls. Our divine healer gently invites the spiritually wounded to come and drink deeply from His chalice of compassion, and to be cleansed in the waters of reconciliation. Jesus is present in the Eucharist to nourish us back to health in mind, body, and spirit.

Do you know anyone who has drifted from his or her faith? How can you treat them with mercy and compassion, and lead them gently to Jesus?

Lord God, you are the healer of all ills. Help me to treat others with the medicine of mercy and compassion.

February 4

The LORD is gracious and merciful,
slow to anger and abounding in mercy.
The LORD is good to all,
compassionate toward all your works. — *Psalm 145:8–9*

As my husband and I raised our kids, our family motto has always been "just to do your best." At times, our children would excel in certain areas, and other times they fell short of their goal; but as long as they tried their best, that is all we asked as parents. We tried to create a loving home environment where the actions of our children were met with mercy and compassion, not anger and unrealistic expectations.

Jesus interacted with people in the same way. Throughout his ministry, he treated the actions of both saints and sinners with mercy and compassion. In giving us the gift of the Eucharist, Jesus offered his mercy to all of humanity for all time. The Lord's love for us in the Eucharist is beyond our comprehension. May the redeeming grace that we receive in the Eucharist strengthen us, that we may do our best to treat all people with the merciful and compassionate love of Christ.

Do you get angry often? Do you find it difficult to be compassionate to some groups of people?

Lord Jesus, you are slow to anger and rich in mercy. Help me to follow your example in my dealings with others.

February 5

But God, who is rich in mercy, because of the great love he had for us, even when we were dead in our transgressions, brought us to life with Christ (by grace you have been saved), raised us up with him, and seated us with him in the heavens in Christ Jesus, that in the ages to come he might show the immeasurable riches of his grace in his kindness to us in Christ Jesus. — *Ephesians 2:4–7*

Have you ever walked away from someone because you were so frustrated with his or her actions? As human beings, we are quick to lose patience with others when they do not act as we think they should; and we find it extremely difficult to offer mercy to someone who has hurt us.

The good news is that God our Father did not walk away from us when our actions severed our relationship with him. Rather, in an act of immense love, God sent his only Son, Jesus, who suffered, died, and rose from the dead to repair our relationship and give us eternal life. Each time we come to the Eucharistic table, we partake in the saving action of Jesus, who nourishes us with his Body and Blood, that we might be rich in his mercy.

Who is in need of your mercy and compassion?

Lord Jesus, may the Eucharist enrich our lives and fill us with mercy and compassion for all people.

February 6

*When he disembarked and saw the vast crowd, his heart was
moved with pity for them, for they were like sheep without a shepherd;
and he began to teach them many things. By now it was already late
and his disciples approached him and said, "This is a deserted place
and it is already very late. Dismiss them so that they can go to the
surrounding farms and villages and buy themselves something to eat."
He said to them in reply, "Give them some food yourselves."*

*But they said to him, "Are we to buy two hundred days' wages
worth of food and give it to them to eat?" He asked them, "How
many loaves do you have? Go and see." And when they had found
out they said, "Five loaves and two fish." — Mark 6:34–38*

Our house was always the gathering place for my children's friends.
One little boy, in particular, loved to eat dinner with us. He said he felt
at home at our table. Hearing this, my mother's heart was moved with
compassion. This little guy ate dinner with us more times than I can
remember.

The merciful heart of Jesus is present in the Eucharist to satisfy our
spiritual hunger. Let us approach the altar to feast on the bread of angels
and to drink deeply from the chalice of compassion.

How can you live as a compassionate and merciful person?

Lord Jesus, fill me with your mercy and compassion.

February 7

Therefore, he had to become like his brothers in every way, that he might be a merciful and faithful high priest before God to expiate the sins of the people. Because he himself was tested through what he suffered, he is able to help those who are being tested. — Hebrews 2:17–18

Jesus took on the form of a human being to teach us how to be human. During his time on earth, Jesus had multiple encounters with people where he offered mercy and compassion to even the hardest of hearts. He became like us in every way but sin, and in doing so, Jesus gave us a model to follow.

Social media platforms have created an environment where people can ridicule and tear down individuals they have not even met. Our life as Christians invites us to turn away from the temptations of this angry world and to follow in the footsteps of Jesus. His life-giving Presence remains with us now in the Eucharist. May our reception of the Body and Blood of Christ help us to treat all people with respect, and with the mercy and compassion of Our Lord Jesus Christ.

How difficult is it for you to treat all people with mercy and compassion? Reflect on your answer in the light of the Eucharistic Presence of Jesus.

Lord Jesus, help me to open my heart to all people, that I may live with mercy and compassion.

February 8

You have been told, O mortal, what is good,
and what the LORD requires of you:
Only to do justice and to love goodness,
and to walk humbly with your God. — Micah 6:8

This Scripture passage is encouraging because it offers us "mortals" a clear and definitive roadmap of what is expected of us as Christians: namely, to do what is good and to live as people of justice and love, walking humbly with Our Lord. When we look at the world around us, we can see clearly that we have lost our way. We have lost our North Star; we have taken our eyes off Jesus. As a result, hateful acts of violence rage in our city streets and in our schools, and countless acts of injustice are enacted everywhere. How are we ever again to walk humbly with God?

In the Eucharist, Jesus continues to pour out his mercy upon our broken world. When we receive Communion, we encounter our Jesus, whose Body and Blood strengthens us in our resolve to do all that the Lord requires of us. His Real Presence invites us to immerse ourselves in his mercy, that we may once again walk humbly with our God, offering justice and love to all.

Who is one person in your life you can offer the love and mercy of God to this day?

Lord God, our world is in turmoil. May the Eucharistic Presence of Jesus help us to live as people of mercy and love.

February 9

*Stop judging, that you may not be judged. For as you judge, so
will you be judged, and the measure with which you measure
will be measured out to you. — Matthew 7:1–2*

We all grew up with wonderful words of wisdom from our parents
and teachers, such as "Actions speak louder than words," and "Lead by
example." While both of these phrases might be a blast from the past,
they carry a poignant message for all of us today: namely, that our actions are important. If we profess to be followers of Christ, yet we tear
down others who are different from us, or gossip about people behind
their back, our actions are not worthy of Christ. Jesus clearly tells us to
stop judging, because the rod of righteousness that we shake in the face
of others will someday be the measurement stick by which God will
judge us. He is the just judge.

When we spend time in the presence of the Blessed Sacrament, we
open our hearts to receiving the Lord's mercy and grace. His holy and
Divine Presence has the power to recreate us anew. Let us gaze upon
the Lord in the Blessed Sacrament, fully aware that we are in the presence of Jesus, the just and only judge.

**When you pray before the Blessed Sacrament, how can you open
your heart to God's mercy and grace?**

Lord God, help me to stop judging others, that I may love them in your name.

February 10

"When did we see you ill or in prison, and visit you?" And the king will say to them in reply, "Amen, I say to you, whatever you did for one of these least brothers of mine, you did for me." — Matthew 25:39–40

I met a woman years ago who took this Scripture passage literally. She told me that this text did not apply to her because she did not know anyone who was in jail. Clearly, she failed to understand the meaning of this text. It is not necessary to personally know someone serving time in prison; there are plenty of good people around us who are emotionally imprisoned, such as by an addiction, whether it be alcohol or drug abuse. Do we take the time to reach out and care for them? Jesus will hold us accountable on judgment day for the ways we showed to mercy to those who struggle.

Through our encounter with the merciful heart of Jesus present in the Eucharist, we can gain the strength to care for others in the name of Jesus. Mercy is the lifeblood of the Gospel. Someday, when we meet Jesus face to face, we will humbly share with the Lord the many ways we cared for him.

Do you know anyone suffering from addictions? Prayerfully consider how you can minister to them.

Lord Jesus, help me to see your Presence in all people, that I may recognize and respond to their needs.

February 11

Bear one another's burdens, and so you will fulfill
the law of Christ. — *Galatians 6:2*

There is a social media post that depicts an illustration of an elephant and a little cat sitting on a bench in the pouring rain. The elephant is holding an umbrella over the kitty. The text says, "I'm not interested in whether you've stood with the great. I'm interested in whether you've sat with the broken." Our life with Christ invites us to do just this: to be there for one another, to carry one another's burdens. It is not important how successful we are, or who considers us great in the eyes of this world. Jesus cares that we live as people of mercy and compassion, offering our help to all, most especially the vulnerable.

Our communion with Jesus at the Eucharistic table unites us to the living Body of Christ, and reawakens our call to fulfill the two great commandments of Jesus, "Love God and love your neighbor as yourself." The Eucharistic Presence of Jesus helps us to refocus our attention on those we can help, and not on the glory of ourselves. May the Eucharist give us the strength and courage to faithfully fulfill the law of Christ.

What are some ways you can care for the vulnerable in your life?

Lord Jesus, help us to recognize and respond with mercy to the needs of our neighbors.

February 12

*Put on then, as God's chosen ones, holy and beloved, heartfelt compassion,
kindness, humility, gentleness, and patience, bearing with one another
and forgiving one another, if one has a grievance against another; as
the Lord has forgiven you, so must you also do. And over all these put
on love, that is, the bond of perfection.* — Colossians 3:12–14

Heated debates seem to be the norm nowadays, even within families. When I scroll through social media, the rhetoric and vitriol used by some individuals is hardly Christlike. It makes me wonder if people would treat others like this if they were in person, and not on social media. The Lord calls us to bear with one another, and to forgive each other, because the Lord has forgiven us. How often do we need to be reminded of this?

Our encounter with Jesus in the Eucharist offers us an opportunity to turn from the ways of this world, that we may immerse ourselves in the sacrificial love of Christ. His Real Presence in the Eucharist has the power to wash away our imperfections, that we may put on the bond of his perfect love. Let us approach the Eucharistic table with hearts seeking transformation, that we may become God's chosen ones, holy and beloved, forgiving one another with the mercy of God.

Do you find forgiveness difficult? Why do you think that is?

Lord Jesus, help me to imitate your love and compassion.

February 13

But the wisdom from above is first of all pure, then peaceable,
gentle, compliant, full of mercy and good fruits, without inconstancy
or insincerity. And the fruit of righteousness is sown in
peace for those who cultivate peace. — James 3:17–18

Our world is polarized, and we are suffering from a lack of mercy. Certain individuals or groups of people with strong viewpoints violently condemn others in an attempt to convince them that they are wrong. Other people just refuse to enter into a peaceful dialogue. Where is the wisdom and mercy of God in all of this? Our Christian faith calls us to live as a peaceful people, full of mercy and compassion, with kindness toward others. Where do we find the strength to turn from the inconsistent wisdom of this world, to embrace the wisdom from above, which is pure and peaceable? It is at the Eucharistic table.

Each time we come to Mass, the Church invites us to place our attitudes, our anger, and our lack of compassion on the altar. We are to join them to the perfect sacrifice of Jesus in the hope of experiencing transformation. The Holy Spirit has the power to change us, helping us to be pure of heart, and full of mercy.

Are you open to seeking the wisdom of the Spirit, that you might live as a person of mercy and peace?

Lord Jesus, help me to cultivate a more peaceful world by offering mercy to all who I meet this day.

February 14

*For the judgment is merciless to one who has not shown
mercy; mercy triumphs over judgment.* — James 2:13

My mom was my best friend. On the night she died, I had the privilege of being with her when she was taken to the emergency room. As I waited for my other family members to arrive, the chaplain of the hospital asked me if there was anything he could do for me. I asked him to pray for my mom, that she would receive God's gift of bountiful mercy at this pivotal time in her life. As he held my mom's hand and prayed for her, I felt a sense of peace wash over me, even in this darkest of moments; and I realized that God had sent an angel of mercy to minister to me and my mom that night.

Jesus wants to minister to us. May his Eucharistic Presence fill us with mercy and help us to live in this world with his love and compassion for all people.

To whom can you offer mercy this day?

Lord Jesus, help me to live as a person of mercy and not judgment.

February 15

Blessed are the merciful,
for they will be shown mercy. — Matthew 5:7

"Random acts of kindness" is a phrase in our contemporary culture that describes the little acts of kindness people do for complete strangers. While these acts of kindness are inspiring, and, at times, newsworthy, they are no replacement for living the Beatitudes. Jesus teaches that if we offer mercy to others, the Lord will be merciful with us. Jesus identified sin when he saw it, but always offered a pathway to salvation, by treating people with mercy and compassion, inviting all to follow him. Our world is in trouble, and families are in crisis. Polarization within the Church is pitting people of good will against one another over religious viewpoints. What are we to do? Take time to respectfully listen to others, pray for them, and invite them back to Mass, where they can encounter the merciful heart of Jesus, present in the Eucharist.

The mercy of Jesus is without measure. Each time we receive his Body and Blood, we unite our hearts to the merciful heart of Christ, who works in us and through us to bring about healing to all those he sends our way. Let us approach the table of the Lord, confident of God's gift of love and mercy for all.

Is there a person you can show mercy and compassion to this day?

Lord Jesus, help me to treat others with mercy and not condemnation.

February 16

Since the LORD, your God, is a merciful God, he will not abandon or destroy you, nor forget the covenant with your ancestors that he swore to them. — Deuteronomy 4:31

This passage from the Old Testament was penned at the time of Moses, just before the Lord delivered the Israelites into the Promised Land after they had spent forty years wandering in the desert. Moses is reminding a new generation of Israelites of the abundant mercy and faithfulness of the Lord their God. The covenant that Moses speaks of had been created between God and Abraham some five hundred years earlier. Jesus is the fulfillment of the Old Testament promise. At the Last Supper, Jesus shared his very self in the gifts of bread and wine. As he shared the cup with the apostles, Jesus said, "This is my blood of the covenant, which will be shed on behalf of many for the forgiveness of sins" (Mt 26:28).

The Eucharist is the visible presence of our invisible God, who is rich in mercy and compassion. The Lord never forgot his promise to Abraham and Moses, for he sent his only Son, Jesus, who suffered and died on the cross, so that our covenant relationship with God could be restored forever. Let us live as people of the new and everlasting covenant.

Does your heart desire a covenant relationship with Jesus?

Lord Jesus, your mercy is without end. Help me to follow your example of faithfulness and love in all of my endeavors.

February 17

Have mercy on me, God, in accord with your merciful love;
in your abundant compassion blot out my transgressions.
Thoroughly wash away my guilt;
and from my sin cleanse me.
For I know my transgressions;
my sin is always before me. — Psalm 51:3–5

Some of the greatest saints in our Church history were once sinners who struggled with many of the same temptations that we experience on a daily basis. While the conversion stories of these reformed sinners may vary, there is one common thread in all. Once they repented of their sins, they experienced the mercy and compassion of God, and they understood that God had forgiven their sins. No one's sin is greater than the love and mercy of God. We simply cannot limit God's mercy to our human standards.

We experience the mercy of God at the Eucharistic banquet of the Lord. If we are in the state of grace, when we partake of the consecrated bread and wine, we receive the Real Presence of Jesus, who thoroughly washes us from our guilt and cleanses us from our venial sins, if we come before him with a repentant heart. The mercy of God helps us to live as people of love, freed from our past transgressions.

How has God's mercy transformed your life?

Lord Jesus, shower me with mercy, that I may live in the light of your love.

February 18

*When he returned to his disciples he found them asleep. He said
to Peter, "So you could not keep watch with me for one hour?
Watch and pray that you may not undergo the test. The spirit is
willing, but the flesh is weak." — Matthew 26:40–41*

This Scripture passage has always troubled me. Peter and the apostles
had to have some inclination that serious trouble was on the horizon
for Jesus, yet they fell asleep and left him all alone at night in the Garden of Gethsemane. How could his beloved disciples demonstrate such
a lack of concern for Jesus? Indeed, their spirits were willing, but their
flesh was weak. Yet despite their actions, Jesus showed them mercy and
compassion even in his darkest of days.

Jesus speaks this same message to us today. He is present in the
Blessed Sacrament, and he is inviting us to keep watch with him, to
spend time in prayer, that we may be able to overcome any temptations
that come our way. Are we like the apostles, too busy to keep watch
with Jesus for an hour? The Blessed Sacrament is a fountain of God's
mercy. Jesus desires us to come, be with him, and pray that we may not
undergo the test, for the spirit is willing but the flesh is weak.

**Is it possible to spend time with Jesus in the presence of the Blessed
Sacrament? If not, can you close your eyes and imagine you are
sitting in front of the tabernacle? Speak to Jesus.**

Lord Jesus, help me to keep watch with you, that I may overcome all temptations.

February 19

The LORD protects the simple;
I was helpless, but he saved me.
Return, my soul, to your rest;
the LORD has been very good to you. — *Psalm 116:6–7*

When we travel, we experience new cultures, enjoy local cuisine, and participate in adventurous activities that we would not normally do at home. For my daughter's sixteenth birthday, she and I had a mother-daughter weekend in New York. After touring the city all day, it was getting dark and we were unable to hail a taxi, so we began to walk back to our hotel. We soon realized we were lost, and we felt helpless. We passed by a Catholic church, so we went in to say a prayer. I felt safe. We prayed before Jesus in the tabernacle, and then returned to our quest to walk back to the hotel. Coming out of church, we spotted a cab parked on the street. We got in and, minutes later, we were at the hotel.

There is such power in prayer. When we come before Our Lord in the Blessed Sacrament, he is here to listen to us. Nothing we have to say is insignificant to the Lord. He is here to help us in every facet of our life. The Lord is gracious and merciful, and he will save you, and return your soul to rest.

How has the Lord answered your prayer?

Lord Jesus, thank you for helping me when I needed it most.

February 20

Who is a God like you, who removes guilt
and pardons sin for the remnant of his inheritance;
Who does not persist in anger forever,
but instead delights in mercy? — Micah 7:18

God is love, pure love. Unfortunately, for many of us, our image of God is one of judgment; we imagine that the Lord is up in heaven with a divine clipboard, watching us and recording all of our sins and transgressions. We are tempted to believe that the Lord is waiting for us to make a mistake so he can inflict punishment on us. This is not who God is. The Lord delights in mercy and wants nothing more than to pardon the sins of his people.

When we partake of the Eucharistic Body and Blood of Jesus, we receive the fullness of God's mercy and love. The Real Presence of Jesus in the Eucharist invites us to drink deeply from the chalice of mercy, for Jesus shed his Blood on the cross for the salvation of all. Let us seek pardon for our sins as we approach the table of life, that we may unite our hearts to our compassionate Lord.

What is your image of God?

Lord Jesus, your mercy and compassion are without measure. Pardon my sins, that I may live in union with you.

February 21

*If you return to the LORD, your kinfolk and your children will
find mercy with their captors and return to this land. The LORD,
your God, is gracious and merciful and he will not turn away his
face from you if you return to him.* — 2 Chronicles 30:9

When a loved one hurts or betrays us, the Lord calls us not to turn
our face from them, but to offer mercy and compassion, as the Lord
does with us. The Lord is gracious and merciful, and he desires that
we imitate his actions in our lives. This can be difficult for many, because the problems of today's society are complex and divisive.

If we are looking to become people of mercy and compassion, Jesus is here in the Blessed Sacrament to help us. Taking prayer time in
adoration gives us a unique opportunity to connect with Our Lord at
a deeply personal level. He is present to us, and he seeks to help us live
gracious and merciful lives. Let us not turn away, but return to the Lord
with open hearts.

Do you find it difficult to offer mercy to others?

Lord Jesus, help me to be merciful in my dealings with my family and friends.

February 22

Truly, the LORD is waiting to be gracious to you,
truly, he shall rise to show you mercy;
For the LORD is a God of justice:
happy are all who wait for him! — Isaiah 30:18

The Lord is waiting to be gracious to us. Our Creator God, who made the heavens and the earth, who created all life, desires to show us mercy. What are we waiting for? Surely, there are things in our lives we are not proud of, actions from our past or present where sin has tempted us and won. Our God is not judging us, he is encouraging us to repent, and he will shower us with his mercy, for he is a God of justice. Our Lord loves us so much that he sent his only Son, Jesus, to redeem us for all eternity.

When we receive Jesus in the Eucharist with sincere hearts, the mercy and compassion of God fills us with his redeeming grace, strengthening us not to sin again. Jesus is waiting for us; let us approach the table of salvation with open hearts, that the Lord may be gracious and show us mercy and love.

What in your life needs God's mercy today?

Lord Jesus, help me to seek you with a sincere heart each day, that I may receive the abundant mercy you have waiting for me.

February 23

Remember your compassion and your mercy, O LORD,
for they are ages old.
Remember no more the sins of my youth;
remember me according to your mercy,
because of your goodness, LORD. — Psalm 25:6–7

As human beings, we cannot possibly understand the mind of God; for we live in a fallen world. God is pure love, and he desires for us to live with him in love. He does not remember the sins we have confessed, nor does he remind us of the many ways we have hurt him by our actions. The Lord's mercy is without measure; his faith is steadfast. The Lord is calling us to himself, that he may grant us mercy and compassion.

When we partake of the Eucharist, we encounter Jesus, the Son of God, sent to redeem us. His Body and Blood are spiritual food for our journey, and provide us with the grace to turn away from sin, that we may experience the mercy and compassion of God. Let us partake of the Real Presence of Jesus with hearts that are repentant of our past sins and with the resolve to sin no more.

The Lord has forgiven you; can you forgive yourself for past actions?

Lord Jesus, pour out your mercy upon me, that I may turn from sin and be faithful to you.

February 24

LORD, may you not withhold
your compassion from me;
May your mercy and your faithfulness
continually protect me. — Psalm 40:12

All of us, at one time or another, feel unworthy of God's love. For some, sins of the past may still torture us, and perhaps we feel that God can never forgive us. For others, maybe our present bad habits and sinful actions keep us from feeling close to the Lord. Whatever our situation may be, we are at the mercy of God, but the Lord is rich in mercy and compassion, and he desires only our faithfulness. God is here to hold our hands and guide us through the days that lie ahead; he remembers not the sins of the past.

When we encounter Jesus in the Eucharist, we are bathed in his mercy and compassion. By his death and resurrection, Jesus freed us from sin and opened the gates of paradise to us. Salvation is ours. Should we fall into sin, we need only to turn to the Lord seeking forgiveness, for God's mercy and faithfulness continually protect us each day.

Does your past prevent you from embracing the mercy of God each day?

Lord Jesus, do not withhold your mercy from me. Help me to live each day in your loving Presence.

February 25

I praise you, LORD, for you raised me up
and did not let my enemies rejoice over me.
O LORD, my God,
I cried out to you for help and you healed me. — *Psalm 30:2–3*

We often find ourselves waiting for answers to our prayers, and during that time, anxiety and stress fill our heart. When we do finally receive an answer to our prayers, is our first response to thank the Lord for his goodness, or do we simply relish the good news? The Lord is with us always, and he is rich in mercy and compassion; yet we should never take his abundant mercy for granted. We should live with gratitude in our hearts.

Spending quiet time in the presence of Our Lord in the Blessed Sacrament can help us refocus our attention on praising God for his goodness and mercy, rather than always asking the Lord for favors. Our Lord knows what we need, and in his mercy, he will bless us accordingly. Let us come before Jesus in the Blessed Sacrament with grateful hearts open to receiving God's abundant mercy.

Do you remember to thank the Lord for his tender mercies each day?

Lord Jesus, thank you for hearing my prayers. Your mercy and compassion are without measure.

February 26

Let the wicked forsake their way,
and sinners their thoughts;
Let them turn to the LORD to find mercy;
to our God, who is generous in forgiving.
For my thoughts are not your thoughts,
nor are your ways my ways. — *Isaiah 55:7–8*

In my life, when something happens and I just cannot understand why, I always say that "when I see God, I am going to ask him to explain." While said in jest, there is an underlying truth, for God's ways are not our ways; as fallen human beings, we will never understand how the mind of God works. With the wicked and sinful, the Lord looks for a contrite heart; but we, as human beings, demand justice and seek restitution. Truly, God's ways are not our ways.

When we sit in prayer in the presence of Jesus in the Blessed Sacrament, we can gain the strength to imitate the ways of God. We cannot do this by ourselves; Jesus is waiting for us to seek his divine help, that we may turn from our sinful ways and follow the ways of the Lord, who is rich in mercy and compassion. Let us resolve to be imitators of our God, that we, too, may be generous in forgiving.

How can the Eucharist help you cultivate the practice of offering mercy instead of judgment to those who offend you?

Lord Jesus, help me to follow the ways of the Lord, that I, too, may live with mercy and forgiveness.

February 27

For to you has been granted, for the sake of Christ, not only to believe in him but also to suffer for him. — Philippians 1:29

I met an elderly person years ago who was quite angry with God. He explained that he was a faithful and practicing Catholic, attending daily Mass, praying the Rosary several times a week, and volunteering at the local food bank on a weekly basis. He did not understand why God made him suffer, since he followed all the rules of being a good Christian. I fear that this man is not alone in his view of Christianity. But the truth is, we do not earn our way into God's good graces. Suffering is part of the human condition; no one escapes the cross.

As followers of Christ, we join our sufferings with Jesus, walking with him as we carry our crosses with renewed faith in the Lord. Each time we receive the Eucharist, we participate in the death and resurrection of Jesus, made present on the altar. Our suffering is redemptive, for it will lead us to the glory of eternal life won for us by Jesus Christ.

What role does suffering play in your life? Do you view it as redemptive?

Lord Jesus, help me to embrace my sufferings with the hope and promise that they will lead me to a new life in Christ.

February 28

Go, proclaim these words toward the north, and say:
Return, rebel Israel — oracle of the LORD —
I will not remain angry with you;
For I am merciful, oracle of the LORD,
I will not keep my anger forever. — Jeremiah 3:12

Raising a family can be stressful. Juggling work and school schedules can put pressure on all family members, and often times disagreements and animosity arise between parents and children. Although it is good to have consequences for bad behavior and attitudes, families that love one another do not remain angry for long. They forgive each other and move on. God acts with us in much the same way. God is ever faithful, and he does not remain angry with us; rather, he treats us with mercy and compassion.

When we encounter Jesus in the Eucharist, we experience God's divine mercy poured out upon us. The Body and Blood of Christ that we share is given to us for the forgiveness of sins. The Eucharist helps us to grow in grace, that we may love the Lord with our whole being, and our neighbor as ourselves.

Can you be patient and offer forgiveness to those who hurt your feelings?

Lord Jesus, help me to withhold my anger from others, that I may imitate you in mercy and compassion.

~ HEALING ~

March 1

Jesus heard this and said to them [that], "Those who are well do not need a physician, but the sick do. I did not come to call the righteous but sinners." — Mark 2:17

The Gospels contain numerous accounts of Jesus dining with saints and sinners alike. Clearly, Jesus did not judge people based on their exteriors; rather, he invited them into a relationship where they could experience his spiritual healing and transformation. Many of us feel unworthy of God's grace, and believe we have to be perfect in order for Jesus to love us. The reality is that we cannot achieve perfection without the divine help of Jesus. He is the divine healer, and his love and mercy will heal us of our imperfections if we come to him for help.

Our reception of the Eucharist offers us a wonderful opportunity to experience the divine healing grace of Jesus. When we approach the altar with hearts seeking healing, Jesus will give us the strength and courage to overcome our sinful ways, so that we may willingly follow Him. Let us be mindful of the Lord's healing touch each time we come to the Eucharistic table.

What is one aspect of your life that needs healing? Ask the Lord to give you the grace and strength to overcome these imperfections.

Jesus, may your Divine Presence in the Eucharist help me to turn away from sin and follow you all the days of my life.

March 2

*This is … the blood of the new and eternal covenant, which
will be poured out for you and for many for the forgiveness
of sins.* — Institution Narrative, Eucharistic Prayer I

These life-giving words spoken by Jesus at the Last Supper, and proclaimed again and again at every Eucharistic liturgy, renew for us the covenant relationship with God and his people. It is a relationship which began with Abraham and Sarah, was renewed again and again with the Israelites, and was brought to fulfillment and perfection through the death and resurrection of Our Lord Jesus Christ.

Years ago, someone asked me why the text in the Sacramentary states that Jesus shed his Blood for the *many*, and not for all people. Our Catholic Faith teaches that Jesus suffered and died for all people, yet not all embrace the faith of Christ. For us to receive the healing graces of the Eucharist, we have to be in a relationship with Our Lord. If we are, then we have an opportunity to restore our covenant relationship that perhaps has been broken through our own failings and sinful actions. Let us approach the altar with repentant hearts mindful of the graces and spiritual healing that await us through our encounter with Jesus in the Eucharist.

How can your reception of the Eucharist strengthen your covenant relationship with Jesus?

Lord Jesus, help me to be faithful to the new and everlasting covenant that was forged by the precious Blood of your cross.

March 3

*Have no anxiety at all, but in everything, by prayer and petition,
with thanksgiving, make your requests known to God. Then the
peace of God that surpasses all understanding will guard your
hearts and minds in Christ Jesus.* — Philippians 4:6–7

Recently, my parish invited me to offer a reflection on the Eucharist following the celebration of First Friday daily Mass. While I love presenting on the Eucharist, I must admit I was surprisingly a little anxious and uncomfortable doing this presentation because of the exposition of the Blessed Sacrament occurring during my talk. I did not want to be disrespectful. In the days leading up, I prayed that the Lord would calm my nerves and use me to touch the hearts of all those in attendance. My anxiety, however, continued even during the Mass. It was not until I received Communion and returned to my pew that I felt a sense of peace wash over me. It was palpable; as if Jesus put his arms around me, and whispered, "I am with you."

When we encounter Jesus in the Eucharist, we have an opportunity to experience a physical healing of our fears and anxieties. Let us come before the Real Presence of Jesus, making our requests known.

What is making you anxious today? Pray that the Eucharistic Presence of Jesus may restore peace to your soul.

Lord Jesus, thank you for never leaving me to face my fears alone. I love you.

March 4

"As he passed by, he saw Levi, son Alphaeus, sitting at the customs post. He said to him, "Follow me." And he got up and followed him. While he was at table in his house, many tax collectors and sinners sat with Jesus and his disciples; for there were many who followed him." — Mark 2:14–15

Levi, called Matthew, was a tax collector, and was considered by the Jewish people to be a sinner. This Gospel story highlights that we do not have to be perfect for Jesus to love us. He is the divine healer, who calls the unworthy, the wounded, and the broken; he invites the sinful, the lost, and the forsaken to leave their posts and to join him at his sacred banquet, where he offers the gift of spiritual healing. Jesus desires that we be one with him.

When we dine at table with Jesus, we receive the grace to turn our lives around, and to follow him. Jesus invites us to drink deeply from the chalice of spiritual transformation. Let us leave our posts and join him at table, seeking healing from all of our imperfections.

What things in your life are preventing you from metaphorically "leaving your post" to follow Jesus?

Lord, may your Eucharistic Body and Blood fill me with the healing grace of transformation and lead me to spiritual wellness.

March 5

"Lord, I am not worthy that you should enter under my
roof, but only say the word and my soul shall be healed."
— Invitation to Communion, Roman Missal

Jesus said the "word": He died for our sins so that we may be healed. Jesus lovingly gave us the gift of his very self in the Eucharist, that we may be one with him for all time. Spiritual healing sits at the heart of our encounter with Jesus in the Eucharist.

Years ago, my mother died of cancer; yet, I had no time to grieve. I had to suppress my feelings, because I had to care for my family and for my father. Every Sunday, when I returned to my pew after receiving Communion, I would begin to cry, because I felt my mother close to me. Through my tears, I also felt a sense of peace gently washing over me. Looking back, I realize that Jesus was healing me of my broken heart and grief when I was united with him in the Eucharist.

Next time you receive the Eucharist, prayerfully reflect upon the words when you say, "Lord, I am not worthy that you should enter under my roof, but only say the word and my soul shall be healed."

What in your life needs healing? a relationship? a broken heart? Seek the Lord's healing each time you receive Communion.

Jesus, may this encounter with you in the Eucharist heal me of my spiritual wounds.

March 6

Come to me, all you who labor and are burdened,
and I will give you rest. — Matthew 11:28

There is a rather unsettling story that is *legendary* in my family. I had two bachelor uncles who grew up in the 1920s during the Great Depression; money was tight, and food was scarce. Both uncles were at a summer family picnic, and there was one piece of watermelon left. One of them wanted it, but the other one ate it; and as a result, the two brothers never spoke again. While I never met my two uncles, I can only imagine the emotional burden they carried inside their hearts all these years. My story is unique to my family, but I am sure there are many family trees filled with similar tales of people carrying the burden of misunderstandings and emotional hurts.

When we partake of the Eucharistic Body and Blood of Christ, we have an opportunity to experience spiritual healing; for our risen Lord, present in the Eucharist, lovingly invites us to bring our burdens to him, and he will give us rest. Jesus is the divine healer. Let us bring all that burdens us to the Eucharistic table as we open our hearts to spiritual healing.

Is there someone you need to make amends with today?

Lord Jesus, you are meek and humble of heart. Help me to find rest in your Eucharistic Presence.

March 7

He gives power to the faint,
abundant strength to the weak,
Though young men faint and grow weary,
and youths stagger and fall,
They that hope in the LORD will renew their strength,
they will soar on eagles' wings;
They will run and not grow weary,
walk and not grow faint. — Isaiah 40:29–31

As we get older, our bodies begin to age, and we experience certain physical limitations. Maybe we are not as flexible as we used to be, and we have a few more aches and pains, especially in the morning. Perhaps we have dietary restrictions, and our list of daily medications increases by the day. It is all part of the aging process.

There are no aging limitations when it comes to our life with Christ. Our participation in the Eucharistic banquet is vitality for our weary soul, and gives us the strength we need to face the daily trials of life. Jesus offers us his eternal Body and Blood as spiritual food for our daily journey, renewing us in mind, body, and spirit each time we come to the table of life. While we may age in our earthly bodies, with the Eucharist, our faith life flourishes in the grace we need for eternal life.

In what ways is your encounter with Jesus in the Eucharist inviting you to reflect on the importance of growing in grace as you age?

Lord Jesus, strengthen me in grace each time I receive you in the Eucharist.

March 8

The LORD is my shepherd;
there is nothing I lack.
In green pastures he makes me lie down;
to still waters he leads me;
he restores my soul.
He guides me along right paths
for the sake of his name.
Even though I walk through the valley of the shadow of death,
I will fear no evil, for you are with me;
your rod and your staff comfort me. — *Psalm 23:1–4*

In this beautiful psalm, we find the image of a Good Shepherd who cares lovingly for his flock, guiding them even through the valley of death, keeping them safe from all harm. He nurtures and gives them comfort.

Jesus is the Good Shepherd; he is the Lamb of God who takes away the sins of the world; and he will guide us along right paths. Jesus is present in the Blessed Sacrament, and he is calling us. Our Eucharistic Lord invites us to rest in his pastures, that he may restore us to spiritual health.

How can the Eucharist help you follow the Lord all the days of your life?

Lord Jesus, you are present in the most Holy Sacrament. Help me to follow you all the days of my life.

March 9

Jesus, aware at once that power had gone out from him, turned around in the crowd and asked, "Who has touched my clothes?" But his disciples said to him, "You see how the crowd is pressing upon you, and yet you ask, 'Who touched me?'" And he looked around to see who had done it. The woman, realizing what had happened to her, approached in fear and trembling. She fell down before Jesus and told him the whole truth. He said to her, "Daughter, your faith has saved you. Go in peace and be cured of your affliction." — Mark 5:30–34

Movie stars enjoy interacting with huge crowds of admirers. As they model their clothes on the red carpet, fans press in, attempting to reach out and touch them so they may tell others about their "personal experience" with their favorite star. In this Gospel story, as Jesus moves through the crowds, the woman with the hemorrhage reaches out and touches his garment. In spite of the crowds pressing in, Jesus immediately felt that healing power had gone out from him. Her faith had saved her.

Metaphorically, each time we come to the Eucharistic table, it is as if we are reaching out to touch the hem of Jesus, so that we may receive healing. May our faith in the Real Presence of Christ save us as we go in peace, cured of our afflictions.

When have you spiritually touched the hem of Jesus' garment, seeking healing and wholeness?

Lord Jesus, may your Eucharist heal me of my afflictions and restore me to health.

March 10

On hearing this, Jesus answered him, "Do not be afraid; just have faith and she will be saved." When he arrived at the house he allowed no one to enter with him except Peter and John and James; and the child's father and mother. All were weeping and mourning for her, when he said, "Do not weep any longer, for she is not dead, but sleeping." He took her by the hand and called to her, "Child, arise!" Her breath returned and she immediately arose. He then directed that she should be given something to eat. — Luke 8:50–52, 54–55

After the miraculous healing of Jairus's daughter, Jesus directed that the little girl be given something to eat. Jesus often used food as a way of ministering to those in need of healing, both spiritually and physically.

Our spiritual healing links us to the table ministry of Jesus, for the Eucharistic Body and Blood of Christ is our spiritual nourishment, and a healing for our afflictions. Praying in the presence of Jesus in the Blessed Sacrament gives us an opportunity to thank the Lord for his miraculous healings in our life. Jesus is present in the Eucharist. Let us spend time in prayer before the Blessed Sacrament asking the Lord to increase our faith, that we may believe in the healing power of Christ.

Have you experienced a healing from Jesus? Reflect on that time.

Lord God, increase my faith, that I may experience the healing power of the Eucharist.

March 11

He will wipe every tear from their eyes. — *Revelation 21:4*

My mother had terminal lung cancer, and the doctors told us she had a few weeks to live. It was late October. I decided to cook an entire turkey dinner for what would be my mother's last Thanksgiving meal. As we gathered at the table and bowed our heads to say grace, I understood the gift of this moment. Looking back, no one had an appetite that day, and the turkey dinner was hardly touched. What we did feast on was a mother's love, and gratitude for cherished family memories. I was profoundly grateful God had given us a chance to gather for one last family meal. As we drank deeply from the chalice of love and offered gratitude for my mother's life, we broke bread, giving thanks to God for her presence. It was a healing experience for all of us.

The Last Supper was much like our Thanksgiving meal. Jesus, fully aware of his impending death, gathered at table one last time with his beloved apostles, and during the meal, he gave us the gift of his Body and Blood in the elements of bread and wine, that he might be with us for all time. His Presence in the Eucharist offers healing to the brokenhearted, and dries the tears of those who grieve.

How has the Eucharist accompanied you in grief and sadness?

Lord Jesus, thank you for the gift of your life that we receive in the Eucharist.

March 12

And Jesus wept. — John 11:35

This is the shortest passage in Scripture, but its profound meaning speaks volumes to our human experience. Jesus, who wept at the death of his friend, Lazarus, experienced the same raw human emotions of grief and loss as we do. In Jesus, we have a Savior who understands when we are sad, lonely, or depressed. His Sacred Heart desires to comfort us in our sorrow and to wipe away our tears. Jesus takes us by the hand and walks us through the dark valley of anguish and grief to the radiant light of new life.

Our Lord is waiting for us to join him in the presence of his Blessed Sacrament, that we may receive his divine gifts of healing and renewed hope. Jesus desires that we bring our wounded and broken hearts to him in the Eucharist, so that his grace can comfort and heal us, wiping away every tear. Let us take a moment today to visit with Jesus in the Blessed Sacrament, praying that our relationship with him may deepen and grow into one that will last us a lifetime.

What painful situation in your life can you bring to Jesus today, seeking healing and hope?

Lord God, thank you for caring for me in my time of distress. Heal me, that I may be renewed in heart and mind.

March 13

To you who hear I say, love your enemies, do good to those who hate you, bless those who curse you, pray for those who mistreat you. To the person who strikes you on one cheek, offer the other one as well, and from the person who takes your cloak, do not withhold even your tunic. Give to everyone who asks of you, and from the one who takes what is yours do not demand it back. Do to others as you would have them do to you. — Luke 6:27–31

This Scripture passage challenges us to live in a manner contrary to the reality of what we see unfolding in the world around us. What would the nighttime news report if there were no acts of violence waged against another, if people blessed those who hurt them, and if people treated others as they wanted to be treated? It is almost impossible to imagine, because our world is in such dire need of healing.

When we come to the Eucharistic table, Jesus is there to give us extraordinary graces to live a life worthy of the Gospel message. Jesus is the divine healer, and each time we receive Communion, he can heal us of our inclination toward violence and restore us to a peaceful spirit. Let us seek spiritual healing from our Eucharistic Lord.

How can you cultivate a peaceful presence this day?

Lord Jesus, help me to turn away from violence and embrace a life of peace.

March 14

Be kind to one another, compassionate, forgiving one another
as God has forgiven you in Christ. — Ephesians 4:32

The call to holiness begins with forgiveness, yet many of us find it so difficult to forgive those who have hurt us. Throughout his ministry, Jesus preached a Gospel of forgiveness. His message was not set within the context of a courtroom so as to first prove who is right and who is wrong; Jesus simply preached forgiveness. We are to forgive one another because God has forgiven us in Christ. Jesus gave his life on the cross so that our sins may be forgiven.

At every Mass, we celebrate the perfect sacrifice of Jesus. When we partake of the Eucharistic bread and wine, we encounter the Real Presence of Jesus, who has the power to forgive our sins, and gives us the grace to forgive others. The Eucharist is first a sacrament of spiritual healing. If we seek holiness, let us bring our innermost desires to the table of the Lord, asking him for the grace of forgiveness and the spiritual strength to forgive those who have hurt us in any way.

Which is easier to do: to offer forgiveness or to ask another for forgiveness?

Lord Jesus, you call us to be compassionate and forgiving. Grant me the grace to live the Gospel message of forgiveness.

March 15

Do not ignore this one fact, beloved, that with the Lord one day is like a thousand years and a thousand years like one day. The Lord does not delay his promise, as some regard "delay," but he is patient with you, not wishing that any should perish but that all should come to repentance. — 2 Peter 3:8–9

We mark our days with a yearly calendar that dates back to the birth of Jesus. We mark the days in the week, weeks in a month, and months in a year. Each segment of time builds upon the other, giving us the past, present, and future. Time is different for God; for today is like a thousand years ago, and a thousand years ago is like today. For God, there are no constraints on time.

The perfect sacrifice of Jesus at Calvary is made present on the altar at every liturgy; that is why the Mass is called the Holy Sacrifice. The church invites us to participate in the perfect sacrifice of Jesus by offering ourselves in the hopes of transforming our fears into hope, our anxiety into peace, and our disbelief into trust. Jesus gave his life on the cross so that no one would perish. Let us join in the perfect sacrifice of Christ and offer to God all that needs healing in our life.

What would you like to offer up to God at Mass?

Lord Jesus, help me to offer up all that keeps me from loving you completely.

March 16

I urge you therefore, brothers, by the mercies of God,
to offer your bodies as a living sacrifice, holy and pleasing
to God, your spiritual worship. — *Romans 12:1*

Many people live out their faith by doing charity work, volunteering their time, and donating money to worthy causes. While these are all worthwhile endeavors, our merciful God is looking for us to dedicate our entire being as a holy and pleasing spiritual sacrifice, and not just facets of our life. The Lord desires our mind, body, and soul.

In the Holy Sacrifice of the Mass, the mercy of God invites us to unite ourselves to the perfect sacrifice of Jesus. The love of Christ we encounter at the Eucharistic altar has the power to heal us of our tendency to sin, and fill us with the grace to overcome future temptations. In faith, let us join ourselves to the sacrifice of Jesus celebrated at the Eucharist, that we may be holy and pleasing to the Lord.

What is easier? To dedicate your life's work to God, or your heart?

Lord Jesus, I offer my entire self to you; may your love heal me of all of my imperfections.

March 17

The LORD *is close to the brokenhearted,*
saves those whose spirit is crushed. — Psalm 34:19

On the night my mother died, I was keeping vigil at her bedside as she slipped into a coma and became non-responsive. About three o'clock in the morning, the doctor came in and told me her organs were shutting down. He suggested I say my goodbyes. As I gently took her frail hand in mine, I expressed my love, and I told my mom how grateful I was that the Lord has blessed me with the best mom in the world, and that I would hold her in my heart forever. I gently kissed her on the forehead and sat back down. Looking up at my mother's face, I saw one little tear roll down her cheek, and I knew that in that moment she had heard me. The words of the psalmist spoke to my heart that night, for the Lord was with me in my sorrow.

The presence of Jesus in the Blessed Sacrament is waiting for us to bring our broken hearts and crushed spirits to him, that he may tenderly embrace us with his love, and heal our broken hearts. His merciful heart cries with us in our sorrow and pain. Come, keep vigil before our Eucharistic Lord, and allow the love of Jesus to heal you.

What situation is causing you grief? Bring this to the Lord.

Lord Jesus, comfort me in my sorrow and heal my broken heart.

March 18

*Know this, my dear brothers: everyone should be quick to
hear, slow to speak, slow to wrath.* — *James 1:19*

The Italians have a saying: "The tongue has no bones, but it breaks bones." We can do great damage to others with our words. Without ever touching another human being, we can literally destroy him or her with our malicious talk, gossip, and slanderous words. Saint James warns us that we should be slow to speak, and slow to anger, for once we hurt another it is difficult to make amends. We need the help of Jesus to turn our hearts around.

The Eucharist is a healing balm for our souls. The Body and Blood of Jesus we receive at the altar can help us find the courage to apologize to those we have hurt, and to grow in spiritual maturity, so that we can better control our emotions and our feelings, so that we do not lash out at others. Jesus is here to help us. Seek his healing grace and strength each time you to come to the Eucharistic table.

Do you lash out with words of anger and bitterness toward others? Seek the Lord's help to control your speech.

Lord Jesus, grant me the grace to control my tongue, that I may not tear down others with my words.

March 19

In those days when there again was a great crowd without anything to eat, he summoned his disciples and said, "My heart is moved with pity for the crowd, because they have been with me now for three days and have nothing to eat." — Mark 8:1–2

The sight of the large crowd who had not eaten in days moved Jesus with compassion. He knew they were hungry, and he miraculously fed them with a few loaves of bread and some fish. Jesus healed the crowd of their physical hunger, yet their spiritual hunger remained, because they did not understand what he offered them.

Each time we receive Communion, we have an opportunity for Jesus to heal us spiritually. So much of what we do in life depends upon our relationship with others, and many times, our efforts are unsuccessful; then our hearts become wounded and broken. In the Eucharist, Jesus fills us with his healing grace, and binds up the emotional wounds of rejection and betrayal that we carry. With Jesus, we have everything we need.

How have you experienced the compassion of Jesus?

Lord Jesus, heal me of my insecurities and help me to offer mercy to all those I meet.

March 20

The righteous cry out, the LORD hears
and he rescues them from all their afflictions. — *Psalm 34:18*

As human beings, we are composed of both a physical and spiritual nature. If one of these facets in our life suffers an affliction, the entire body cries out. When we are physically sick, or are suffering from mental distress, it is common for us to pray to God for healing, since our affliction prevents us from enjoying life. However, many times, we neglect to care for our spiritual well-being; sometimes we might not even be aware of the impairments that afflict the health of our soul.

Our life on earth is fleeting, and our spiritual life with Christ is eternal; so, our spiritual well-being should be a priority. Each time we receive the Eucharist, we encounter Jesus, the divine physician, who will heal us of our afflictions if we cry out to him. He is here to shower us with mercy and compassion, and restore our souls to spiritual wellness. Let us look to Jesus to heal us of our afflictions, that we may be spiritually fit for all eternity.

What is the condition of your spiritual life? What afflictions do you suffer from spiritually?

Lord Jesus, heal me from all afflictions that keep me from loving and serving you.

March 21

Though my flesh and my heart fail,
God is the rock of my heart, my portion forever. — Psalm 73:26

The older we get, the more aches and pains we experience. Our bodies have a way of letting us know that we are not as young as we used to be. Some people go to extremes to reverse the aging process, undergoing plastic surgery, receiving injections, and trying fad diets all in an effort to be eternally young. Even though our bodies may fail, God is our rock and our salvation; our spirit is eternal, and our home is with God in heaven. What are we doing to care for our souls?

Following the statutes of our Faith makes and keeps us Catholic; yet, if we desire more for our spiritual lives, cultivating a personal relationship with Jesus is key. Our Lord is present in the Blessed Sacrament. When we spend time in his Presence, Our Lord can heal us of spiritual wounds. Jesus loves us unconditionally; and the time we spend in prayer before the Blessed Sacrament can help us to create and deepen bonds of love and trust in God. Jesus desires our hearts and souls, that he may heal us of all that keeps us from him.

Can you spiritually place yourself before the presence of Jesus in the tabernacle to pray for spiritual healing?

Lord Jesus, my spirit desires to love you more each day. Remain with me and heal me of my faults.

March 22

LORD, be gracious to us; for you we wait.
Be our strength every morning,
our salvation in time of trouble! — Isaiah 33:2

Waiting is never fun, especially if we are waiting on important news concerning a loved one or ourselves. It is important for us to remember that we are never alone in our waiting; the Lord is with us. Every morning, as we awaken to a new day, let us be grateful for the gift of this day and the abundant blessings the Lord has planned for us. The Lord will never give us more than he can help us handle. In times of joy, let us praise the Lord; in times of sorrow, let us turn to Jesus for strength, for he is our salvation in time of trouble.

Jesus is present to us in the Eucharist. His Divine Presence, mediated in the consecrated bread and wine, is a healing balm for our weary souls. Jesus will not leave us, especially in times of distress. Let us come to the altar with hearts seeking spiritual healing, with hearts seeking Jesus, for he is our strength and salvation.

Are you in a season of waiting for something? Turn to the Lord for his divine help.

Lord Jesus, thank you for never leaving me. May your Eucharistic Presence bring me comfort and healing all the days of my life.

March 23

My God will fully supply whatever you need, in accord with his glorious riches in Christ Jesus. To our God and Father, glory forever and ever. Amen. — Philippians 4:19–20

People like to take advantage of all-you-can-eat buffets. The opportunity to fill their plates with a wide variety of soups, salads, entrées, and desserts is very satisfying, plus the fact that you can refill your plate at no extra cost. While this may be appealing to many people, these buffets offer more food than any of us need. Our society idolizes excess and abundance; yet Scripture reminds us that God will fully supply whatever we need in accord with the glorious riches of Christ Jesus. If we can refocus our priorities, we will slowly discover that Jesus is really all we need; and he will provide us with the necessary graces to live in right relationship with him, that we may gain eternal life.

Each time we partake of the Body of Christ and drink from the chalice of his precious Blood, Our Lord assures us we will never hunger or thirst again. Jesus satisfies our wants, and his Eucharistic Presence has the grace to heal us of our desire to live in excess abundance.

Are you satisfied with the blessings Our Lord has given you, or do you desire more?

Lord Jesus, help me to prioritize my life, that my relationship with you will supply me with whatever I need.

March 24

The LORD gives sight to the blind.
The LORD raises up those who are bowed down;
the LORD loves the righteous. — Psalm 146:8

Spiritual blindness can affect even the most successful of us. We can be tempted to see our financial and personal successes as self-made achievements accomplished through hard work and good luck. We seek the accolades and awards that come with our success, for they build up our egos, and they place the emphasis of our lives directly on our performance. When we do this, though, we are blinded to the spiritual reality that all gifts come from God. If we are successful at what we do, the Lord desires that we use these gifts to help others, and not just for our own gratification.

When we partake of the Eucharist, we encounter the Real Presence of Jesus, who gave sight to the blind and raised up those who are bowed down. These spiritual gifts of healing await us at the Eucharistic table, if we desire them. Jesus is here to remove the scales from our eyes, that we may clearly see that all of our life is gift from God, and that we are to share our gifts with others, for the Lord loves the righteous.

Does your spiritual sight need adjustment so that you might see and respond to the needs of others?

Lord Jesus, help me to see all that you created me to be, that I may use my gifts to help others.

March 25

Do not fear: I am with you;
do not be anxious: I am your God.
I will strengthen you, I will help you,
I will uphold you with my victorious right hand. — Isaiah 41:10

As J. R. R. Tolkien wrote, "Not all who wander are lost." Our quest for knowledge can take us from the comforts of our current lifestyle down a myriad of pathways, all in search of spiritual truth. The road is different for each one of us, and as long as we wander in search of the truth, we are not lost. When we finally find the truth, who is Jesus, we discover that he has been with us our entire life; we simply failed to have the eyes to see, or the ears to hear his loving Presence, because our priorities were elsewhere. Nevertheless, he was with us, is with us, and will always be with us. We have nothing to fear, for the Lord will uphold us with his victorious right hand.

Pursuing truth will lead us to Jesus present in the Eucharist. Spending time before the Blessed Sacrament will help us to fine-tune our attention on following Jesus. His gentle Presence directs our steps that we might not lose our way, that we might not fear.

What is preventing you from discovering the presence of Jesus in your life?

Lord Jesus, dispel my fear, that I may faithfully follow you all the days of my life.

March 26

He will wipe every tear from their eyes, and there shall
be no more death or mourning, wailing or pain, [for] the
old order has passed away. — Revelation 21:4

Years ago, a cherished friend of mine lost her two-month-old son to SIDS, sudden infant death syndrome. She was inconsolable, and I felt helpless. All I could do was to enfold her in love and prayer. They say that time heals all wounds, and in some way that is true, yet when grief takes root in the human heart it is difficult to remove; it often lies dormant in the recesses of our emotions. Jesus has the healing grace to restore us to spiritual wellness.

The Lord is waiting for us to bring our grieving hearts to him, that he may transform our sadness into hope. Spending time before Jesus in the Blessed Sacrament is therapeutic, for the Lord meets us in our frailty and loss. Our Lord loves us unconditionally, and he desires to heal us of our grief. Christ can restore the light back into our lives. Let us bring our broken hearts to Jesus, that he may wipe away every tear from our eyes, for the old order has passed away, and through Jesus, we have life eternal.

Are you grieving the loss of a loved one? Turn to Jesus, seeking healing from your sorrow.

Lord Jesus, you are the divine healer. Help me to let go of my grief, that I might experience your grace of healing and transformation.

March 27

I have heard your prayer;
I have seen your tears.
Now I am healing you.
On the third day you shall go up
to the house of the LORD. — *2 Kings 20:5*

The Lord uses the ordinary events of our daily life to help us recognize our human need for dependence upon him. When faced with challenges, rather than turning to the Lord in prayer, we sometimes wander away from God in search of instant gratification and self-praise, which blind us to the spiritual reality that Our Lord is never far from us. His loving Presence guides our steps even in difficult times. The Lord listens to our prayers, wiping away our tears and healing our wounded souls.

In the Blessed Sacrament, we encounter Jesus in a deeply personal way. The Lord is present to us, and he desires that we turn to him with our spiritual needs and petitions. His loving Presence in the Eucharist invites us to visit with him, that we may share our concerns of life, and seek his help with all of our needs. Let us take time to be with Our Lord in adoration, that his healing Presence may restore us to spiritual health.

What was a recent event where you were able to see God's hand at work in your life?

Lord Jesus, thank you for hearing my prayers, and for delivering me from all evil.

March 28

Heal me, LORD, that I may be healed;
save me, that I may be saved,
for you are my praise. — *Jeremiah 17:14*

The prophet Jeremiah, aware of his inability to heal himself of his sins and failings, sought healing from God. He understood sin to be a disease of his soul from which only God could save him. Today, many of us believe we have the power to heal ourselves. Instead of turning to God, we consult with self-help books, astrological charts, and meditative techniques to fill the void that sin carves out in our souls. The truth is that we cannot spiritually heal ourselves; only the Lord can heal us of our sins and restore our souls back to health.

When we partake of the Eucharistic Body and Blood of Jesus, our wounded souls are bathed in God's mercy, cleansing us of our venial sins and giving us the grace to sin no more. Jesus, present to us in the Eucharist, desires that we seek his help, that we may be saved. Let us turn to the Lord for healing, that we might experience his gift of salvation.

Whose help do you seek when you are in need of spiritual healing?

Lord Jesus, you are the divine healer. Heal me of my sins, that I might praise you all the days of my life.

March 29

*Everyone in the crowd sought to touch him because power came
forth from him and healed them all. — Luke 6:19*

Have you ever attended a sold-out performance where people are
packed in tightly; and those in the front rows flail their arms in an
attempt to touch the celebrity? Jesus must have experienced similar
scenarios with the crowds that followed him. Unlike the multitudes at
a rock concert, the people trying to touch Jesus knew he could help
them. They recognized Jesus as the person who casts out demons, and
who cures people of their physical ailments; and they desired to reach
out and touch him. Physical touch plays an important role in the healing process, for we are physical beings, and the power of touch has
therapeutic properties.

When we encounter Jesus in the Eucharist, we experience the Real
Presence of Jesus, the divine healer, the one who healed the crowds. Jesus is present to us, and he seeks to heal us; we simply need to reach out
and touch him by receiving his Body and Blood in Communion. Each
time we come to the Eucharistic table, let us seek healing from Our
Lord through the Eucharist.

What in your life is in need of healing? Give this over to the Lord.

*Lord Jesus, heal me of my spiritual wounds, that I may lovingly serve you all
the days of my life.*

March 30

For I will restore your health;
I will heal your injuries — Jeremiah 30:17

Our world is in crisis, and people are suffering physically, mentally, and spiritually. While we all experience difficulties, some can choose to ignore or avoid a painful situation completely. In the process of healing, it is necessary for us to name the problem, and to admit we need help in dealing with it. If we do not acknowledge what is bothering us, we will never take our first step toward healing.

Jesus is the divine healer, and he desires to restore us to health. Each time we partake of the Eucharistic, we have a graced opportunity to receive healing as the Lord renews us in mind, body, and spirit. It is important to name what needs healing in our life, and then to bring these heartfelt needs to Our Lord as we receive Eucharist. Seek his healing and grace, and trust that the Lord will heal our injuries and restore us to health.

What particular issues do you still struggle with? Seek the Lord's help.

Lord Jesus, pour your healing grace upon me, that I may experience a healing of my afflictions.

March 31

He himself bore our sins in his body upon the cross, so that, free from sin, we might live for righteousness. By his wounds you have been healed. For you had gone astray like sheep, but you have now returned to the shepherd and guardian of your souls. — *1 Peter 2:24–25*

Jesus took on the sins of humanity when he died for us on the cross. He did not die just for those living in Jerusalem at that time; Jesus' saving act of salvation paid for our sins and the sins of God's people for all time. The death of Jesus heals us, giving us a share in the eternal covenant of love in the kingdom of heaven. Our fallen nature is weak, and without a strong faith in Jesus, we fall back into sin. We wander like lost sheep, eventually straying to another pasture. Jesus seeks out the lost, and his love will find us and bring us back to him.

When we encounter the Eucharistic Presence of Jesus, we experience the unconditional love of our crucified Christ. There is no greater love. As faithful followers of Our Lord, let us turn away from sin, that we may receive fully the love of Christ that awaits us each time we receive him in the Eucharist.

How can Jesus heal you of your sins today?

Lord Jesus, may your love, visible in the Eucharist, lead me to my heavenly home.

~ HOPE ~

April 1

Blessed be the God and Father of our Lord Jesus Christ, who in his great mercy gave us a new birth to a living hope through the resurrection of Jesus Christ from the dead. — 1 Peter 1:3

I live in the Midwest, and springtime is my favorite season, because it heralds the end of winter. Trees are budding after their snowy sleep, flowers are blossoming, and a renewed sense of hope blankets the earth. While nature bestows new life upon us, as Christians, our true hope springs forth from the resurrection of Jesus, which we celebrate every springtime at Easter.

When I am weary, I spend time before the Blessed Sacrament. For there, in the presence of the risen Lord, I can hear him whisper to me in the depths of my heart, "Do not worry, this too shall pass. Have faith in me, and I will lead you through the darkness to the light of a new day." Our lives are incredibly busy. Taking the time to pray before the Lord in the Blessed Sacrament can restore our weary souls and give us the gift of hope that we need each day.

What is causing you to worry? Ask the Lord to fill you with the radiant light of his hope.

Lord Jesus, help me to live with a heart filled with the life-giving hope of your resurrection.

April 2

For God so loved the world that he gave his only
Son, so that everyone who believes in him
might not perish but might have eternal life. — *John 3:16*

At times, we all experience particular moments of sickness and loss, and for many, it is a daily challenge to remain hopeful in the face of such uncertainty. This Scripture passage, however, should be of great comfort, for it is a beautiful reminder that we should never lose hope, for we are not alone to face our trials. God sent his only Son, Jesus, that we may not perish. The presence of the Son of God dawns brightly on a darkened world.

We encounter Jesus in a most intimate way when we receive Communion. Jesus willingly gave his life for us, that we may live eternally; let us never forget the sacrifice he made for our salvation. May the Eucharistic Body and Blood of Christ we receive at the table fill us with hope and lead us to everlasting life.

Are you struggling with a lack of hope? With despair? Place your needs before the table of Our Lord, seeking hope and renewal.

Lord Jesus, may we live as people of hope, glorifying you and our Father in heaven.

April 3

The Spirit itself bears witness with our spirit that we are
children of God, and if children, then heirs, heirs of God and
joint heirs with Christ, if only we suffer with him so that we
may also be glorified with him. — Romans 8:16–17

We live in difficult times. Whether we are watching the news on television, or scrolling through social media posts, acts of violence bombard our senses, and people's comments are rude and disagreeable. It appears the world has lost its moral compass, and even people of goodwill can fall into despair. As followers of Jesus, we have to resist the ways of the world, and to keep our eyes focused on Christ. He is our hope and promise for new life. Jesus invites us to seek the things above, not the things of this world.

In the Eucharist, we find respite and hope as we join ourselves to Christ, who offers us the strength to turn away from all that is not of God. We are heirs to the Kingdom, and our hope is in the risen Lord.

Can you fast today from watching all forms of media? Instead, spend time in prayer reflecting on the Eucharist as you open your heart to the Lord's gift of hope.

Lord Jesus, help me to live in this world with a peaceful heart filled with hope.

April 4

*For I am already being poured out like a libation, and the
time of my departure is at hand. I have competed well; I have
finished the race; I have kept the faith. From now on the crown
of righteousness awaits me.* — *2 Timothy 4:6–8*

Every year, our city sponsors a marathon. The skilled athletes who
participate undergo rigorous training for months at a time. While win-
ning is ideal, their ultimate goal is to complete the race. Endurance is
key. No matter how long it takes, their hope lies in competing well and
finishing the race. Our life with Christ is similar to that of a marathon
runner. Some of us may be sprinters leading the pack and finishing early; while others of us may grow weary, but we keep going because our
eyes are fixed on our heavenly goal. We persevere and never lose hope.

Our training for life begins at the Eucharistic table, where we draw
strength and spiritual nourishment to complete the race and to keep
the faith. Jesus is with us as we conquer the hills and valleys of life, and
his grace will give us endurance to finish the race, for the crown of
righteousness awaits us.

**Do you seek the gift of perseverance and endurance to carry your
crosses with the hope of gaining eternal life?**

*Lord Jesus, you are the just judge. Help me to keep the Faith, that I may be
awarded the crown of righteousness.*

April 5

Trust in the LORD and do good
that you may dwell in the land and live secure.
Find your delight in the LORD
who will give you your heart's desire. — *Psalm 37:3–4*

Our faith lives do not involve only our spiritual side; clearly, this Scripture instructs us to trust in the Lord and do good that we may dwell in the land. Faith is holistic, and it involves prayer to God and action on our part. For example, if a loved one is sick, and we pray for healing, yet never bother to visit or call our loved one, how are we helping our prayers to be answered? If we pray for employment, yet fail to apply for new positions, how are we participating in our life of prayer? We are to trust in the Lord and do good, that we may dwell in the land and live secure.

When we bring our prayer requests before Jesus in the Eucharist, he listens to the desires of our hearts. The Body and Blood we receive are spiritual food for our journey and give us the grace to help serve the needs of those we offer up in prayer.

Call to mind a prayer request you have recently made to the Lord. How are you helping to bring a resolution to this prayer petition?

Lord Jesus, help me to trust in your providence, that I may take great delight in doing good for others.

April 6

Cast all your worries upon him because he cares for you. — *1 Peter 5:7*

It is humanly impossible for us to comprehend the love that the Lord has for us. None of us deserves God's love, yet the Lord desires that we come to him with all of our concerns because he deeply cares for us. No problem in our lives is too insignificant for the Lord, for his love will help dispel all of our fears. As Christians, why then are we so anxious? Why do the children of God seek earthly things to soothe their anxieties rather than cast their worries upon the Lord?

Jesus is present to us in the Eucharist. His Eucharistic Body and Blood, given up for us, is medicine for our weary souls. Each time we receive Our Lord in Communion; Jesus invites us to cast all of our worries upon him, for he cares for us, and he will restore hope to our troubled souls. Let us come before Jesus in the Eucharist with hearts seeking spiritual healing and wholeness, as we drink deeply from the chalice of hope and trust in the Lord.

How do you process stress and anxiety? Bring these problems to Jesus; seek his help, that you might experience healing.

Lord Jesus, may your Presence in the Eucharist heal my troubled soul and restore me to spiritual wellness.

April 7

He fulfills the desire of those who fear him;
he hears their cry and saves them. — Psalm 145:19

Fear of the Lord is a gift of the Holy Spirit, and it does not mean that we should be terrified of God. On the contrary, fear of the Lord calls us to have reverence and awe of almighty God. Because we are created in his image and likeness, our worship of God is our response to his gift of love. Only sin can put a wedge between God and us. God loves us and he sent his only Son, Jesus, to redeem us from the consequences of sin, that we may experience salvation for all eternity. The Lord hears the cries of his people and restores hope to their hearts. We have nothing to fear.

Our encounter with Jesus in the Eucharist reaffirms our need and desire to be in awe of almighty God. Jesus is the visible expression of the love of God our Father. On the night before he sacrificed himself for our sins, Jesus instituted the Eucharist that his saving Presence would be with us for all time. The presence of Jesus in the Eucharist fulfills the desires of all those who fear the Lord.

How does the term *fear of the Lord* speak to your spiritual experience?

Lord Jesus, help me never to lose my sense of awe and reverence for the Holy Trinity.

April 8

Behold, I tell you a mystery. We shall not all fall asleep, but we will all be changed, in an instant, in the blink of an eye, at the last trumpet. For the trumpet will sound, the dead will be raised incorruptible, and we shall be changed. — 1 Corinthians 15:51–52

When my children were little, I lost both of my parents in the same year, and it was very difficult for me to explain where Nanny and Poppy were. My children were familiar with heaven as a place where God lived, but it was hard for them to understand that their beloved grandparents were also with God. While it was a sad time, I remember they had great hope that we would all be together again; because someday we, too, can be in heaven with God. The death and resurrection of Jesus restored hope to our forsaken world. By his rising from the dead, Jesus conquered death, opening the gates of heaven to all who believe in him.

At every Mass, we celebrate this great mystery of our Faith, the death and resurrection of Jesus. Jesus redeemed us by his innocent Blood, and we are people of the Resurrection. When we partake of the Body and Blood of Jesus, we unite our hearts to the Risen Christ with the hope and promise that we shall be with him in paradise.

What is your vision of heaven?

Lord Jesus, may your Eucharistic Presence give me hope that I may join you in heaven.

April 9

Set your hopes completely on the grace to be brought to you at the revelation of Jesus Christ. Like obedient children, do not act in compliance with the desires of your former ignorance but, as he who called you is holy, be holy yourselves in every aspect of your conduct, for it is written, "Be holy because I [am] holy." — 1 Peter 1:13–16

Whether we are cradle Catholics or have come into the Faith recently, our belief in Jesus Christ challenges us to keep our sights set on heaven. Like obedient children, we are to obey our heavenly Father in every aspect of our behavior, with the hope and assurance that Jesus will come back and take us to himself.

The Eucharist bathes us in the holiness of Christ, and reinforces our desire to follow Jesus. Our encounter with the Real Presence of Jesus helps us to remain hopeful even when things are not going our way. We are hopeful because Jesus is with us in every aspect of our lives. Let us seek to be holy as he is holy.

What do you long for in your relationship with Jesus?

Lord Jesus, thank you for calling us to yourself. Help us to be holy because you are holy.

April 10

We give thanks to God always for all of you, remembering you in our prayers, unceasingly calling to mind your work of faith and labor of love and endurance in hope of our Lord Jesus Christ, before our God and Father, knowing, brothers loved by God, how you were chosen. — *1 Thessalonians 1:2–4*

Doing the work of God is not always easy, and sometimes we encounter obstacles and ridicule for our Christian belief, even from friends and family members. Our modern society attempts to erase the mere mention of God from the fabric of life; yet we, who have found favor with God, must persevere in our work of faith and labor of love because we have hope in Jesus Christ.

Our encounter with Jesus in the Eucharist provides us with grace to remain steadfast in our hope that the Lord will return for us. By eating and drinking of his Body and Blood, we are strengthened in our resolve to bring to fruition the work of faith begun in us by Christ Jesus.

Have you ever lost hope in God? What brought you back to the Lord?

Lord Jesus, may the Eucharist bring me the grace of endurance in my faith.

April 11

*May the eyes of [your] hearts be enlightened, that you may
know what is the hope that belongs to his call, what are the
riches of glory in his inheritance among the holy ones,
and what is the surpassing greatness of his power for
us who believe.* — Ephesians 1:18–19

In high school, I took a class in shorthand to help prepare me to take notes in college. For the first three weeks of class, I struggled to understand the abbreviated symbols, and I was beginning to lose hope that I would ever succeed in learning. Then one day, for reasons I still cannot name, I had an awakening. My eyes became enlightened, and suddenly I began to understand the concept of shorthand. At last, my hope and confidence in learning was restored. In many ways, our lives as Christians are akin to my experience of taking shorthand. At first, our Faith may seem hard to understand and we may lose hope if we feel that our prayers are not being heard.

Our encounter with Jesus in the Eucharist can help restore our hope and renew in us our gift of faith. Jesus died for our sins so that we might enjoy the riches of glory that await his holy ones. Let us bring our hopes and desires and place them before the altar.

What are the longings of your heart? Offer them in prayer to God.

Lord Jesus, strengthen me, that I may never waver in my faith and hope in you.

April 12

For I know well the plans I have in mind for you ... plans for your welfare and not for woe, so as to give you a future of hope. — Jeremiah 29:11

This Scripture passage from Jeremiah offers great comfort, for the Lord is reassuring us that he has a plan for our lives. No matter what difficulties we encounter, the Lord is with us, and he will help us overcome everything, because he has our best interests at heart. Amid the hardships of life, we will prosper and not give in to trials and tribulations. God has promised a plan for our welfare; we should not give up or give in to sin.

God's plan came to fruition when he sent his only Son, Jesus, to redeem us of our sins and gain for us eternal life. The Blood of the innocent Lamb of God won for us a future of hope. Each time we partake of the Body and Blood of Jesus, we participate in the saving action of Christ; we are renewed in our hope for eternal life.

Have you ever felt like God has forgotten about you?

Lord Jesus, help me to trust in you, that I may be renewed in my hope for a future with you in the glorious kingdom of heaven.

April 13

I am confident of this, that the one who began a good work in you will continue to complete it until the day of Christ Jesus. — Philippians 1:6

God is at work in each one of us. How does that make you feel? From the moment of our baptism, our sanctification process began, with the sole purpose of recreating us into the image and likeness of Our Lord. While life can have its challenges, it gives us hope to know that we are not alone in our struggles. Jesus is with us. Sanctification is the work of God; our role is to follow the Lord as he leads us through the narrow gate to the glorious kingdom of heaven that awaits all those who hope in Christ.

Each time we partake of the Eucharist, we have an opportunity to strengthen the work that God has begun in us. Christ's Body and Blood can cleanse us of our venial sins and help us to turn away from sin, if we come before the Lord with repentant hearts. Jesus is waiting for us at the altar to unite us to himself, that he may continue the good work in us until we meet him on the day of resurrection.

In what ways do you cooperate with the grace of salvation that is in you?

Lord Jesus, help me to follow you every day, that I may be with you on the day of resurrection.

April 14

*I will always hope in you
and add to all your praise. — Psalm 71:14*

We have all witnessed natural disasters on television. News correspondents on the scene interview survivors immediately afterward, and we hear stories of heroic efforts of people saving themselves and others. In the midst of losing everything, there are always those individuals who praise God for saving them. Their faith is firm and steadfast, and their hope rests in the Lord. Their testimony in the midst of the cross invites us to do some soul searching. How would we react in a similar situation? Our Christian faith calls us to praise God in all ways, and in all times, for he is ever-present, and his love for us is eternal.

When we partake of the Eucharist, the saving power of Jesus fills us with his love and gives us the grace to stand firm in our faith, that we may live as people of hope. Jesus is present in the Eucharist. Let us find spiritual nourishment at the table of Lord, praising God for his act of salvation.

Are you able to see God's Presence in difficult moments?

Lord Jesus, my hope is in you, and I will praise you all the days of my life.

April 15

I wait for the LORD,
my soul waits
and I hope for his word. — Psalm 130:5

Despite our on-demand culture, there are still times when we must simply wait. We wait for results from medical tests; we wait to hear back about a job interview; we wait to hear news about a loved one. No one likes to wait. Whatever the situation is that we are waiting for, it is important for us to hope in the Lord, for he is with us, and will help us through every event in life.

Spending time in prayer before the Blessed Sacrament can help quiet our hearts, calm our nerves, and restore hope to our weary spirits. Jesus is present in the Blessed Sacrament, and he is here to hold us while we wait for whatever is troubling us. Let us resolve to wait in hope as we pray in the presence of Jesus in the Eucharist.

How do you handle waiting? Do you get impatient, or do you place your hope and trust in the Lord?

Lord Jesus, help me wait in joyful expectation, as I place all my trust in you.

April 16

We know that all things work for good for those who love God,
who are called according to his purpose. — Romans 8:28

If asked, most people have no idea as to why God created them. Some might respond that they are to carry on the family lineage; others that they have something to contribute to society; while others that they are here to love and care for their family. These are all wonderful responses; the spiritual truth, however, is that we all have a higher calling from God. The Lord has created us with a purpose in mind, and when we love God, we can rest in the assurance that he loves us even more, and that he desires only goodness for us. Our understanding of goodness might differ from what God envisions, for the Lord created us to love and serve him and our neighbor. If our neighbor is in need, our calling from God is to help them, not to simply focus on our own comfort and happiness. We know that all things work for good for those who love God.

When we partake of the Eucharist, Jesus fills us with his Body and Blood and gives us the grace and strength to carry out our purpose in life. The Eucharist is our spiritual sustenance for doing the work of God.

What do you envision your purpose in life to be?

Lord Jesus, help me to fulfill my calling in life according to God's plan.

April 17

May the God of hope fill you with all joy and peace in believing, so that you may abound in hope by the power of the holy Spirit. — Romans 15:13

As Christians, we have great cause to be joyful, for Jesus has won for us the glorious crown of eternal life; all we must do is hold on to this precious gift. Our human inclination to sin is great, and often we stumble and fall. Perhaps we have even walked away from Jesus, believing that there is something better than life eternal. Jesus loves us, and he is always here to forgive us and to fill us with the hope that we can try again.

Jesus gave us the gift of himself on the night of the Last Supper. Mediated through the sacramental gifts of bread and wine, the Eucharist fills us with the hope of the resurrection, and nourishes us with the grace to renew our faith in the Lord. The Eucharist is our source of joy. May we abound in hope and peace each time we receive our precious Lord in holy Communion.

Does your faith bring you joy? Why?

Lord Jesus, help me joyfully live my faith, that I may have hope for each new day.

April 18

For in hope we were saved. Now hope that sees for itself is not hope. For who hopes for what one sees? But if we hope for what we do not see, we wait with endurance. — Romans 8:24–25

Football fans are familiar with the Hail Mary pass, a one-in-a-million toss with little or no chance of success. This maneuver, carried out at the end of a game, is enacted with the hope that a "miracle" win might occur. It is hoping against hope that things will turn out well. In a way, this football scenario speaks to us. The death and resurrection of Jesus instilled the hope of salvation within our hearts; but we have not yet achieved our goal of eternal salvation. Christian hope is rooted in miracles, for hope is in what we cannot see and have not yet experienced. We hope that Jesus is with us always, and at the same time, we wait with hope and expectation for his return.

Our encounter with Jesus in the Eucharist solidifies within us the hope that we will someday be with Jesus in heaven. His gift of the Eucharist gives us spiritual nourishment to carry on each day as we wait in hope for the fulfillment of our salvation.

Are there areas in your life where you struggle to remain hopeful?

Lord Jesus, help me to live in the hope that one day I will be with you in heaven.

April 19

Remember not the events of the past,
the things of long ago consider not;
See, I am doing something new!
Now it springs forth, do you not perceive it? — Isaiah 43:18–19

Every saint has a past, and every saint in our Church is a reformed sinner. Our hope in God invites us to let go of the baggage we carry from our past. Many of us struggle, thinking that God can never forgive us for our past mistakes. We are limiting God's immense power to forgive and to heal us of past wounds. Our Lord loves us so much that he sent his only Son, Jesus, who suffered and died for our sins to restore our covenant relationship with God. Our merciful Lord encourages us not to remember the events of our past, but to repent and to see that he is doing something new. Hope springs forth in our souls.

We draw spiritual strength from our encounter with Jesus in the Eucharist. Our Eucharistic Lord is here to help us move forward from the sins of our past, and to place our hope and trust him. Christ has saved us, and his Eucharist fills us with the hope and promise that all things are new in our life, and grace springs forth.

Do you still carry the burdens from your past? Give them over to the Lord.

Lord Jesus, help me to move forward from past mistakes, as I place my hope in you.

April 20

If then you were raised with Christ, seek what is above, where Christ is seated at the right hand of God. Think of what is above, not of what is on earth. For you have died, and your life is hidden with Christ in God. When Christ your life appears, then you too will appear with him in glory. — *Colossians 3:1–4*

Individuals who struggle with addictive behavior and who are in rehab have, in a way, died to their old way of life and rose to a new life free of addiction. It is not an easy journey, and takes great daily determination on the part of the participant. Our lives with Christ are similar. Through the waters of baptism, we died to our sinful ways, and we rose to a new life in Christ. Our new life as a Christian challenges us to focus our determination on what is above, and not on reversion to old habits, including enticements of money, power, and prestige.

The spiritual nourishment we receive at the Eucharistic table fills our heart with the love of Christ, and strengthens us to follow the Lord. As we partake of the Body and Blood of Jesus, let us seek what is above, and not what is on earth, that we too may share in the life of Christ when he appears in glory.

What bad habit do you need to let go of today?

Lord Jesus, help me to follow you every day of my life.

April 21

Therefore, we are not discouraged; rather, although our outer self is wasting away, our inner self is being renewed day by day. For this momentary light affliction is producing for us an eternal weight of glory beyond all comparison, as we look not to what is seen but to what is unseen; for what is seen is transitory, but what is unseen is eternal. — 2 Corinthians 4:16–18

Cataracts impact the way we see the world. As less light enters the retina, our vision becomes cloudy or blurred. Cataract surgery gives hope, for it involves removing the cataract and replacing it with an implant. The momentary affliction from the surgery pales in comparison to the restoration of vision one achieves. With implants, the colors of the world are vivid; red, blue, yellow, and white are crisp, clear, and bright; and the beauty of creation is once again visible to our human eye.

Our experience of the Eucharist offers us restoration of our spiritual sight, renewing our inner self day by day. Our encounter with Jesus gives light to our weary spirits, and helps us to place our hope in not what is seen, but what is unseen: the glory of eternal life with Christ.

Today, how can you look to what is of Christ, and not of this passing world?

Lord Jesus, help me to wait with patience for the unseen glory of eternity that awaits all those who hope in you.

April 22

"Jesus, Son of David, have pity on me!" Then Jesus stopped and ordered that he be brought to him; and when he came near, Jesus asked him, "What do you want me to do for you?" He replied, "Lord, please let me see." Jesus told him, "Have sight; your faith has saved you." He immediately received his sight and followed him, giving glory to God. When they saw this, all the people gave praise to God. — Luke 18:38, 40–43

The blind man in this Gospel story sat by the side of the road every day, begging. As Jesus walked by, the blind man cried out for help, for he wanted to see. Jesus restored his physical sight, and the man immediately got up and gave praise to God. This Gospel story reminds us that we should never give up, never give way to discouragement. Life can be difficult, and in the midst of suffering and pain, we are to call out to the Lord in prayer.

The Body and Blood we receive offers us the gift of hope in the midst of our daily trials. Jesus is present to us. Let us come to the table of Our Lord with hearts seeking the Lord's help, asking him to let us see his Presence at work in our lives, that we may have hope.

Do you struggle to see God's Presence? Seek his help in prayer.

Lord Jesus, help me to have the spiritual sight to know that you are with me always.

April 23

*Therefore, my beloved brothers, be firm, steadfast, always fully
devoted to the work of the Lord, knowing that in the Lord
your labor is not in vain.* — 1 *Corinthians* 15:58

I think that at one time or another, we have all experienced the feeling that the no one is listening to us. Parents, especially, understand this. Raising children in this polarized world takes a steadfast faith, and the resolve not to give in to feelings of defeat, not to lose hope. It is not easy, for each day temptations from the outside world entice our children, yet our call is to remain firm, and steadfast, and always fully devoted to the work of raising our children in the Faith, for we believe that our work is not in vain.

When we encounter Jesus in the Eucharist, he offers us the necessary graces to persevere in our mission. His mercy and compassion are here to help us if we are weary, and to raise us up in hope, for the Lord is with us always.

**Do you sometimes feel that you labor in vain? Bring your cares
and concerns before Jesus in the Eucharist. Seek his help.**

*Lord Jesus, help me to remain steadfast in my faith, that I may always be fully
devoted to the work of the Lord.*

April 24

Where then is my hope,
my happiness, who can see it? — Job 17:15

At one time or another, we have all felt like Job, perhaps asking the question "Why do bad things happen to good people?" Job's life was a series of incredible hardships and losses, yet Job never lost hope in the Lord, even in the face of tragedy. The life of Job invites us to do some soul searching; when life gets difficult, do we put our faith in God or walk away in despair? Hope is essential to our life with Christ. I can only imagine what the apostles experienced when they witnessed the crucifixion of Jesus. Were they tempted to lose hope? Or did they remember the life-giving actions of Jesus at the Last Supper, and how he gave us the gift of himself in the elements of bread and wine, that we may have eternal life?

Each time we receive the Eucharist, we receive the gift of hope given to us by Jesus. His Real Presence in the Eucharistic bread and wine fills us with the promise of eternal life won for us by his Blood. The Eucharist is our hope and our happiness. May we always cherish this gift of life from Jesus.

What is your initial reaction when your life is confronted with difficulties and trials?

Lord Jesus, may the Eucharist fill my heart with the hope and promise of eternal life that await all who believe in Christ.

April 25

Oh, that I may have my request,
and that God would grant what I long for. — Job 6:8

So much of our lives are spent waiting and hoping for something we desire. We wait on medical tests, we wait on the economy to improve, we wait on God to answer our prayers. Job was no different; however, despite experiencing a series of tragedies, Job never lost hope in God. The Lord was his anchor in the turbulent seas of life. On this side of heaven, we will experience difficulties and challenges, and our faith in God will be tested. Nevertheless, the Lord invites us to place our hope in him, and not in the events of this fallen world.

Jesus satisfies all of our longings. When we place our hope and trust in him, we have nothing to fear. Partaking of the Body and Blood of Jesus helps us to refocus our priorities, that we may seek what is above, and not what is of this world. Jesus is with us. Let us turn to him in faith, that we may live as people of hope.

What challenges are you facing right now? Turn to the Lord with a hopeful heart as you wait for the Lord to answer your prayers.

Lord Jesus, increase my faith, that I might place my hope in you with each passing day.

April 26

Rather the LORD takes pleasure in those who fear him,
those who put their hope in his mercy. — Psalm 147:11

Movies featuring action heroes attract the most attendance these days at theaters. The underlying theme in all of these action films is that superheroes do not rely on anyone; they are larger-than-life people who rely only on their own individual strengths. While these movies are entertaining, they subliminally suggest to our culture that we do not need anyone, that we can accomplish everything in life on our own. Our Christian life is the complete opposite, for the Lord takes great delight in those who put their hope in his mercy. Our dependence upon God for all our needs is the very thing that draws us closer to him.

When we receive Jesus in holy Communion, our hearts are united with him, and this mystical moment invites us to place our complete hope and trust in the Lord. Without Jesus, we have no hope. We are not superheroes; we are people in need of Christ's mercy. Let us approach the Eucharistic table with hearts open to receiving God's grace and mercy, for we will never be disappointed.

In what ways do you depend upon God each day?

Lord Jesus, help me to place my hope and trust in you, that I may always depend upon you.

April 27

My soul, be at rest in God alone,
from whom comes my hope.
God alone is my rock and my salvation,
my fortress; I shall not fall. — *Psalm 62:6–7*

My father was in the hospital suffering from heart failure. Late one night, I received a call from the attending doctor informing me that my father was failing quickly, and that I should come over now. As I drove, I prayed that the Lord would not take my dad on this particular day, since it was my birthday. It was a simple prayer of hope offered to the Lord. As I walked down the hallway to my dad's room, I noticed a sign at the nurse's station that said, "Expect a Miracle." I did not think anything of it. I stayed with my dad for hours, keeping vigil and praying. Without cause, his breathing began to improve. Soon, he was sitting up and talking with me. Relieved and exhausted, I went home to get some rest. As I walked back down the hallway, I looked for the sign, but it was not there.

Hope is foundational to our faith in Jesus. Our Lord, present in the Blessed Sacrament, invites us to be with him. Every situation in our lives is important to him. Let us come before the Blessed Sacrament with hearts open to the miracles that the Lord has waiting for us.

Is God your rock and your salvation?

Lord Jesus, in you alone is my soul at rest.

April 28

Rejoice in hope, endure in affliction, persevere in prayer. — *Romans 12:12*

I never imagined there would be a time in my life where I could not receive Eucharist; yet that was a reality for all of us for many months. During that time, I persevered in prayer, hoping it would all end soon. Yet, the affliction continued, so I persevered in prayer, remaining hopeful. As the world slowly began to reopen, hearts rejoiced with hope as we reunited with loved ones, returned to schools and workplaces, and our churches reopened. I remember attending my first Mass after lockdown. I could not wait to receive the Eucharist. My spirit rejoiced, for I reunited with the Lord, although I knew he had been with me always.

Jesus is present to us in the Eucharist. When we partake of his Body and Blood, we receive him into our heart, and he is with us to help us endure our afflictions so that we may rejoice in hope. Let us never take the gift of Jesus in the Eucharist for granted.

What did you feel when you received your first Communion after the churches reopened?

Lord Jesus, in the midst of afflictions, help me to persevere in prayer and rejoice always in hope.

April 29

We who have taken refuge might be strongly encouraged to hold fast to the hope that lies before us. This we have as an anchor of the soul, sure and firm, which reaches into the interior behind the veil, where Jesus has entered on our behalf as forerunner. — *Hebrews 6:18–20*

When life gets difficult, and darkness is hemming round, it is our hope in Jesus that will carry us through. Jesus is our anchor, our light in the darkness, and we must hold fast to him, especially when we are afraid or anxious, lest we fall into despair. Jesus is beside us, holding our hands and guiding us through the rough waters of an uncertain future. We need to trust in the Lord, for he will help us to rediscover the virtue of hope that we desperately need in difficult times.

Jesus is present in the Blessed Sacrament, and he is waiting for us to come to him, that his loving Presence may comfort us and restore hope to our weary souls. We have nothing to fear; for Jesus invites us to hold fast to the hope that lies before us. Let us place ourselves in his loving and compassionate Presence, asking for the strength to carry our crosses with faith and hope.

What are your greatest fears? Give them over to Jesus, that you might find hope in the midst of life's challenges.

Lord Jesus, help me to have hope this day. May I never waver in my faith, and always trust in you.

April 30

A clean heart create for me, God;
renew within me a steadfast spirit. — Psalm 51:12

This beautiful passage from Scripture should be on the lips of every Christian; for we are continually in need of spiritual renewal, because our fallen nature tempts even the best of us to sin. We need to seek the Lord's help to create within us a clean heart and to renew us in spirit each day. Holiness is a process, and with the Lord's help, we can draw closer to God.

The Eucharist unites us to Jesus. Through this union with Christ, we have the graced opportunity to ask the Lord to renew us in spirit and create within us a clean heart, that we may become all that he desires us to be. Let us receive Our Lord in the Eucharist with hearts that are worthy of this spiritual encounter, as we strive for holiness and peace all the days of our life.

How does this Scripture passage speak to your spiritual life?

Lord Jesus, create in me a new heart, that I may live with your guiding peace and love all the days of my life.

~ PEACE ~

May 1

While they were still speaking about this, he stood in their midst and said to them, "Peace be with you." But they were startled and terrified and thought that they were seeing a ghost. Then he said to them, "Why are you troubled? And why do questions arise in your hearts? Look at my hands and my feet, that it is I myself. Touch me and see, because a ghost does not have flesh and bones as you can see I have." And as he said this, he showed them his hands and his feet. While they were still incredulous for joy and were amazed, he asked them, "Have you anything here to eat?" They gave him a piece of baked fish; he took it and ate it in front of them. — Luke 24:36–43

Fear, in its many forms, can prevent us from experiencing the peace of Christ. Spiritual fear often goes undetected, and can leave us feeling unsettled. It can stir up feelings of unworthiness, guilt, and even a lack of trust in the workings of the Lord. In this story, Jesus alleviates the fears of the apostles by sharing a meal with them.

Each time we come to the altar, Jesus is present to feed us with his Eucharistic Body and Blood, spiritual nourishment to calm our fears and anxieties. The Lord himself nourishes us with the peace of the Risen Christ.

What troubles your spirit today?

Lord Jesus, help me to overcome my fears, that I may lovingly serve you with a peaceful heart.

May 2

Rejoice in the Lord always. I shall say it again: rejoice! Your kindness should be known to all. The Lord is near. Have no anxiety at all, but in everything, by prayer and petition, with thanksgiving, make your requests known to God. Then the peace of God that surpasses all understanding will guard your hearts and minds in Christ Jesus. — Philippians 4:4–7

Years ago, I was at a summer barbecue, where I met a Catholic woman whose heart was greatly troubled. As we talked, she told me she was angry because her adult children no longer listened to her, and her house needed updating, even though she had just had a new roof installed. She finished her conversation by telling me that she hated her life, because she had no control over anyone or anything. Sadly, this woman had no relationship with Jesus, and no sense of gratitude. Her happiness and emotional well-being were rooted in her need to control people and the events of her life.

Scripture tells us to have no anxiety at all, for Jesus Christ will guard our hearts and minds and bring us peace. Our encounter with Jesus in the Eucharist can help us experience the peace that surpasses all understanding. In faith, let us bring our needs before our Eucharistic Lord, trusting in his goodness.

Do you feel a need to control people or the events of your life?

Lord, help me to find peace in the midst of my daily struggles.

May 3

The people who walked in darkness
have seen a great light;
Upon those who lived in a land of gloom
a light has shone.
For a child is born to us, a son is given to us;
upon his shoulder dominion rests.
They name him Wonder-Counselor, God-Hero,
Father-Forever, Prince of Peace. — Isaiah 9:1, 5

The prophet Isaiah shares his vision of the coming of the Messiah, who will usher in the dawn of a new era for humanity, a time filled with God's light and peace. Two thousand years later, our world still needs the Prince of Peace. We need Jesus to help us reject the godless ways and worldly desires of our sinful world, so that we may live and move and have our being in the radiant light of the Prince of Peace.

The Eucharist reminds us that the Prince of Peace is with us now. His Presence is vast, and we no longer walk in darkness. Christ lives among us and in us. Each time we partake of the banquet of Our Lord, Jesus fills us with his radiant light and his gift of peace, and he invites us to take his glorious light to the darkened corners of our world.

How can you share the light and peace of Christ with those you meet this day?

Lord Jesus, help us to walk in your radiant light, that we may live as people of peace.

May 4

He said to [his] disciples, "Therefore I tell you, do not worry about
your life and what you will eat. ... Can any of you by worrying
add a moment to your life-span?" — Luke 12:22, 25

At some time or another, we have waited for the results of medical tests, whether it be for us or for a loved one, and that time of waiting can be one of great anxiety. We worry about an unknown future. Jesus is reassuring us that worrying will not add one single moment to our life. He is calling his followers to place their trust in him, and not the passing things of this world; for only in Jesus will we find peace.

Our relationship with Jesus in the Eucharist can calm our anxious hearts, and help us to stay afloat during the turbulent times of our life. The grace we receive at the Eucharistic table enables us to stay focused on living in the present, and not to worry about tomorrow. With Jesus by our side, we can overcome anything that tomorrow will bring. Let us bring our worries and concerns to our Eucharistic Lord, seeking the peace of heart that only he can give.

What is causing you concern today? Give this problem to the Lord, seeking his divine gift of peace.

Lord Jesus, I place all my trust in you. Help me not to worry, that I may have peace in my heart.

May 5

The LORD bless you and keep you!
The LORD let his face shine upon you, and be gracious to you!
The LORD look upon you kindly and give you peace! — Numbers 6:24–26

In the last days of my mother's life, her best friend of thirty years came over to our house to see her for one last time. Before her visit, she and I agreed that it would be too painful to say goodbye, so she would simply wish my mom peace. At the end of her visit, with tears in her eyes, she kissed my mom on the forehead and wished her peace. Unable to speak, my sweet mother squeezed her hand. That beautiful moment between my mom and her best friend remains in my memory and in my heart forever.

Peace is a tangible feeling; it is a spiritual awareness that God is with us. Jesus' gift of peace awaits us at the altar. When we partake of the Body and Blood of Jesus, we encounter the Risen Christ, who after the Resurrection greeted his apostles with "Peace be with you." When we are in the presence of the Eucharistic Jesus, we are in the presence of the Prince of Peace.

If you knew you were seeing someone for the last time, how would this change your experience of being with each other?

Lord Jesus, thank you for granting us your divine gift of peace. May your Eucharistic Presence bring light to the darkened areas of my life.

May 6

Peace I leave with you; my peace I give to you. Not as the world gives do I give it to you. Do not let your hearts be troubled or afraid. — John 14:27

My dad suffered from heart failure. A few days before he passed, I asked a priest to give him last rites. The priest came and anointed my dad with holy oil and gave him his final Communion, food for his journey home to heaven. I felt so relieved that I was able to give my dad this final gift. Days later, the Lord gave me the gift of being present with my dad at his bedside when he passed away. While I grieved his passing, and felt his loss, I experienced an extraordinary feeling of peace at that moment. The Lord's Presence was palpable; I knew that Jesus had come to take my father home to heaven. I had nothing to fear.

When we partake of the Eucharist, we encounter the Real Presence of Jesus, who heals the brokenhearted and offers us his gift of everlasting peace. Our Lord reassures us: Do not let your hearts be troubled or afraid. His Presence is with us in the Eucharist. We have nothing to fear.

Have you ever experienced the peace of Christ in the midst of a stressful situation?

Lord Jesus, may your Eucharistic Presence fill me with your gift of peace, that my heart might not be troubled.

May 7

I have told you this so that you might have peace in me. In the world you will have trouble, but take courage, I have conquered the world. — John 16:33

Have you ever felt defeated? As if you have nowhere to turn and you have no hope? This is not a good place to be. Our Christian faith invites us to turn to the Lord, especially in the midst of our trials, for Jesus assures us that he has conquered the world, and through him we will find peace.

Where do we find the courage to overcome our troubles, that we may experience the peace that Jesus promises? Spending prayer time in the presence of Our Lord in the Blessed Sacrament affords us the opportunity to center ourselves, and to rest in the peace that only Jesus can bring. In the silence of our prayer, we can hear the Lord speak to us, as he takes us by hand and leads us through the tribulations of life. Jesus is present to us in the Eucharist. Let us seek his Divine Presence, that we may experience his gift of peace.

What situation in life is causing you stress and anxiety? Seek the Lord's help, that you may be at peace.

Lord Jesus, thank you for helping me through difficult situations. May your peace live in my heart this day.

May 8

Finally, brothers, rejoice. Mend your ways, encourage one another,
agree with one another, live in peace, and the God of love
and peace will be with you. — 2 Corinthians 13:11

We have all heard the saying "Never burn a bridge." There is great wisdom in this sentiment. Why? Permanently holding on to a grudge serves no one and creates disharmony in our spirit. Who knows if in the future, our paths might cross again with someone, and we might need their help in some way? If we burn a bridge, there is no way to cross over, and reconciliation becomes extremely difficult. The Lord calls us to mend our ways and to live in peace with one another. This is a challenge for many of us.

At Mass, before we receive the Eucharist, we offer our brothers and sisters a sign of Christ's peace. The Lord desires that we live in harmony with one another, and that we carry no grudge with us to the altar. Partaking of the Body and Blood of Christ gives us grace to mend our ways and live in peace with our neighbor and with Our Lord. Let us bring our hardened hearts before our Eucharistic Presence of Jesus, seeking his mercy, love, and pardon.

Do you find it difficult to forgive and forget?

Lord Jesus, help us to live as people of peace, encouraging one another on our journey in life.

May 9

In peace I will lie down and fall asleep,
for you alone, LORD, make me secure. — Psalm 4:9

Have you ever fallen asleep while saying your prayers? This has happened to me countless times. While I do not recommend waiting until you are tired to pray, there is a sense of peace and tranquility that comes over us as we gently fall asleep in the arms of Jesus. He is our life; we should think about Jesus upon waking and as we close our eyes to sleep. For in him alone shall we find peace.

Our days are hectic, and our responsibilities and obligations are vast and varied. No wonder we are exhausted at the end of the day. Jesus invites us to rest in his Presence; to spend quality time with him in prayer before the Blessed Sacrament.

If your days are ruled by your calendar, then pencil in time for Jesus. Make your relationship with Our Lord a priority in your busy life. Visit him in the Blessed Sacrament. In the quiet of the adoration chapel, Jesus is here to help you find rest from your burdens, and to make you feel secure in the midst of your day. Seek his peaceful and gentle Presence today.

Do you find praying a peaceful experience?

Lord Jesus, in you alone do I find rest. Be with me today, that I may feel secure in your Presence.

May 10

May the Lord of peace himself give you peace at all times and in
every way. The Lord be with all of you. — 2 Thessalonians 3:16

It is important for us to live in the spiritual awareness that the Lord is with us always. Rather than stress over what needs to be done next, or wonder how we will accomplish the many tasks of today, our faith in Jesus calls us to be dependent upon him and not on our own agenda. Never get ahead of God. The Lord of peace invites us to follow him. He takes us by the hand and leads us through the myriad experiences that await us each day. His peace is with us at all times and in every way. We simply need to be spiritually attuned to his Presence. We can discover his Presence at the Eucharistic table.

When we partake of the Body and Blood of Jesus, Our Lord is here to open our senses to his abiding Presence. The Eucharist is our communion with Jesus, and gives us the grace to follow the Lord, to walk peacefully with him throughout our day. Let us turn to the Lord with open hearts, that we may receive his gift of abiding peace.

Do you seek the Lord's help and peace throughout your day? Lean on his Presence and let him lead you.

Lord Jesus, you are with me always. Increase my awareness of your peaceful Presence.

May 11

*In contrast, the fruit of the Spirit is love, joy, peace, patience,
kindness, generosity, faithfulness, gentleness, self-control. Against
such there is no law. Now those who belong to Christ [Jesus] have
crucified their flesh with its passions and desires. If we live in the
Spirit, let us also follow the Spirit. — Galatians 5:22–25*

We are earthen vessels, created by God to contain the life of the
Spirit. While experiences of our past may have caused chips or even
cracks in our cups, our lives with Jesus have the power to create us anew.
Through his death and resurrection, our earthen vessels are washed
clean in the Blood of the Lamb, and we are purified. Now, our vessels
can hold the precious fruits of the Spirit, which are love, joy, peace,
patience, kindness, generosity, faithfulness, gentleness, and self-control.

Each time we encounter Jesus in the Eucharist, our earthen vessels
are filled with the graces needed for us to live each day in the Spirit.
Let us bring our wounded and broken selves to the table of the Lord,
seeking the Lord's help, that we may be created anew.

**In what ways does the image of an earthen vessel speak to you in
your spiritual life?**

*Lord Jesus, fill me with the fruits of the Spirit, that I may faithfully follow you
each day.*

May 12

We boast in hope of the glory of God. Not only that, but we even boast of our afflictions, knowing that affliction produces endurance, and endurance, proven character, and proven character, hope, and hope does not disappoint, because the love of God has been poured out into our hearts through the holy Spirit that has been given to us. — Romans 5:2–5

We have all experienced times in our lives when it seems that everything is going wrong. On one particular Friday, many years ago, my mom was at home dying of cancer; my dad, who was her caretaker, fell at home and broke his hip. This necessitated bringing my mom to our house, as the paramedics transported my dad to the hospital for surgery on his hip. On that same day, my husband experienced chest pains, and the doctor admitted him for observations to a different hospital. With my three immediate family members in crisis, I sat in my kitchen and asked the Lord, "What now?" I felt his gentle Presence. These afflictions produced endurance and proven character, and finally hope, but it was not an easy road.

Jesus is here to help us in those moments of darkness. Each time we partake of the Eucharist, we receive his peace and his gift of hope, because the love of God has been poured into our hearts.

When life is overwhelming, what is your first response?

Lord Jesus, fill me with hope, that I may see your Presence in all situations.

May 13

Blessed are the peacemakers,
for they will be called children of God. — *Matthew 5:9*

Sometimes I wonder if peace is even possible. Our world is divided, and we are at odds with one another; there is polarization in politics, the Church, and even within families. Peace seems so elusive. Yet Our Lord calls us to be peacemakers, for then we will blessed, we will be the children of God.

When we encounter Jesus in the Eucharist, we have a graced opportunity to experience the peace of the Risen Christ, in a way that is impossible in our wounded and broken world. The Real Presence of Jesus in the Eucharist is here to nourish and sustain us on our quest to be peacemakers. If peace does not come from us, then who will our loved ones experience it through? When we eat and drink of the Body and Blood of Christ, we unite ourselves to the Prince of Peace, and we become the very mystery we receive. Jesus is with us and in us as we journey in life. Let us turn to him, that we may strive to be peacemakers wherever the Lord calls us.

In what ways can you sow the seeds of God's peace in a volatile situation?

Lord Jesus, help me live as a person of peace, that I may be called a child of God.

May 14

*May the Lord of peace himself give you peace at all times and in
every way. The Lord be with all of you. — 2 Thessalonians 3:16*

Calendars and schedules rule our lives. Smartphones now have the
capability to remind us of upcoming meetings, doctor appointments,
and social engagements; school calendars keep us on track as to when
our child's hot lunch day will be or when the upcoming parent-teacher
conference will occur. Spiral-bound appointment books help us plan
months ahead, just in case we do not have anything else to do. In reality, we all are living supercharged, busy lives where peace is extremely
elusive, if not absent altogether.

Jesus, present in the Blessed Sacrament, invites us to step away from
the busyness of our lives and to spend quality time with him, that we
may immerse ourselves in his peace. Our spiritual lives need quiet time,
for silence enables us to hear the voice of Our Lord speaking to us.
Today, I invite you to take time in prayer before the Blessed Sacrament
in the tabernacle. Ask the Lord to let his peace wash over you, that you
might feel his Divine Presence with you at all times. Seek his divine
help in prioritizing your daily calendar, that you might carve out time
for prayer each day.

**What is one appointment today that you can reschedule, just to
give you time to pray?**

Lord Jesus, help me to center myself in your peaceful Presence every day.

May 15

For as Christ's sufferings overflow to us, so through Christ does our encouragement also overflow. — *2 Corinthians 1:5*

One of my favorite movies is *The Wizard of Oz*. I enjoy the Scarecrow, because he speaks to our spiritual journey. The Scarecrow believed he was a failure because he did not have a brain. Failure is a peculiar concept. Is it that we do not measure up to the "standards" of this passing world? More importantly, to whom do we give the power to tell us that we failed? Although at times we might not do our best — or perhaps we did not even try — we are not failures. Has God ever told us that we failed? No. We sin, we stumble and fall, but we are made in the image and likeness of God; we will never be failures. We belong to Jesus Christ, and he encourages us in our every affliction.

We draw strength to overcome our weaknesses each time we encounter Jesus in the Eucharist, who shed his precious Blood on the cross for us out of love. The Eucharistic Presence of Jesus is here to encourage us and restore peace to our souls.

Have you ever felt like a failure? Spend time in prayer reflecting on the spiritual reality that you are made in God's image and likeness.

Lord Jesus, may your Presence in the Eucharist give me the encouragement I need to overcome my afflictions, that I might live in your peace.

May 16

I have told you this so that you might have peace in me. In the world you will have trouble, but take courage, I have conquered the world. — John 16:33

While we live in this broken world, as Christians, we do not belong to this world; we belong to Jesus. Our relationship with Our Lord, forged in his precious Blood, should bring us a sense of peace in the midst of the trials and tribulations happening around us. Jesus never promised life would be easy; he promised he would never leave us to face our crosses alone. Through his death and resurrection, Jesus conquered sin and death. We are people of the Resurrection.

Jesus is present in the Blessed Sacrament, and he desires for us to bring our troubles and concerns to him. We can grow in our spiritual lives by spending time before the Blessed Sacrament and inviting the peace of Christ to wash over us and bring us comfort in the midst of our trials. Jesus is waiting for you. Come, spend time with our beloved Lord.

Do you readily turn over your crosses to the Lord in prayer, seeking to receive his gift of peace?

Lord Jesus, instill within me your gift of everlasting peace.

May 17

Therefore, from the day we heard this, we do not cease praying for you and asking that you may be filled with the knowledge of his will through all spiritual wisdom and understanding. — *Colossians 1:9*

As I write this reflection, I have just received news that one of the deacons in our parish passed away peacefully last night, after a short illness. I pray that Jesus came and took him by the hand, and escorted him into the glorious kingdom of our God and Father. My friend lived a life worthy of Christ. He encouraged all those he met, and would go out of his way to help someone in need. Although there is a sense of sadness today, there is also a great sense of peace, for anyone who knew him believes that he is now with Jesus.

My friend drew his strength for doing ministry from the Eucharist. Each time he assisted at Mass, the Body and Blood of Jesus nourished him, and it gave him great comfort and peace. Today, I rejoice with God for the life of my friend and for all those whom Jesus has called home to be with him. May they experience the peace of the Risen Christ that we all long to share.

Do you routinely pray for the souls of your loved ones, that they might experience the peace of God's kingdom?

Lord Jesus, help us to be filled with the knowledge of your will, that one day we might join you in the glorious kingdom of peace.

May 18

*He said to them, "Come away by yourselves to a deserted
place and rest a while." — Mark 6:31*

Busyness rules our lives, leaving little or no time for rest. Every day, parents juggle school and work schedules, while others of us put long hours in just trying to make ends meet. The hectic pace of daily life takes its toll on not only our physical well-being, but on our spiritual well-being too. In Scripture, Jesus recognized the need for rest, and he invited his disciples to come away to a quiet place so that they could regain their strength and refocus on their mission.

Like the apostles, Jesus encourages us to come away and rest. He desires that we spend quiet time with him before the Blessed Sacrament. When we choose to step away from the busyness of our lives and spend time in quiet prayer, Jesus renews us in grace and helps us to restore peace to our hectic lives.

Where is your place of respite and solitude?

Lord Jesus, help me to take time each day to sit in silence before your loving Presence.

May 19

Who is like you among the gods, O LORD?
Who is like you, magnificent among the holy ones?
Awe-inspiring in deeds of renown, worker of wonders,
when you stretched out your right hand, the earth swallowed them!
In your love you led the people you redeemed;
in your strength you guided them to your holy dwelling. — *Exodus 15:11–13*

All of us, at one time or another, have been rendered speechless by the awe and power and beauty we experience in nature. Whether it is the majestic gorges of the Grand Canyon, the beauty of a full rainbow after a summer's storm, or freshly fallen snow that adorns the bare tree branches in a forest, God reveals his Presence to us in the beauty of creation, and we respond. We gravitate toward beautiful sunsets and sunrises; we find peace in watching the waves of the seas crash upon the shores. The awe and majesty of God is ever present in creation.

Jesus, the only Son of God, who led us to redemption by the Blood of the cross, is truly present to us in the Blessed Sacrament. Each time we come into his Presence, our hearts should overflow with awe and reverence, for we are in the Divine Presence of Jesus. Take time to reflect upon the indescribable wonder of this moment.

Name your most powerful experience of God. How did it touch your heart?

Lord Jesus, may your Presence in the Eucharist fill me with awe and reverence.

May 20

Conduct yourselves in a way worthy of the gospel of Christ, so that, whether I come and see you or am absent, I may hear news of you, that you are standing firm in one spirit, with one mind struggling together for the faith of the gospel. — *Philippians 1:27*

These words of Saint Paul, written to the Philippian community two thousand years ago, speak to us as clearly today. Spiritual warfare is real; as faithful followers of the Gospel of Christ, we can experience spiritual attacks frequently, although we may be unaware of this happening to us. The forces of darkness attempt to destroy our relationship with Jesus; they seek to destroy our faith in the Lord; and they seek to destroy our peace. We must stand firm in our faith.

Receiving Jesus in the Eucharist is the best way to defend ourselves against the forces of evil. Holy Communion unites us to the heart of Christ and safely defends us against spiritual attacks that seek to undermine our faith in God. Jesus is the Prince of Peace, and his loving spirit will help us turn away from sin and stand firm in our faith. Let us come to the table, with hearts seeking spiritual help from Jesus.

Can you name a time when you experienced a spiritual attack on yourself? How did you respond?

Lord Jesus, save me from the forces of darkness that seek to destroy my faith in you.

May 21

Answer me when I call, my saving God.
When troubles hem me in, set me free;
take pity on me, hear my prayer. — Psalm 4:2

Some days, I am afraid to answer the phone; it seems like someone is always calling with bad news. Recently, several friends of mine have become seriously ill, some have required surgery, and others are undergoing treatment. It is an anxious time for everyone involved. I lift them up in prayer every day, and I call upon God to heal them and grant them peace in their times of suffering.

When I am anxious and worried about things, I find great comfort in receiving Communion. My encounter with Jesus in the Eucharist washes away my anxiety. The Lord's peace enfolds me like a blanket, and I rest in his loving care. When troubles come into your life, turn to Jesus in the Eucharist, and open your heart, that you might receive his gift of peace. The Lord hears our prayers and answers them with love and compassion.

Where do you seek peace in the midst of daily trials?

Lord Jesus, help me to trust in your goodness and to receive your gift of everlasting peace.

May 22

Whoever belongs to God hears the words of God. — John 8:47

Many of us have the bad habit of not listening when people are speaking to us. We might be part of the conversation, and might even nod in agreement, but we are not really hearing what people are saying. Our world is so noisy, and peace is elusive. If we do not listen attentively, we will not hear clearly. When Scripture is proclaimed at Mass, some in the pew appear to be listening, and others are actually thinking of what they need to do after Mass. If we do not listen attentively, we will not hear, for there are many distractions to pull us away from the words of God.

Praying before the Blessed Sacrament is a wonderful way for us to develop our listening skills. Jesus is waiting for us to join him in prayer, so that he can place a word on our hearts that can heal, comfort, or encourage us. The spiritual discipline of praying before Jesus in the Blessed Sacrament will help us to grow in our relationship with the Lord. In the silence of the adoration chapel, we have an opportunity to listen as Our Lord communicates with us. If we do not listen, we will never hear.

Do you struggle with actively listening to others? Seek the Lord's help, that you might hear.

Lord Jesus, open the ears of my heart, that I might hear you speaking to me in prayer.

May 23

*And the one who searches hearts knows what is the
intention of the Spirit, because it intercedes for the holy
ones according to God's will.* — Romans 8:27

Many times, we fail to understand the important work that the Holy Spirit accomplishes in our lives. The Spirit is divine; he is the third Person of the Trinity. The Spirit, aware of God's purpose for us, nudges us along life's path, leading and guiding us to cooperate with the plan God has in place for us. The Holy Spirit searches our hearts and intercedes for us before the throne of our Father in heaven.

Our reception of Eucharist opens us to the power of the Holy Spirit, that we might experience spiritual transformation according to God's will. At the Eucharistic banquet, the priest invokes the Holy Spirit to come upon the gifts of bread and wine, transforming them into the Body and Blood of Christ. This miraculous transformation takes place before our eyes at every liturgy. This day, let us come before Our Lord in the Eucharist, seeking his Holy Spirit to transform our lives, that we might become the very mystery we receive.

How often do you pray to the Holy Spirit?

*Lord Jesus, may your Spirit transform me, that I may experience newness of life
that comes from following God's will.*

May 24

May the God of endurance and encouragement grant you to think in harmony with one another, in keeping with Christ Jesus, that with one accord you may with one voice glorify the God and Father of our Lord Jesus Christ. — *Romans 15:5–6*

Peace and harmony are elusive in our culture. We struggle to agree on anything. How will we ever regain our peace and harmony? We need Jesus, for the voices of our world are determined to draw us away from him. When we encounter Our Lord in the Eucharist, we receive the grace to seek peaceful solutions to disagreements.

In becoming the very mystery we receive in the Eucharist, we have an opportunity to imitate the life of Jesus, offering mercy and compassion to others, forgiving those who hurt us, and loving God and our neighbor. Jesus, present in the Eucharist, has the power to heal the spiritual wounds of division that keep us from one another. Let us come before our Eucharistic Lord seeking his gift of peace, that we may live in harmony with one another, glorifying the God and Father of Our Lord Jesus Christ.

Do you struggle with differences of opinion with others? Bring your experiences to the Lord.

Lord Jesus, help me to live in peace and harmony, that my life might give glory to God.

May 25

Now to him who can strengthen you, according to my gospel and the proclamation of Jesus Christ, according to the revelation of the mystery kept secret for long ages but now manifested through the prophetic writings and, according to the command of the eternal God, made known to all nations to bring about the obedience of faith, to the only wise God, through Jesus Christ be glory forever and ever. Amen. — Romans 16:25–27

Mystery stories are fascinating; the storyline keeps you guessing until the very end until everything is revealed, and you think to yourself, "Why didn't I see that?" The mystery of Christ is unfolding before us every day. Do we have the eyes of faith to see his revelation? Or do we stumble in the darkness, searching for a way out of our misery?

When we encounter Jesus in the Eucharist, we receive the grace to be obedient to the Gospel of Jesus which has been made known to the nations. The gift of Jesus in the Eucharist is for the salvation of all people; yet for some, knowledge of Jesus remains a mystery. As we approach the table of the Eucharist, let us pray that the proclamation of the Gospel might touch the hearts of all people, that in the fullness of time, we may be one in Christ Jesus.

Do you know someone who is unfamiliar with the Gospel?

Lord Jesus, may your Eucharist strengthen me in faith, that I might proclaim your Gospel to all I meet.

May 26

Grace to you and peace from God our Father and
the Lord Jesus Christ. — *Ephesians 1:2*

Growing up, I experienced grace as a commodity. In other words, if my soul was running low on grace, I metaphorically went to the sacramental "gas station" to fill up. Now, I have begun to understand grace as relational, meaning that the closer we are to God, the more we are in the state of grace. Grace binds us to the Lord, which produces peace in our lives. The greeting that Saint Paul cites in Scripture is one that wishes us a deep and loving relationship with God our Father and the Lord Jesus Christ.

When we receive Jesus in the Eucharist, the grace of this encounter strengthens our relationship with the Lord and fills our hearts with peace. Jesus is present to us in the consecrated bread and wine. Let us confidently partake of his Body and Blood, that we may be filled with every grace and blessing.

Have you experienced a time when your reception of Communion filled you with profound peace?

Lord Jesus, pour out your grace upon me, that I may deepen my relationship with you.

May 27

Finally, brothers, rejoice. Mend your ways, encourage one another, agree with one another, live in peace, and the God of love and peace will be with you. Greet one another with a holy kiss. All the holy ones greet you. The grace of the Lord Jesus Christ and the love of God and the fellowship of the holy Spirit be with all of you. — 2 Corinthians 13:11–13

Our faith is not a private matter. Saint Paul invites us to put our faith into action by living in communion with one another, and by treating each other with love and respect, because we are brothers and sisters in Christ. When we see someone struggling, we are to offer encouragement, not belittle him or her. If we imitate the life of Christ, and greet others with love and peace, then the grace of Our Lord Jesus Christ, the love of God, and the fellowship of the Holy Spirit will be with us.

Our reception of the Eucharist can help us to see others as Jesus sees them. By offering our hearts to the Lord and seeking to mend our ways, the Real Presence of Jesus can give us the grace to reawaken our sense of belonging to the Body of Christ and help create bonds of love for our fellow Christians.

What is your experience of a community of faith?

Lord Jesus, grant me the grace to live in peace and harmony with my brothers and sisters in Christ.

May 28

I entrust this charge to you, Timothy, my child, in accordance with the prophetic words once spoken about you. Through them may you fight a good fight by having faith and a good conscience. Some, by rejecting conscience, have made a shipwreck of their faith. — *1 Timothy 1:18–19*

Our world has slipped into a coma of conscience. Acts of violence, sins against humanity, and wars have become so common that many people are no longer disturbed by what is happening in our world. They are laser-focused on their own lives and happiness. Where is our intrinsic sense of good and evil? Our consciences should align with our Christian faith and values, so that we may live in peace and harmony with Christ. In his letter to Timothy, Saint Paul reminds us that rejecting a good conscience can be destructive to our faith. We cannot believe in Jesus and live with a conscience that is contrary to our faith in Jesus.

If we struggle with aligning our conscience with the tenets of our Catholic Faith, we should spend time in prayer before the Blessed Sacrament. Jesus is present to us, and he is here to help us discern what is right and wrong, and will give us ways to align our actions with our Faith. Let us turn to him.

How do you justify actions that conflict with our Catholic Faith?

Lord Jesus, help me to live with a clear conscience, that I may faithfully serve you all the days of my life.

May 29

*Whoever would love life
and see good days
must keep the tongue from evil
and the lips from speaking deceit,
must turn from evil and do good,
seek peace and follow after it.* — 1 Peter 3:10–11

In our Catholic tradition, we believe that if we are fearful, or in need of something, we should call upon the name of Jesus in prayer, for "every knee should bend, / of those in heaven and on earth" (Phil 2:20) at the sound of his name. Nowadays, the name of our Redeemer finds itself battered around in foul and slanderous talk; routinely used in exclaiming excitement or amazement. The third commandment tells us not to take the name of God in vain, yet we continue to do so.

When we receive Jesus in the Eucharist, we encounter the Real Presence of Our Lord, who has the power to help us remove this kind of speaking from our tongue. Jesus, the Prince of Peace, is waiting for us to seek his help. Let us come before Jesus in the Eucharist, asking him for the grace to speak words of goodness and love, affirmation and mercy, and never to use his name in vain as we strive to live as people of peace.

Do you frequently use the name of Jesus in your speech when angry or upset?

Lord Jesus, please forgive me using your name in vain. Help me to call upon your holy name reverently in times of need.

May 30

Keep on doing what you have learned and received and heard and seen in me. Then the God of peace will be with you. — Philippians 4:9

The words *tinsel, silent,* and *listen* are composed of the same six letters of the alphabet, yet each of the three words has very distinct meanings. Most of us live in a tinsel environment. Our lives are driven by the crackling tinsel sounds of overly committed schedules, cell phones that disturb our peace with rings, beeps, or tweets, and the internet at our fingertips. Rearranging the letters from *tinsel* to create *silent* reminds us to seek out peace and quiet. Resting in silent moments of prayer affords us the opportunity to listen. So much of life is tinsel chatter, but it is vital for our spiritual lives to step away from the madness of tinsel to become silent, that we may *listen* with new ears.

Making Jesus a priority involves frequently stepping away from our tinsel existence so as to enter into the silent space of adoration, where we have a graced opportunity to listen as the Lord speaks to us. Today, take time to enter into silent prayer before our Eucharistic Lord, that you may listen and reflect on what you have learned and received and heard from God, for then the peace of Christ will be with you.

Can you take a few minutes today to pray in silence?

Lord Jesus, help me to listen to your life-giving words, that I may have peace.

May 31

May the saving sacrifice of your Son, the King of peace,
offered under sacramental signs that signify peace and unity,
strengthen, we pray, O Lord,
concord among all your children. — Prayer over the Offerings,
Mass for the Preservation of Peace and Justice

Peace is elusive, if not absent, in our world. As people of goodwill, it is difficult for us to stay hopeful when we watch the news on television, and day after day, there are multiple stories of shootings, robberies, and acts of violence against innocent people. At times like this, we must stay razor focused on our relationship with Jesus, for he is the King of Peace, and he will triumph over evil.

Jesus is present in the Eucharist, and as we partake of his Body and Blood, we recommit ourselves to working for peace and unity among all of God's children. We cannot bring about peace in our broken world without Jesus. His grace, given to us in the Eucharist, strengthens us to live each day in harmony with our neighbor. Let us offer our lives to the Lord, that we may foster concord among all the children of God.

Is it difficult for you to live in peace with others? Why?

Lord Jesus, may your Eucharistic Presence lead me to live in peace and harmony with all people.

~ LOVE ~

June 1

This is the chalice of my blood, the blood of the new and eternal covenant, which will be poured out for you and for many for the forgiveness of sins. — Institution Narrative, Eucharistic Prayer II

On St. Patrick's Day, my Irish friend proudly wears a T-shirt inscribed with the phrase "Beer is proof that God loves us." While this humorous sentiment may resonate with many of us, I think a more suitable phrase might be "The Eucharist is proof that God loves us," for it is in the Eucharist that we encounter a tangible expression of God's unconditional love for each one of us.

Sometimes, we forget how much God loves us. We try to limit his bountiful mercy and love to our human standards, which are flawed and imperfect. Each time we receive the Eucharist, we have a wonderful opportunity to give thanks to God for the gift of his only Son, Jesus, who suffered and died, that our covenant relationship be restored. The Lord invites us to come to the table to eat and drink of his Body and Blood, that we may experience the fountain of his mercy, love, and compassion.

Are there areas in your life where you feel unworthy of God's love?

Jesus, help us to grow in our awareness of your loving Presence in the Eucharist.

June 2

Jesus said to Simon Peter, "Simon, son of John, do you love me more than these?" He said to him, "Yes, Lord, you know that I love you." He said to him, "Feed my lambs." He then said to him a second time, "Simon, son of John, do you love me?" He said to him, "Yes, Lord, you know that I love you." He said to him, "Tend my sheep." He said to him the third time, "Simon, son of John, do you love me?" Peter was distressed that he had said to him a third time, "Do you love me?" and he said to him, "Lord, you know everything; you know that I love you." [Jesus] said to him, "Feed my sheep." — John 21:15–17

After Simon Peter's poignant profession of love, Jesus responds by lovingly entrusting the care and feeding of his followers into the hands of Peter. We, too, are disciples of Christ, and each time we come to the Eucharistic table, Jesus spiritually poses the same question and answer to us: "Do you love me?" "Feed my sheep." Our encounter with Jesus in the Eucharist gives us the courage to follow the Lord's commandment.

Who is Jesus asking you to love and care for this day? How will you respond to the Lord's request?

Jesus, may my encounter with you in the Eucharist strengthen me to lovingly serve others in your name.

June 3

Everyone serves good wine first, and then when people have drunk freely, an inferior one; but you have kept the good wine until now. — John 2:10

Jesus performed many miracles in the Gospels, but perhaps his most well-known miracle — even among those who are not Christian — is turning water into wine. This miraculous event took place at a wedding that Jesus, his mother, and apostles were attending. From the guest list, we can surmise that this was a close friend or family member getting married. It must have been a great wedding if the wine ran out. At the behest of his mother, Mary, and out of love for the bridal couple, Jesus changed water into wine so that celebration could continue. This miracle clearly demonstrates the great love and affection that Jesus has for God's people.

Jesus loves us, and if we turn to him for help and guidance, he can turn our scarcity into abundance. Each time we come to the Eucharistic table, Jesus is waiting to transform the muddied waters of our life into pure, choice wine. He desires to bless us abundantly in ways we could never imagine. Let us bring ourselves before the Eucharistic Presence of Jesus, that we may taste and see the goodness of the Lord.

What are some ways your life has been abundantly enriched by the love of Jesus?

Lord Jesus, your love is unconditional. Thank you for blessing me abundantly in ways I can never explain.

June 4

*"I have given you a model to follow, so that as I have done
for you, you should also do." — John 13:15*

At Christmas time, many of us receive greeting cards with typed letters from our friends outlining everything that has happened in their family in the past year. Yet, if they are our friends, shouldn't we already know all of this information? We are losing the personal touch with those we love. Our overscheduled calendars and busy lives are keeping us from loving one another, from being present to those we care about.

Our mission in life is to become the very mystery we receive. Throughout the Gospels, Jesus ministered to people with tender care. He lovingly forgave people of their sins, healed them of their infirmities, and transformed their lives. He has given us a model to follow. Jesus calls us to care for the needs of our friends and family in whatever capacity that entails. In becoming the Body of Christ, we become a new creation; we become spiritual nourishment for all those who long for God. Let us minister to our family and friends this day with love.

Who needs your help and attention this day? Reach out with love and assist them.

Lord Jesus, help me to follow your example of being in loving service to all those you place in my life.

June 5

If there is any encouragement in Christ, any solace in love, any participation in the Spirit, and compassion and mercy, complete my joy by being of the same mind, with the same love, united in heart, thinking one thing. — Philippians 2:1–2

At times, we have all felt unworthy and unloved. Perhaps these negative feelings are the result of a bad relationship or poor self-image. Our Creator God loves us, and nothing we can do or say will change God's love for us. His love is so immense that he sent his only Son, Jesus, to save us. On the night before Jesus died, he gave us the gift of himself in the Eucharist that he might be with us for all time. What great love Jesus has for you and me!

The love of Christ Jesus that awaits us at the altar can transform our darkness into light, our sadness into joy. We simply need to receive him in faith and grace. United with the heart of Jesus, when we receive the Eucharist we are filled with Christ's mercy and compassion, helping us to experience God's love each day.

Do you struggle with feelings of unworthiness? Seek the Lord's Eucharistic love to help you and to heal you.

Lord Jesus, may your Eucharistic Presence fill me with your abiding grace and everlasting love.

June 6

Beloved, let us love one another, because love is of God; everyone who loves is begotten by God and knows God. ... In this way the love of God was revealed to us: God sent his only Son into the world so that we might have life through him. In this is love: not that we have loved God, but that he loved us and sent his Son as expiation for our sins. Beloved, if God so loved us, we also must love one another. — 1 John 4:7–11

We are all guilty of misusing the word *love*. How often have you said, "I love ice cream," or "I love to travel," or "I love this movie"? Our culture has exploited the true meaning of love, diluting it to enjoyment of pleasure, rather than a profound and selfless act of caring for another.

Jesus on the cross shows us the depths of God's love for us. We experience this profound gift of divine love each time we share the Eucharistic banquet. As we partake of Christ's Body and Blood, broken and poured out for us, may we in turn pour out our lives in loving service to our brothers and sisters in Christ.

How have you experienced God's love today?

Lord Jesus, you revealed God's love for us through the sacrifice of the cross. Help me to love others, as you love me.

June 7

God proves his love for us in that while we were still sinners Christ died for us. How much more then, since we are now justified by his blood, will we be saved through him from the wrath. — Romans 5:8–9

Parents love their children unconditionally. Parental love does not fluctuate based on a child's behavior; rather, it is an unbreakable bond between parent and child. So, too, our relationship with God. While we were still sinners, God our Father, out of love for us, sent his only Son, Jesus, to restore our covenant relationship, that we may have eternal life. What great love God has for his children!

We experience the unfathomable depths of the Father's love through Jesus each time we receive the Eucharist. As we partake of the Eucharistic Body and Blood of Christ, we reaffirm our loving relationship with God our Father. Christ, the only Son of God, shed his innocent Blood for us. May we approach the Eucharistic table of sacrifice with hearts filled with gratitude and love for the gift of salvation given to us by our heavenly Father.

How can you show love today to God and to those around you?

Lord Jesus, help me to live each day as a beloved child of God. May my actions always reflect my great love for you.

June 8

"Teacher, which commandment in the law is the greatest?" He said to him, "You shall love the Lord, your God, with all your heart, with all your soul, and with all your mind. This is the greatest and the first commandment. The second is like it: You shall love your neighbor as yourself. — Matthew 22:36–40

The first and greatest commandment — to love God with our whole hearts — is one that most people of faith try to follow. The second commandment, which calls us to love our neighbor as ourselves, appears problematic. How so? The rise in violent crimes, including mass shootings, points to a reality that our modern culture fails to love our neighbor as ourselves. In fact, there is little or no respect for life. How can we reorient our focus from one of violence to one of love of neighbor? Jesus is the way.

The Eucharist is the premier sacrament of love, for when we partake of the Eucharistic bread and wine, we encounter Jesus, who calls us to love God and one another. When we dine at the table of the Lord, we spiritually give our assent to follow all that Jesus has commanded, including this second great commandment. Let us approach the altar with hearts seeking to follow the Lord's commandments of love.

What is more difficult, love of God or love of neighbor? Why?

Lord Jesus, help me to live each day in the light of your love.

June 9

*So faith, hope, love remain, these three; but the greatest
of these is love. — 1 Corinthians 13:13*

Love is a powerful emotion; it has the ability to influence the decisions we make and even the way we live our lives. Often, we confuse the word *love* with the term *loyalty*, and we speak as if these terms are interchangeable. For example, if we love a particular sports team, we will jeer at the opposing team because we are loyal to our team. Loyalty in this sense can be controlling, and it has the ability to stir up feelings of guilt, because we do not want to be disloyal. While loyalty may be a precursor to love, it is not love. With love, there is no guilt, there is no need to control; for God is love, and love never fails.

On the night before he died, Jesus instituted the gift of his unconditional love in the Eucharistic elements of bread and wine, commanding us to do this loving action in memory of him. When we encounter Jesus in the Eucharist, he fills our hearts with pure love, and sends us into the world to share this gift of divine love with others.

How do you perceive the difference between love and loyalty?

Lord Jesus, help me to experience your gift of love when I come to the Eucharistic table.

June 10

*Above all, let your love for one another be intense, because
love covers a multitude of sins. Be hospitable to one
another without complaining. — 1 Peter 4:8–9*

Growing up, we ate dinner together every night as a family. My
mom cooked simple meals, and she would serve dinner family-style.
When we passed the serving plate of food to my mom, she would always take the smallest piece of meat, the wing of the chicken, or just the
broth of the soup. She sacrificed her desires for the good of her family.
She never complained, and her love for us was immense. My mom was
a lot like Jesus.

Love is the strongest of all emotions, and Jesus clearly demonstrated
his great love for you and me when he took upon himself the sins of the
world. There is no greater love than to lay down one's life for a friend.
Jesus loves us intensely, and his gift of love is waiting for us in the Eucharist. In the consecrated elements of bread and wine, we encounter
the pure love of Jesus, who poured out his life for us. Our participation
in the Eucharistic banquet showers us with the grace and strength to
dedicate our lives to the One who willingly died for us.

What sacrifice can you make to the Lord today?

*Lord Jesus, thank you for your immense act of love. May the Eucharist draw us
closer to your Sacred Heart.*

June 11

All the brothers greet you. Greet one another with a holy kiss. I, Paul, write you this greeting in my own hand. If anyone does not love the Lord, let him be accursed. ... The grace of the Lord Jesus be with you. My love to all of you in Christ Jesus. — *1 Corinthians 16:20–24*

One of the most difficult things families can experience is separation from the ones we love. Military families know this, as their loved ones serve in foreign lands. When we are sick, it is emotionally painful to sacrifice holiday celebrations with our families; yet we do it out of love and concern for everyone's well-being. Separation is most difficult, because we are used to expressing love through the physical contact of hugs and kisses. In his letter to the Corinthians, St. Paul encourages us to greet one another with a holy kiss, because we are brothers and sisters in Christ; our love for Jesus unites us as the family of God.

The Eucharist also unites us in love with Jesus and our brothers and sisters in Christ. When we partake of the Body and Blood of Jesus, we encounter Our Lord, who expressed his profound love for us by sacrificing his life that we may have eternal life. Love unites us to Jesus and to all those who love him.

What feelings do you experience when separated from the ones you love? Offer these emotions up to the Lord.

Lord Jesus, help us to recognize and respond to your Presence in our brothers and sisters in Christ.

June 12

Love is patient, love is kind. It is not jealous, [love] is not pompous, it is not inflated, it is not rude, it does not seek its own interests, it is not quick-tempered, it does not brood over injury, it does not rejoice over wrongdoing but rejoices with the truth. It bears all things, believes all things, hopes all things, endures all things. Love never fails. — 1 Corinthians 13:4–8

These verses are the most eloquent in the Bible, for they perfectly describe the life of Jesus through the lens of love. If we are to imitate Our Lord, then our pattern of behavior should reflect the explanation of love in this passage. Love, in its purest form, is an action that focuses on the well-being of another. It is not self-centered, nor does it assume perfection on the part of the other.

We experience the gift of the pure love of Jesus when we receive Eucharist. In an act of selfless love, Jesus gave his life on the cross for us; and before he died, he passed on to us the gift of his pure love mediated in the elements of bread and wine. May we approach the altar with hearts open to receiving this gift of divine love.

How have you experienced the pure love of Jesus?

Lord Jesus, your entire life is a reflection of love. Help me to love others as you have loved me.

June 13

Jesus, however, called the children to himself and said, "Let the children come to me and do not prevent them; for the kingdom of God belongs to such as these." — Luke 18:16

After my children made their first holy Communion, they enjoyed counting each time they went to Mass and received Eucharist. They looked forward to their second Communion, third Communion, fourth Communion, and so on. Finally, we lost count because going to Mass and receiving the Eucharist were part of the fabric of our Sunday family routine. My children always felt welcome at the Lord's table.

Unlike other sacraments, which we receive only once, or periodically, the Sacrament of the Eucharist is here for us to receive every day of our lives. Jesus' love for us is so great that he gave us his life in the elements of bread and wine, that we would never hunger or thirst again. His Body and Blood are spiritual nourishment for our journey to heaven. As children of the Lord, let us come to Jesus in the Eucharist as often as we can, for the kingdom of God belongs to such as these.

How can you help the children in your life draw closer to Jesus in the Eucharist?

Lord Jesus, we are your children. Help us to feel welcome to come to you with all of our needs.

June 14

And that Christ may dwell in your hearts through faith, that you, rooted and grounded in love, may have strength to comprehend with all the holy ones what is the breadth and length and height and depth. — Ephesians 3:17–18

Have you ever driven through the redwood forests in northern California or viewed pictures of the sequoias? These giant trees have stood for hundreds of years, and their root systems are massive. They can withstand any storm. St. Paul reminds us that our faith in Christ is likened to a tree, and our faith must be rooted and grounded in love, so that we may fully live out our lives as followers of Christ. Love is the essential nutrient that feeds our Christian faith.

The Eucharist is love, and it is our nourishment in life. The presence of Jesus we receive in the Eucharistic bread and wine feeds our souls with the essential nutrients of love, stabilizing our faith and trust in God. Jesus' love for us is endless. Let us approach the altar with open hearts seeking to receive Christ's gift of love, that our faith may grow strong.

How can I deepen my roots of love for God and my neighbor?

Lord Jesus, pour out your divine love upon me, that I may comprehend with all the holy ones the depth of your love for humanity.

June 15

If anyone says, "I love God," but hates his brother, he is a liar; for whoever does not love a brother whom he has seen cannot love God whom he has not seen. This is the commandment we have from him: whoever loves God must also love his brother. — *1 John 4:20–21*

The words of this Scripture give us good reason to pause and do some soul-searching. Why do we often find it easier to say, "I love God," whom we have not physically seen, while we exhibit contempt toward our neighbors, co-workers, and family members, who we see each day? The spiritual reality is that God is in every single person; we *do* see the Lord every day. He is present in the homeless person living on the street, and in the annoying neighbor who lives next door. How are we to love those who are made in the image of God?

Our encounter with Jesus in the Eucharist can help us overcome our lack of charity toward our brothers and sisters. Jesus is pure love, and when we partake of his Body and Blood, his love can help us see others in a new light. Let us receive his transforming love.

Do you struggle with loving your neighbor as yourself?

Lord Jesus, help me to see your Presence in the faces of those I meet each day, that I may love them as I love you.

June 16

For this is love, that we walk according to his commandments;
this is the commandment, as you heard from the beginning,
in which you should walk. — 2 John 6

At times, we burden ourselves with countless rules and regulations to the point that the pure essence of the Gospel is almost lost. Jesus gave us two commandments: love God above all else, and love our neighbor as ourselves. It is that simple, and yet humanity has made it so complicated. Today, let us peel back our faith to reveal the pure essence of loving God and our neighbor. Who will be the recipient of your love and concern today? How will your actions demonstrate your love for God this day?

One of the most fruitful ways we can show our love for the Lord is to spend time with Jesus in the Blessed Sacrament. Here, in the solitude of the adoration chapel, Jesus waits for you, and he showers you with his love the moment you walk into his Presence. This day, put these two commandments of love into action, as you offer love and kindness to those you meet, and to offer your heart to Jesus.

How will the simplicity of this rule of love affect your life today?

Lord Jesus, help me to wrap my entire day in love of neighbor and love of God.

June 17

In the morning let me hear of your mercy,
for in you I trust.
Show me the path I should walk,
for I entrust my life to you. — *Psalm 143:8*

Years ago, when I was trying to develop a deeper daily prayer life, I created what I call "prayer triggers." In other words, I took routine tasks that I did each day and attached a prayer to each one; for example, when I make my morning coffee, I thank God for the safety of my home. When I sit down at the computer, I thank God for the gift of technology. It took some spiritual discipline on my part, but now my entire day is wrapped in prayer. Before my feet hit the ground in the morning, I thank the Lord for the gift of this day and the abundant blessings it will hold, and I ask him to show me the path I should walk this day. I entrust my life into his hands.

When we spend time in prayer before the Blessed Sacrament, the Lord is present to listen to our concerns, and to answer our prayers with love and mercy. Jesus is waiting for us to come to him, and to spend even five minutes with him. With love, Jesus will show us the path he has planned for us. Let us entrust our lives to him.

Do you find it difficult to pray throughout your day?

Lord Jesus, thank you for the gift of your enduring love that leads and guides me every day of my life.

June 18

Rather, when you hold a banquet, invite the poor, the crippled, the lame, the blind; blessed indeed will you be because of their inability to repay you. For you will be repaid at the resurrection of the righteous. — Luke 14:13–14

So much of what we do for others might not have the best of intentions. We might give someone a gift in the hopes that we will receive a gift in return; or perhaps we do a favor for another, knowing that we can receive a favor in return. We call this type of behavior *quid pro quo*, and it is a reciprocity of giving and receiving. This is not the kind of giving that Jesus speaks of in the Gospel. Giving is its own reward. In other words, we are to give kindness to others, to assist those in need, and to care for the poor without expecting any compensation in return. This kind of selfless conduct on our part takes grace, for it is difficult to act this way on our own.

The grace we receive in the Eucharist can help shift our attention onto the needs of others, and not our own self-interests. In the Eucharist, Jesus gives us the vision to see those in need and the courage to help them, without expecting anything in return.

What are your motives when you lend a helping hand?

Lord Jesus, help me to serve others in your name, without expecting any compensation in return.

June 19

No one can serve two masters. He will either hate one and love the other, or be devoted to one and despise the other. — *Matthew 6:24*

God has given us everything we need in life. He has blessed us with bountiful gifts and blessings. Unfortunately, our enjoyment of material goods often takes precedence over our relationship with God, resulting in our being enslaved to our personal passions, addictions, and need for money and power. Jesus warns us that we cannot serve two masters. We need to choose who we will love and serve in this life. We need to choose life over death.

The Eucharist is our spiritual nourishment. It is our strength for overcoming the pitfalls of this passing world. As we partake of the Body and Blood of Christ, the life-giving presence of Jesus fills our heart and helps us to refocus our priorities. Jesus is present in the Eucharist, and he desires for us to love and serve him every day of our lives.

Who is the master of your life?

Lord Jesus, strengthen me in faith, that I may place my love for you above all else in my life.

June 20

For the whole law is fulfilled in one statement, namely, "You shall love your neighbor as yourself." — Galatians 5:14

Shortly after my parents passed away, I was at the monument store with my two young children ordering my parents' gravestone. It was a hot summer day. After finishing my transaction, the kids and I got back into the car — and it would not start. This was before cell phones, so the kids and I walked to the local drug store to use the public phone. I called my husband, but he did not answer his pager. Stranded, we returned to the monument store to cool off. The shopkeeper asked me what was wrong, and I told him. He immediately went into the back room and came out with the keys to his car. He said, "Use my car and take your kids home." I was speechless, and I will never forget his kindness. For me, this was the fulfillment of the law "You shall love your neighbor as yourself."

When we pattern our life after that of Jesus, miraculous things can happen. Kindness grows, love flourishes, and people care about one another. Each time we partake of the Eucharist, we receive Jesus, who pours his love into our hearts that we may imitate his life of love for others.

Have you ever gone out of your way to help a stranger?

Lord Jesus, help me to be ready and willing to help all those you send my way.

June 21

Love does no evil to the neighbor; hence, love is the
fulfillment of the law. — Romans 13:10

Organ donors are people who are willing to donate one of their organs to a complete stranger in order to save the life of this person. These individuals are acting out of sacrificial love for neighbor, with no expectations in return. They are examples of the love that Jesus speaks of in the Gospels. God is pure love, and it is impossible for us to truly love God and not love our neighbor as well. Jesus came into this world to reestablish God's covenant of love with humanity; a covenant which had been severed by sin. Jesus, in fulfillment of the law of love, instituted the Eucharist, that his love would be with us for all time.

Our participation in the Eucharistic banquet fills us with the unconditional love of Jesus and helps us to redirect our actions toward loving our neighbor as ourselves. The grace we receive in Communion strengthens our ability to think and act in love. Let us bring our hearts to Christ at this Eucharistic table, that he may pour out his pure love into our lives.

In what ways can you live with charity in your heart for all people?

Lord Jesus, help me to follow your example of loving God and my neighbor as myself.

June 22

*Whoever eats my flesh and drinks my blood has eternal life,
and I will raise him on the last day. For my flesh is true food,
and my blood is true drink. Whoever eats my flesh and drinks
my blood remains in me and I in him. — John 6:54–56*

Communion with Jesus is an intimate and loving encounter with our risen Lord. When we eat of the bread of life and drink from the chalice of salvation, we are receiving inside us the sacramental, Real Presence of Jesus, who sacrificed his life on the cross for the forgiveness of our sins. Many of us have lost the sense of the Real Presence of Jesus, and our experience of Communion has been diminished to a mere symbolic representation of the Last Supper. Nothing could be further from the truth. In Jesus' own words, we have his testimony, "Whoever eats my flesh and drinks my blood remains in me and I in him." The Eucharist is the Real Presence of Jesus, given to us out of love.

If you struggle with belief in the Real Presence, seek his mystical Presence each time you partake at the altar. Reception of the Eucharist will transform your life into the very mystery that you receive; that you are the living Body of Christ, consecrated and holy.

What does the Eucharist mean to you?

Lord Jesus, may the Eucharist be my spiritual sustenance and bring me to eternal life.

June 23

Before the feast of Passover, Jesus knew that his hour had come to pass from this world to the Father. He loved his own in the world and he loved them to the end. The devil had already induced Judas, son of Simon the Iscariot, to hand him over. So, during supper, fully aware that the Father had put everything into his power and that he had come from God and was returning to God, he rose from supper and took off his outer garments. He took a towel and tied it around his waist. — John 13:1–4

Jesus loved his disciples until the end. On the night before he died, fully aware that Judas would betray him, Jesus took a towel and washed the feet of his betrayer alongside those of his faithful apostles. He made no distinctions, washing the feet of all who were present in the Upper Room.

Each time we come to the altar, Jesus challenges us to model our lives after his. We are to love as Jesus loves, and to serve the needs of all people, friends and strangers alike. We draw our strength for mission from our encounter with Jesus in the Eucharist.

Do you struggle with offering loving service to certain groups of people?

Lord Jesus, help me to love and serve all people, for they are made in the image and likeness of our God.

June 24

They devoted themselves to the teaching of the apostles and to the communal life, to the breaking of the bread and to the prayers. — Acts 2:42

The Church comprises a community of believers who devote themselves to following the teachings of Christ. We are not individuals who journey alone on our private spiritual pathways; we are here to love and support one another. Our shared belief in the Eucharist unites us as one family of faith that gathers to celebrate the Eucharist in remembrance of Jesus who died for our sins.

The love of Jesus that we receive in the Eucharist empowers us to reach out to the needy members of our parish and community, and to mentor others in the Faith. We belong to a community of believers, and through our reception of Eucharist, we can collectively devote ourselves to the teachings of Christ and to breaking bread with our neighbors.

Do you actively participate in the life of your parish, or do you prefer to keep your faith a private matter?

Lord Jesus, help me to be a loving member of my parish family, that I may serve others in your name.

June 25

> *Then Moses stretched out his hand over the sea; and the* LORD *drove back the sea with a strong east wind all night long and turned the sea into dry ground. The waters were split, so that the Israelites entered into the midst of the sea on dry land, with the water as a wall to their right and to their left.* — *Exodus 14:21–22*

The beloved Scripture story of Moses and the Israelites passing through the Red Sea, as they fled enslavement from the Egyptians, calls to mind God's enduring love for his people. Like the Israelites, we often find ourselves enslaved to sin, and through the death and resurrection of Jesus, God has led us through the waters of hopelessness to a new life in Christ. We have crossed over to the land of salvation, having been redeemed by the Blood of the innocent Lamb of God.

When we encounter Jesus in the Eucharist, we experience the fullness of redemption won for us by Christ. The Body and Blood of Jesus that we receive in the Eucharist strengthens us to turn away from sin and readies our steps to follow Our Lord to the new life that awaits us. Let us come before Our Lord with hearts ready to cross over from sin to the glory of a life in Christ.

In what ways do you feel enslaved to sin?

Lord Jesus, may your Eucharist lead me safely through the waters of life.

June 26

In the morning there was a layer of dew all about the camp, and when the layer of dew evaporated, fine flakes were on the surface of the wilderness, fine flakes like hoarfrost on the ground. On seeing it, the Israelites asked one another, "What is this?" for they did not know what it was. But Moses told them, "It is the bread which the LORD has given you to eat." — Exodus 16:13–15

God has always provided for his people. In the Old Testament, Our Lord sent manna each morning as food for the Israelites. They trusted in God to provide for them, and he was ever faithful.

Jesus is ever faithful to us, and the consecrated bread that we eat at Mass provides us with food for our spiritual journey. Jesus gives us His flesh to eat and His precious Blood to drink. The Eucharist is our spiritual food for eternal life, for Jesus promised that "whoever eats my flesh and drinks my blood has eternal life" (Jn 6:54). The living bread that Jesus gives us is his flesh for the life of the world.

In what ways can the Eucharistic Lord feed your spirit today?

Lord Jesus, thank you for giving us your Body and Blood as food for our spiritual journey. May your Eucharist nourish me and lead me to the gates of heaven.

June 27

Now the men there numbered about five thousand. Then he said to his disciples, "Have them sit down in groups of [about] fifty." They did so and made them all sit down. Then taking the five loaves and the two fish, and looking up to heaven, he said the blessing over them, broke them, and gave them to the disciples to set before the crowd. — Luke 9:14–16

There is an old saying, "Many hands make light work." In other words, the more people we have helping with a project, the more easily things can be done. We all know this to be true, and Jesus understood it as well. At this miraculous meal, Jesus had the people sit in groups of fifty, then he took the loaves and fishes, said the blessing, and then gave the pieces of bread and fish to the disciples to set before the crowd. Jesus fed the thousands with the help of his heavenly Father and his apostles. Our Lord invites us to help him, too.

Jesus needs our voices and our hands to accomplish his work in our world. When we receive his Body and Blood at the Eucharistic table, Jesus nourishes us with the graces needed to love and care for all those he sends our way. Let us receive this grace with open hearts and hands.

How might you nourish another's soul today?

Lord Jesus, help me to share your message of love with my family and friends, and all those you send my way.

June 28

I am the bread of life. Your ancestors ate the manna in the desert, but they died; this is the bread that comes down from heaven so that one may eat it and not die. I am the living bread that came down from heaven; whoever eats this bread will live forever; and the bread that I will give is my flesh for the life of the world. — John 6:48–51

As human beings, we need the two basic elements of water and food to survive. In this Gospel passage, Jesus reminds his disciples that their ancestors ate the manna from heaven, but they still died. Jesus tells them that he is the bread of life, sent from heaven, and anyone who eats this bread will live forever. What Jesus means is that — just like ordinary food and water, but in a more profound way — we cannot live without him. He is our spiritual sustenance needed to survive. Jesus sacrificed his flesh for the life of the world.

Each time we come to the Eucharistic table, we receive Jesus, the bread of life, whose life fulfills all of our spiritual desires. Partaking of the Real Presence of Jesus fills us with the spiritual nourishment we need to live in this world as faithful and loving disciples of Jesus.

How can the Eucharist nourish your spiritual life?

Lord Jesus, may the Eucharist fill me with your life-giving Spirit, that I may never hunger or thirst again.

June 29

It is the spirit that gives life, while the flesh is of no avail. The words I have spoken to you are spirit and life. — John 6:63

Our bodies are truly temples of the Holy Spirit that enable us to move and have our being in this physical world. The Holy Spirit gives us life, and prompts us to do the work of God through the words we speak and the actions we accomplish. The work of God is firmly rooted in loving the Lord above all else, and our neighbor as ourselves.

At the Last Supper, in an act of love, Jesus took bread into his holy hands, said the blessing, and broke the bread, saying, "Take and eat; this is my body" (Mt 26:26). In a similar manner, Jesus took a chalice filled with wine, said the blessing, and shared the chalice, saying, "This is my blood of the covenant, which will be shed on behalf of many for the forgiveness of sins" (v. 28). At this moment, the earthly gifts of bread and wine were transformed by the power of the Holy Spirit into his Body and Blood. When we partake of the Eucharist, we experience the transforming love of Jesus poured out for us for all eternity.

What is your understanding of the Holy Spirit?

Lord Jesus, may the Eucharist I receive fill me with your Spirit of truth and life.

June 30

A person should examine himself, and so eat the bread and drink the cup. For anyone who eats and drinks without discerning the body, eats and drinks judgment on himself. — *1 Corinthians 11:28–29*

I met a woman estranged from her family, who confided that she had not seen her parents or siblings in years. Differences in lifestyle choices had built a wall of separation between them. One day, to her amazement, she received an invitation to her sibling's wedding, and she struggled to decide whether she should attend or not. While she was still part of the family, she had not had a relationship with them for years, and now felt like an outsider. The invitation was a gesture of love and reconciliation from her family. She seized the opportunity and returned to her loved ones.

We are all part of God's family, yet if we have been living our lives without Jesus, how can we partake of him? The Eucharist is a sacrament of love. Jesus invites us to reconcile with and return to him that we may enjoy his Presence in the Eucharist. When we eat and drink of the Body and Blood of Christ, our hearts should be in a loving relationship with Our Lord. His love invites us to the table; may our hearts be ready to accept his invitation.

Do you feel alienated from Our Lord? Seek his forgiveness and love.

Lord Jesus, help me to receive you into my heart with love.

~ FORGIVENESS ~

July 1

Behold the Lamb of God; behold him who takes away the sins of the world. Blessed are those called to the supper of the Lamb. Lord, I am not worthy that you should enter under my roof, but only say the word and my soul shall be healed. — Invitation to Communion

Do we understand the significance of what we are saying at each Mass when we recite these words? Jesus is the Word-made-Flesh. He is the Lamb of God who suffered and died for our sins. The once-and-for-all perfect sacrifice of Christ has saved us.

It is important for us to seek forgiveness from God and from one another when we sin. It is equally important for us to believe that God has forgiven us, if we have confessed our sins and we are sorry. As human beings, we are so hard on ourselves, remembering only our imperfections and our past sins. Our reception of Jesus in the Eucharist gives us the wisdom and grace to experience forgiveness, for Jesus, the Lamb of God, gave his life for us, and we believe we are healed.

Do you struggle with believing God has forgiven you? Spend some time in front of the Blessed Sacrament asking the Lord for the grace of repentance, reconciliation, and spiritual healing.

Jesus, may my Eucharistic encounter heal me of my imperfections and give me the grace to sin no more.

July 2

*If one has a grievance against another; as the Lord has
forgiven you, so must you also do. — Colossians 3:13*

Years ago while driving down a gravel road, I came across a little
country church, with a road sign that said, "Bless your enemies: After
all, you created them." While humorous at first, this powerful statement
invites us to reflection. God has given us the gift of free will; we have
the freedom to choose our friends, and to choose our enemies. Our life
with Christ, however, calls us to choose a pathway of forgiveness and
reconciliation, not alienation.

As Jesus took his last breath on the cross, he cried out, "Father, forgive them, they know not what they do" (Lk 23:24). If Our Lord can
forgive those who crucified him, who are we to withhold forgiveness
from another? Our participation in the Eucharistic banquet strengthens
us to follow the way of Jesus, and not the ways of this world; to forgive
as we have been forgiven. Our challenge is not to bless our enemies, but
to forgive them so that they are no longer enemies, but friends.

May the Real Presence of Christ in the Eucharist give us the grace
to forgive all those we have a grievance against.

Do you desire the grace to forgive others? Ask Jesus to help you.

Lord Jesus, help me to offer mercy and compassion to all who have hurt me.

July 3

He reclined at table with the Twelve. And while they were eating, he said, "Amen, I say to you, one of you will betray me." — Matthew 26:20–21

The Last Supper was the culmination of three years of public ministry in which Jesus healed the sick, forgave sinners, and transformed the lives of people. While gathered at table with his trusted apostles the night before he died, Jesus announces that one of them would betray him. In a strange twist of faith, it is not only Judas, but all of the apostles, except John, who betray Jesus by abandoning him at his crucifixion. It is in this context of sin and betrayal that Jesus institutes the Eucharist.

The Eucharist is a sacrament of healing. The unconditional love Jesus has for his people remains a mystery beyond our human comprehension. To this day, Jesus continues to invite the betrayers, the sinful, the pompous, and the broken to dine at his table. Our crucified Lord lovingly offers us the mystery of his Body and Blood, shed for the forgiveness of sins, to all who believe in him. Let us seek his mercy and forgiveness as we come to the table of the Lord.

When in your life have you betrayed Jesus? Take a moment and pray for the grace of forgiveness.

Lord Jesus, forgive me for the times I have betrayed you. May your Eucharistic Body and Blood heal me and lead me to life everlasting.

July 4

Now one of the criminals hanging there reviled Jesus, saying, "Are you not the Messiah? Save yourself and us." The other, however, rebuking him, said in reply, "Have you no fear of God, for you are subject to the same condemnation? And indeed, we have been condemned justly, for the sentence we have received corresponds to our crimes, but this man has done nothing criminal." Then he said, "Jesus, remember me when you come into your kingdom." He replied to him, "Amen, I say to you, today you will be with me in Paradise." — Luke 23:39–43

We cannot even begin to understand the depth of the Lord's mercy and forgiveness. When someone hurts us, our human inclination is to seek revenge, but this is not the way of Jesus. Our Lord invites us to reconciliation.

Will our response be like that of the good thief, who sought God's abundant mercy, or like the bad thief, who reviled Jesus? When we approach the Eucharistic table with repentant hearts, we have an opportunity to receive a fountain of mercy, a foretaste of life to come in his kingdom.

To whom can you offer mercy and forgiveness this day?

Lord Jesus, help me cultivate a heart that is rich in mercy and forgiveness.

July 5

The next day he saw Jesus coming toward him and said, "Behold the Lamb of God, who takes away the sin of the world." — John 1:29

In the opening chapter of the Gospel of John, St. John the Baptist sees Jesus and proclaims to his followers that Jesus is the Lamb of God. In chapter 19, Pilate hands over Jesus for crucifixion at the exact time that the Jewish people sacrifice an unblemished lamb for the Jewish feast of Passover. Over and over, John's Gospel portrays Jesus as the Lamb of God who takes away the sins of the world. This is a powerful Eucharistic image.

Each time we come to the table, the priest invites us to receive Jesus with this invitation: "Behold the Lamb of God, who takes away the sin of the world." In our reception of the Eucharist, we receive Jesus, the Lamb of God, who not only takes away our sins, but also gives us the grace to forgive others. In inviting us to become the very mystery we receive, Jesus calls us to live as people of mercy and compassion, forgiving all those who have hurt us.

Is forgiveness difficult? Ask the Lord to fill your heart with the saving grace to forgive those who have hurt you.

Lord Jesus, you are the innocent Lamb of God. Help me to forgive the sins of others, as you have forgiven me.

July 6

The body of Christ we receive in Holy Communion is "given up for us," and the blood we drink "shed for the many for the forgiveness of sins." For this reason the Eucharist cannot unite us to Christ without at the same time cleansing us from past sins and preserving us from future sins. — Catechism of the Catholic Church (CCC) 1393

I must admit that for a long time, I was oblivious to the great gift of forgiveness that awaits us at the Eucharistic table. It is important to understand that in order to receive this divine gift of forgiveness at the altar, we must be in the state of grace; we must be in right relationship with Jesus. If we are in the state of grace and sorry for our venial sins, our encounter with Jesus in the Eucharist can heal us of our sins and preserve us from future sins.

Forgiveness of sins invites us to do some soul-searching. Who are the people you love the most in life? Do you intentionally hurt them? No. Why? Because you are aware of what makes them happy, and you do not want to hurt them. If Jesus is the one we love the most, then our behavior will begin to reflect this loving relationship. We will want to please Jesus because we love him. The grace we receive in the Eucharist will help us to do this.

What is preventing you from loving Jesus unconditionally?

Lord God, help me to turn from the temptation of sin and follow you.

July 7

*If you forgive others their transgressions, your heavenly
Father will forgive you. — Matthew 6:14*

We have an enormous capacity to forgive, but all too often we choose to remain bitter. Offering forgiveness can be one of the most difficult choices we make in life because it involves overcoming emotional obstacles like anger, pride, and the desire for revenge. None of these qualities are of God. Throughout the Gospels, Jesus called us to live as people of forgiveness, to turn the other cheek, to forgive seventy times seventy times. Holding a grudge against another can only harden our hearts and turn us away from Jesus.

If God has forgiven us, why can't we forgive those who have hurt us? What good can come from us carrying a grudge for years or lashing out intentionally? Our Lord, who we encounter in the Eucharist, summons us to forgive, as we have been forgiven by our heavenly Father. We find the strength to forgive at the table of the Lord; for the grace of forgiveness sits at the heart of the Eucharist.

What is preventing you from living as a person of forgiveness?

*Lord Jesus, I need you. May your Eucharistic Presence heal me of my weaknesses
and lead me to live a life worthy of your Gospel.*

July 8

So he got up and went back to his father. While he was still a long way off, his father caught sight of him, and was filled with compassion. He ran to his son, embraced him and kissed him. — *Luke 15:20*

There's an old saying, "To err is human, to forgive divine." All too often, we are only human. In the story of the Prodigal Son, the Father waited each day for his son to return. One day, he caught sight of his son coming up the road, and filled with compassion, he ran out to welcome him home with an embrace of complete love. The father celebrated the fact that his son, while still imperfect, was now home. Often, we find it is easier to chastise and alienate those whose actions are unacceptable to us, rather than forgive them. The story of the Prodigal's Father challenges us to live as people of forgiveness.

The grace we receive in the Eucharist can help us model our actions after that of the Prodigal's Father: to offer love and forgiveness instead of anger and judgment. Let us come before the Eucharistic table, seeking the Lord's grace to forgive others.

Who are the prodigals in your life? Do you treat them with love and compassion or harsh condemnation and judgment?

Lord Jesus, may the Eucharist nourish me with the grace to follow the example of the Father in the Prodigal Son story and to live as a person of forgiveness.

July 9

Put on then, as God's chosen ones, holy and beloved, heartfelt compassion, kindness, humility, gentleness and patience, bearing with one another and forgiving one another … as the Lord has forgiven you, so must you also do. — *Colossians 3:12–13*

After college, I worked with an individual who was morally corrupt. He had no code of ethics, and his behavior was reprehensible. What was most upsetting about this situation is that I found myself hating him, which was uncharacteristic of me. Luckily, after a few months, he moved on; but my emotional wounds remained. Every Sunday, when I went to Mass, I asked the Lord to forgive me for the feeling of hatred I still carried for this individual. Over time, the negative feelings washed away and I knew it was time to forgive him, for the Lord had forgiven me.

The grace we receive in the Eucharist helps us put on heartfelt compassion and kindness toward others, and invites us to live as people of forgiveness, bearing with one another. Our Lord Jesus has forgiven us, and through our reception of his Eucharistic Body and Blood, we, too, gain the grace to forgive others.

Who are some people who have wounded you? Jot down their names on paper. Read each name aloud and say, "I forgive you."

Lord Jesus, thank you for the gift of forgiveness. May I have the strength to forgive others as I have been forgiven.

July 10

All bitterness, fury, anger, shouting, and reviling must be removed from you, along with all malice. [And] be kind to one another, compassionate, forgiving one another as God has forgiven you in Christ. — Ephesians 4:31–32

When someone treats us unfairly or unjustly, our first inclination is to react with anger. Yet as Christians, our Faith invites us to live as people of peace, forgiving one another, bearing our grievances with one another, and to love others as Jesus loves us. These actions are not easy to do, especially when we are upset. The call to holiness challenges us to see these difficult situations as moments to grow in grace, for they present us with an opportunity to act Christlike in the face of difficulties, to forgive others as Jesus has forgiven us.

Where do we find the strength to live in this manner? Our encounter with Christ in the Eucharist gives us grace to imitate Jesus, so that we can act Christlike in all of our endeavors. Let us ask our Eucharistic Lord for the grace of becoming the very mystery we receive at this altar.

How do you react when treated unfairly? How could you respond with love, instead?

Lord Jesus, help me to turn to you for help in all circumstances, that I may walk in your ways.

July 11

"Let the one among you who is without sin be the first to throw a stone at her." And in response, they went away one by one, beginning with the elders. So he was left alone with the woman before him. Then Jesus straightened up and said to her, "Woman, where are they? Has no one condemned you?" She replied, "No one sir." Then Jesus said, "Neither do I condemn you. Go, [and] from now on do not sin any more." — John 8:7, 9–11

There is an old saying "Hate the sin, love the sinner." Jesus puts this saying into practice in this Gospel scene by giving us an example of how to relate to others when confronted with sin. Instead of siding with the woman's accusers, Jesus challenges them to look inward, to stop their self-righteous behavior, and to examine their own lives. We are all sinners, and we hope that God treats us with mercy and compassion. Should we not do the same for others?

The spiritual practice of praying before the Blessed Sacrament can renew our focus in life. Jesus is present to us, and his merciful Presence can help us reassess our inclination to sin, so that we can work on overcoming our temptations. His grace can help us put our energies on deepening our relationship with God, so that we can go and sin no more.

Are you judgmental toward others? How could you look at others with an attitude of mercy?

Lord Jesus, help me to offer mercy and not judgment to others.

July 12

Lord, you are good and forgiving,
most merciful to all who call on you. — Psalm 86:5

When our feelings are hurt, the human response is to forgive another *only if* we receive an apology first. In a way, there is an exchange of actions: hurt feelings, apology offered, response of forgiveness. God is not like this. He did not wait for us to atone for our sins before acting in mercy; he sent his only Son, Jesus, to restore our covenant relationship with him. We did nothing to deserve redemption. Our Lord is good and forgiving, and his mercy is without measure. The Blood of Jesus freed us from sin and opened the gates of paradise to us. This saving act of redemption from Jesus invites us to reexamine our behavior toward others.

Praying before the Blessed Sacrament is a wonderful way for us to enter into deeper reflection on the mystery of salvation. Jesus is present to us and he desires us to be with him, in quiet prayer. Spending time in the presence of the Jesus in the Blessed Sacrament empowers us to transform our behavior, that we may imitate Our Lord, who is good and forgiving, merciful to all.

Are you quick to forgive, or do you wait for others to apologize first?

Lord Jesus, help me to imitate you by offering mercy and forgiveness to people, even if they have not atoned for their actions.

July 13

*Those who conceal their sins do not prosper,
but those who confess and forsake them obtain mercy.* — *Proverbs 28:13*

We cannot hide our sins from God; he knows everything. Concealing our sinful actions from the Lord only serves to hamper our spiritual growth. We live in a fallen world with a fallen human nature, and only by admitting our sins and seeking forgiveness from God can we hope to grow in our spiritual life. The Lord is rich in mercy, and he desires for us to turn to him for help, that we may prosper in our relationship with him.

Encountering Jesus in the Eucharist offers us an opportunity to transform our lives and to grow in holiness before Our Lord. Jesus is present to us in the Eucharist, and his transforming grace empowers us to turn away from sin, that we may fully live each day in his redeeming love. We simply need to choose reconciliation. Let us come before our Eucharistic Lord, seeking mercy for our sins, for Jesus desires to transform our hearts.

Have you ever deliberately withheld specific sins from your confession? Ask the Lord for the grace to confess all of your sins, that you might become a new creation in Christ.

Lord Jesus, help me to turn from my sinful ways and embrace a life rich in your love and mercy.

July 14

The LORD protects the simple;
I was helpless, but he saved me.
Return, my soul, to your rest;
the LORD has been very good to you.
For my soul has been freed from death,
my eyes from tears, my feet from stumbling.
I shall walk before the LORD
in the land of the living. — Psalm 116:6–9

At times, we are all struck by feelings of helplessness. When this happens, we need to turn to the Lord for help by placing our complete hope and trust in him. These negative feelings will slowly dissipate and our soul will find rest. The Lord will never leave us to fend for ourselves; he is with us always, and he desires only our well-being.

God's love is so intense that he sent his only Son, who suffered and died to free us from the bonds of death. The Church celebrates this redemptive action of Jesus at every Mass. The Eucharist, given to us by Jesus at the Last Supper, is medicine for our sinful souls. Partaking of the Body and Blood can fill us with hope, and help restore us to spiritual wellness. When we receive Communion, let us hand over our emotional wounds to Jesus, that he may heal us and settle our souls in his peace.

Have you ever felt helpless? How did you cope?

Lord Jesus, restore me to spiritual health, that my soul may rest in your goodness and mercy.

July 15

Therefore, confess your sins to one another and pray for one another, that you may be healed. The fervent prayer of a righteous person is very powerful. — James 5:16

It takes spiritual courage to own up to our actions and confess that we were at fault, that we caused another's emotional pain and suffering. Taking responsibility for our sinful behavior is key to beginning the process of healing; praying for the well-being of those we have hurt is also essential in bringing about reconciliation. Unfortunately, instead of confessing our sins, we often try to shift the blame to others, in an attempt to cover up the truth. We are concerned only about our own welfare, and not the good of the people we have hurt.

When we partake of the Body and Blood of Christ, Jesus gives us the spiritual strength to take ownership of our actions, and the grace to confess with contrition to those we have hurt. His redeeming Presence in the Eucharist invites us to pray for one another, that we may all experience reconciliation and healing.

Have you ever admitted your transgressions to another person? What reaction did you receive?

Lord Jesus, may the Eucharist I receive at the altar fill me with the grace to reconcile with all those I have hurt in word and deed.

July 16

If we say, "We are without sin," we deceive ourselves, and the truth is not in us. If we acknowledge our sins, he is faithful and just and will forgive our sins and cleanse us from every wrongdoing. — 1 John 1:8–9

Jesus came to save all sinners. If we deceive ourselves into thinking that we are without sin, then where is our redemption? The truth is that we are all sinners; and it is only through Jesus that we can hope to experience forgiveness of sins and eternal redemption. Jesus is ever faithful and forgiving, and he will cleanse us from every wrongdoing.

When we encounter Jesus in the Eucharist, we experience his saving power and his forgiveness, and we gain the clarity to see how our actions might hurt others. Let us approach the Lord seeking forgiveness for our venial sins, and the grace to sin no more.

Do you feel in need of redemption?

Lord Jesus, may our participation in the sacred mysteries of the Eucharist free us from sin and cleanse us from every wrongdoing.

July 17

Repent, therefore, and be converted, that your sins may be wiped away, and that the Lord may grant you times of refreshment and send you the Messiah already appointed for you, Jesus. — Acts 3:19–20

In order for us to repent, we must first recognize that our actions are sinful, that our behavior is not in alignment with the Gospel of Jesus. Unfortunately, we live in a society where virtually anything goes. Sin does not exist in the minds of many people nowadays. We hear comments like "If it feels good, do it," or "As long as you are not hurting anyone, who cares?" God cares, and the Lord knows our sins; yet he loves us anyway. God sent his only Son, Jesus, who gave his life that we may be saved. Repenting of our sins requires more than being sorry; it entails converting our lifestyle from actions that hurt Our Lord to living in the light of God's mercy and grace.

When we receive Jesus in the Eucharist, his Divine Presence fills us with the grace needed to turn our lives around, to repent of our venial sins, and to live as children of God. Let us come before the Lord in the Eucharist with repentant hearts, seeking God's mercy and love.

Are there actions in your life that do not correspond to the Lord's message of love?

Lord Jesus, help me to turn away from sin, that I may live in the light of your love.

July 18

In him we have redemption by his blood, the forgiveness of transgressions, in accord with the riches of his grace that he lavished upon us. In all wisdom and insight, he has made known to us the mystery of his will in accord with his favor that he set forth in him. — Ephesians 1:7–9

Jesus paid the price for our redemption with his own precious Blood. Through Jesus, our sins are forgiven, our covenant with God is restored, and salvation is ours; all we have to do is hold on to it by remaining in his grace. Grace is relational, and is a gift lavished upon us from God that helps us to follow Jesus every day. We simply need to receive it, embrace it, and live it.

Each time we come to the Eucharistic table of Our Lord, we partake of the consecrated bread and wine, Christ's Body and Blood given for the forgiveness of sins. May the Lord lavish us with the grace of his Eucharistic Presence, that we may find favor with God as we seek to do his will.

When have you felt God's grace working in your life?

Lord Jesus, thank you for redeeming us with your precious Blood. May I never stray from your Divine Presence.

July 19

"This is the covenant I will establish with them after those days, says the Lord:
'I will put my laws in their hearts,
and I will write them upon their minds,' "
he also says:
"Their sins and their evildoing
I will remember no more."
Where there is forgiveness of these, there is no longer
offering for sin. — Hebrews 10:16–18

We often hear the sayings "Forgive and forget," or "Let bygones be bygones." Although we may forgive others, often in subsequent arguments we will bring up actions of the past, reopening old wounds. The Lord does not treat us like this. When we repent of our sins, Jesus will never remind us of past transgressions. We are the ones who imprison ourselves in the past, believing that the Lord can forgive but not forget.

Our encounter with Jesus in the Eucharist offers us healing for our venial sins, and strengthens us to sin no more. Jesus loves us; he shed his Blood on the cross for the forgiveness of our sins. Each time you receive Communion, ask the Lord to heal you of all that keeps you from loving him. Seek his grace, that you might look to the future with hope and not remember the sins of the past.

Do you struggle with forgetting the past sins of others?

Lord Jesus, thank you for your gift of forgiveness we receive at the altar. Help me to love you more each day.

July 20

But to the Lord, our God, belong compassion and forgiveness, though we rebelled against him and did not hear the voice of the LORD, our God, by walking in his laws given through his servants the prophets. — Daniel 9:9–10

Have you ever hurt someone's feelings without knowing it? It is not a good experience — it is difficult to apologize when you are unaware of how and why your actions hurt another. It is even more stressful if the person whose feelings are hurt refuses to tell you what you have done, and instead chooses to remain silent and withdrawn. We call this type of immature behavior "giving someone the cold shoulder," and it is a sign of an unhealthy relationship. The bond we share with the Lord is not like this, for our God is compassionate and merciful, and quick to forgive.

As an act of unconditional love, God sent Jesus to restore the covenant relationship with us that had been broken through sin. Jesus, out of love for us, offered us forgiveness for all time by gifting us with his Body and Blood as spiritual sustenance. Jesus will never turn his back on us. At this table, let us humbly receive his gift of forgiveness.

What are some ways you can be more compassionate and forgiving in your dealings with others?

Lord Jesus, grant me the grace to walk in your ways, that I may never rebel against you.

July 21

Then he took a cup, gave thanks, and gave it to them, saying, "Drink from it, all of you, for this is my blood of the covenant, which will be shed on behalf of many for the forgiveness of sins. I tell you, from now on I shall not drink this fruit of the vine until the day when I drink it with you new in the kingdom of my Father." — Matthew 26:27–29

These actions of Jesus at the Last Supper are redemptive in nature. He is foreshadowing his impending death on the cross, where he will shed his Blood for humanity for the forgiveness of sins. Jesus ends his discourse making mention of the end times, when all of his followers from all ages will share in the Supper of the Lamb in the glorious kingdom of his Father.

We experience a foretaste of the heavenly banquet each time we receive Communion. Jesus is present in the consecrated bread and wine, and he invites us to eat and drink of his Body and Blood, shed for the forgiveness of sins.

Are you aware of the gift of forgiveness that awaits you at the table of the Lord?

Lord Jesus, may your Eucharist fill me with your Divine Presence and cleanse me of my faults.

July 22

Therefore I tell you, all that you ask for in prayer, believe that you will receive it and it shall be yours. When you stand to pray, forgive anyone against whom you have a grievance, so that your heavenly Father may in turn forgive you your transgressions. — Mark 11:24–25

We have all heard the phrase "Forgiveness is a two-way street." We cannot expect people to forgive us if we do not offer forgiveness to others. Yet sometimes, we are stubborn and refuse to forgive another, because it might imply that we were in the wrong. Or, we might not offer forgiveness because the "principle" of the argument is at stake — regardless of the fact of a human heart that might be suffering from lack of forgiveness. Jesus challenges us to act differently: to forgive anyone against whom we have a grievance, so that our heavenly Father in turn may forgive us.

Our reception of Jesus in the Eucharist unites us to the merciful heart of Christ and offers us the grace to forgive others, as we desire our heavenly Father to forgive us. It is a free choice we must make. Forgiving others will free us from the baggage of carrying grudges and will open our hearts to salvation in Christ.

Is there anyone you need to forgive today?

Lord Jesus, help me to live with a merciful heart, that I may offer forgiveness in your name.

July 23

*Repent, therefore, and be converted, that your sins
may be wiped away. — Acts 3:19*

We all know someone in our family or circle of friends who has drifted away and no longer practices their Catholic Faith. Preaching only alienates our loved ones even more. What are we to do? To be honest, I do not know how conversion of heart takes place, since I have been a practicing Catholic my entire life. What I do know is that with God all things are possible, and prayer is our best tool in leading our loved ones back to the Church.

Praying for our loved ones in the presence of Our Lord in the Blessed Sacrament is a powerful way to help bring about conversion of their souls. Jesus is present to us in a most intimate way in the Eucharist, and he is like a trusted friend who holds our hands as we pour out our hearts to him. Jesus is listening to our prayers for conversion, and he will help our loved ones come back to their Faith. When and how this will occur is in the hands of Jesus. We must trust in his redeeming grace, and hold fast that one day, our loved ones will repent and their sins will be forgiven.

Are there people in your life who are no longer practicing their Faith? Bring these individuals to prayer and trust that God is in control.

Lord Jesus, help me to pray fervently for all those in need of conversation, trusting that your grace will lead them back to the Church.

July 24

Strive for peace with everyone, and for that holiness without which no one will see the Lord. — *Hebrews 12:14*

Peace seems so elusive. We hear stories in the news of violence in our streets, mass shootings in schools and places of work, wars, persecution, acts of terrorism, hate crimes; the list is endless. Is it even possible for people of goodwill to find peace? The death and resurrection of Jesus won for us eternal salvation. Redeemed by the Blood of the innocent Lamb, we must strive to be holy, as Our Lord is holy. This is not easy, for we are tempted on a daily basis by the forces of our sinful world. To achieve peace and holiness, we need the help of Jesus in the Eucharist.

When we partake of the Body and Blood of Christ, we are strengthened in our resolve to live as peaceful people. The Eucharist is our spiritual nourishment and sustenance for carrying on the work of Christ. In striving to live as people of peace, we will grow in holiness, as we become the very mystery that we receive at this Eucharistic table.

Do you lash out at others when you are angry? Cultivate the habit of prayerfully calling out to Jesus to help you remain peaceful.

Lord Jesus, help me to strive for peace, that I may live in grace and holiness.

July 25

Be on your guard! If your brother sins, rebuke him; and if he repents, forgive him. And if he wrongs you seven times in one day and returns to you seven times saying, "I am sorry," you should forgive him. — Luke 17:3–4

Calling others out for their actions is a very delicate thing to do, for there is always a risk that our words will alienate the person, which can result in a division in families or a breakup in a relationship. Although the Lord calls us to admonish another, we are to do so with mercy, love, and compassion, never with judgment or condemnation. If someone begins to change their behavior, or attempts to make amends, we are to forgive them and never bring up their past actions, for the Lord remembers not the sins of old. It is not easy to forgive and forget; we can only accomplish this with the help of Our Lord.

When we receive Communion, our hearts are united to the merciful heart of Christ, who shed his Blood on the cross for the forgiveness of our sins. May the Eucharist we receive give us the grace to forgive others.

Is there someone you need to forgive? Is there someone you need to ask forgiveness from? Seek the Lord's help in this endeavor.

Lord Jesus, fill me with your grace, that I may offer forgiveness to those who wrong me.

July 26

*Therefore if you bring your gift to the altar, and there recall that
your brother has anything against you, leave your gift there
at the altar, go first and be reconciled with your brother, and
then come and offer your gift.* — Matthew 5:23–24

The exchange of peace at Mass, immediately before we receive Communion, is based upon this Scripture passage. The Lord is telling us that we need to be in right relationship with our neighbor before we can bring the gift of ourselves to the altar. Forgiveness sits at the heart of being a Christian. The Lord is looking for the gift of our heart, pure and undefiled, without any blemish of anger or disagreement.

Our Lord shed his Blood on the cross for the forgiveness of sins. He gave us the gift of himself in the elements of consecrated bread and wine, that we may be one with him for all time. United to the merciful heart of Christ, how can we withhold forgiveness from another human being? Let us be mindful of the divine call to be in right relationship with our neighbor before we come forward to receive Jesus in the Eucharist.

With whom do you need to reconcile before you come to the table of the Lord?

Lord Jesus, help me to live in this world as a person of peace.

July 27

Indeed, if, while we were enemies, we were reconciled to God through the death of his Son, how much more, once reconciled, will we be saved by his life. — Romans 5:10

To be honest, I have never thought of myself as an enemy of God. Yet this text from Romans suggests that because of sin, God may have considered us as enemies. But through the death of his only Son, Jesus, we have become reconciled and we now have the opportunity to enter into a loving relationship with our God.

There is no limit to how deep our relationship with the Lord can grow. Each time we receive the Eucharist, we receive grace to deepen our love and commitment to follow the Lord. That commitment is a choice we must make on a daily basis. Christ's Body and Blood gives us strength to choose God over the sins of our past. Let us resolve to live each day in gratitude for the gift of reconciliation won for us by Jesus.

What impact does sin have on your relationship with the Lord?

Lord Jesus, help me to turn away from sin, that I may be in a loving relationship with you.

July 28

To live in a manner worthy of the Lord, so as to be fully pleasing, in every good work bearing fruit and growing in the knowledge of God, strengthened with every power, in accord with his glorious might, for all endurance and patience, with joy giving thanks to the Father, who has made you fit to share in the inheritance of the holy ones in light. — Colossians 1:10–12

God has created us for a specific task and purpose. We are to live in a manner worthy of the Lord, bearing good fruit for the kingdom of God. As we grow in knowledge of Our Lord, we align ourselves to the mission of Jesus, who came to save all people from sin. We are to share this Good News, of salvation, with others.

The Eucharist strengthens us with every power we need to carry on the mission of Christ. Let us come before the table of the Lord with joyful hearts, filled with gratitude to God for the gift of salvation we have received through Jesus.

In what ways does your life bear fruit for the kingdom of God?

Lord Jesus, may I grow in knowledge and wisdom of God, that I may give thanks for all of my blessings.

July 29

And all this is from God, who has reconciled us to himself through Christ and given us the ministry of reconciliation. — 2 Corinthians 5:18

Have you ever watched a relay race? The first runner takes off and then passes the baton to the next runner, and so on, until the last runner crosses the finish line. Our life with Christ is similar to a relay race. In sacrificing his life on the cross, Jesus reconciled us to God. Every generation since the time of Jesus has passed down the baton of reconciliation to the next generation. As followers of Jesus, we, too, are charged with the mission of bearing witness to others of the saving power of Jesus. He died for the sins of all people, not just the ones who were living at the time of the crucifixion. The Lord needs us to be faithful disciples who lovingly share the Good News with everyone we meet.

It takes courage and strength to pass on the baton of discipleship to a new generation. The Eucharist is our spiritual nourishment for carrying on the work of Christ. Each time we receive Communion, let us ask the Lord to fill us with his grace, that we may relay his message of reconciliation to all those the Lord sends our way.

How often have you shared the Good News of salvation and reconciliation with your family and friends?

Lord Jesus, may the Eucharist give me strength to share in your ministry of reconciliation.

July 30

For our sake he made him to be sin who did not know sin, so that we might become the righteousness of God in him. — 2 Corinthians 5:21

While we were still sinners, Jesus, the sinless Son of God, took on human form, sacrificing his life on the cross so that our sins would be forgiven. This saving act of Jesus constitutes the greatest love story of all time. For our sake, Jesus took on our sinful nature to save us that we may become the righteousness of God in him.

Our experience of Jesus in the Eucharist brings us into the heart of our Savior, whose love for us is so great that he offered his life to God in exchange for our eternal salvation. Each time we partake of his Body and Blood, the grace of righteousness fills our hearts. Let us approach the altar grateful for our redemption, firmly resolving to live each day in the light of God's healing grace.

How does your life feel righteous in the eyes of God?

Lord Jesus, help me to turn away from sin, that I may be worthy of your saving act of redemption.

July 31

But now in Christ Jesus you who once were far off have become near by the blood of Christ. So then you are no longer strangers and sojourners, but you are fellow citizens with the holy ones and members of the household of God. — Ephesians 2:13, 19

When my daughter, Lauren, was little, she liked to dress up like Cinderella and pretend she had glass slippers. She loved the story of the handsome prince rescuing Cinderella. When Lauren had her first daughter, she purchased a plaque for the nursery that said, "One shoe can change your life." This whimsical statement speaks to us on many levels. Before Jesus came into the world, we were far-off people without hope, for sin had broken our covenant with God. At the proper time, God sent his only Son, Jesus, who shed his Blood on the cross for the forgiveness of our sins. Through Jesus, redemption is ours and we have hope of eternal life. One could say that our Savior changed our life forever.

On the night before he suffered and died, Jesus chose to give us the gift of his whole self in the elements of bread and wine, for he desired to be with us for all time. As we receive the Eucharist, let us be mindful: We are now consecrated and holy, members of the household of God.

What does redemption mean to you?

Lord Jesus, help me to live as a fellow citizen of the household of God.

~ SELF-GIFT ~

August 1

"Father, if you are willing, take this cup away from me; still, not my will but yours be done." — Luke 22:42

When life is difficult, our response is to pray. But what do we do when it seems that God is not hearing us? The reality is that God hears and answers all of our prayers; often, we fail to see his hand at work in our life because we focus on what we want, and not what God wants for us.

On the night before he was crucified, Jesus prayed in the garden of Gethsemane, asking the Father to take this cup away; then he followed up his petition with the most powerful prayer of all: "Not my will but yours be done." Prayer is not about getting your own way; rather, it is about aligning your heart and mind to the will of God. When we receive Jesus in the Eucharist, we have an opportunity to offer up our difficult situations into the hands of the Lord in an act of self-gift. In this intimate moment of Communion, Jesus is present to you. Bring your prayers to him, and surrender the situation into his loving hands. Ask the Lord to give you the strength to carry your cross, for it is not your will, but the Father's that shall be done.

What crosses are you willing to surrender to the Lord?

Jesus, may the Eucharist give me the courage to unite my will to the Father's in heaven.

August 2

I urge you therefore, brothers, by the mercies of God, to offer your bodies as a living sacrifice, holy and pleasing to God. — Romans 12:1

Growing up, I remember the good sisters at my Catholic grammar school telling us kids that we should "offer up" everything that was difficult or painful in life. From my perspective, "offering up" seemed like a good way to keep me from complaining. As I grew into adulthood, and became a wife and mom, I forgot about this spiritual concept and tried to solve things on my own. I soon found myself overwhelmed and exhausted.

Jesus is here to help us take up our crosses, and to look at life through the perspective of his dying and rising, through him, with him, and in him. Offering up our crosses takes courage and trust in God. When we encounter Jesus in the Eucharist, we receive the grace to grow in spiritual awareness that we are not alone, that the Lord, who gave his life for us, is here to help us every step of the way.

What situation in life can you offer up to God this day?

Lord Jesus, I offer my life to you. Help me to draw closer to you, that I may discern your will for me.

August 3

In the Eucharist the sacrifice of Christ becomes also the sacrifice of the members of his Body. The lives of the faithful, their praise, sufferings, prayer, and work, are united with those of Christ and with his total offering, and so acquire a new value. Christ's sacrifice present on the altar makes it possible for all generations of Christians to be united with his offering. — CCC 1368

Each time we celebrate the Eucharist, the paschal mystery of Christ invites us to transform our fears into strength, our despair into hope, and our crosses into opportunities for new life. The Eucharistic liturgy shapes our view of reality, for it challenges us to look at our lives from the perspective of Christ's paschal mystery.

The Holy Spirit, who transforms the gifts of bread and wine into the Body and Blood of Christ during the consecration, has the power to transform our lives too. At every Eucharistic celebration, we are invited to offer up all that needs transformation in our lives, as we join them to the perfect sacrifice of Christ.

What are you willing to offer up to the Lord in the hopes of transforming your spiritual life?

Lord Jesus, help me to have the faith to believe that my life can be transformed each time I receive you in the Eucharist.

August 4

The way we came to know love was that he laid down his life for us;
so we ought to lay down our lives for our brothers. If someone who
has worldly means sees a brother in need and refuses him compassion,
how can the love of God remain in him? Children, let us love not
in word or speech but in deed and truth. — 1 John 3:16–18

Christian discipleship calls us to imitate Jesus, who, out of love for us, laid down his life that we may have eternal life. To model our lives after Our Lord requires stepping out of our comfort zones to care for the needs of all those the Lord sends our way. This is not easy — it requires a self-emptying, a giving up of our selfish desires, that we may refocus our precious resources of time, talent, and treasure to serve our brothers and sisters in Christ.

When we partake of the Eucharistic Body and Blood, we unite our lives to the heart of Christ, and we receive the necessary graces to love our brothers and sisters outwardly, not just in word or speech, but also in truth and deed. May the love of God remain in us as we serve in the name of Christ.

What do you need to give up in order to follow the Lord?

Lord Jesus, help me to use my gifts and talents at the service of those in need.

August 5

Then Jesus said to his disciples, "Whoever wishes to come after me must deny himself, take up his cross, and follow me. For whoever wishes to save his life will lose it, but whoever loses his life for my sake will find it." — Matthew 16:24–25

There is a story about a man was who was angry with the Lord because he thought he had a difficult life. The man asked God if he could exchange his cross for something different. God led him into a room, and said, "Pick your cross, and it is yours." Inside the room were huge heavy crosses, many towering over the man. Overcome with fear, he thought to himself, "My cross is nothing compared to these." Turning to God, the man said, "Lord, I will gladly take up my cross, for I know now that I can bear it."

Jesus will never give us a cross we cannot bear, for he is with us to help carry our heavy burdens of life. Our participation in the sacrifice of the Eucharist unites us to the cross and resurrection of Jesus, and gives us the grace and strength we need to carry our crosses with the hope and promise of new life.

What is weighing heavy on your heart today? Ask the Lord to help you carry this cross.

Lord Jesus, help me to take up my crosses and lovingly follow you each day.

August 6

So be imitators of God, as beloved children, and live in love, as Christ loved us and handed himself over for us as a sacrificial offering to God for a fragrant aroma. — Ephesians 5:1–2

Years ago, while attending my twentieth reunion from grammar school, I had an experience that changed my faith life forever. In a casual conversation about the Eucharist with a fellow classmate, my friend told me that he would be willing to sacrifice his life to protect the presence of Jesus in the Eucharist. I was speechless and profoundly sad, for I realized I did not share the same zeal for the Eucharist that he did. From that moment, everything changed for me. I prayed fervently before the Blessed Sacrament; I wanted a loving relationship with Jesus in the Eucharist, one that I, too, would be willing to die for. Over time, Jesus answered my prayers.

Encountering the Real Presence of Jesus in the Eucharist radically changed my life, for I went from being a practicing Catholic who loved God to a disciple of Jesus who is in love with God. My awareness of Jesus in the Eucharist transformed my faith life from one of passivity to active discipleship. Today, without a doubt, I would give my life for Jesus.

Do you desire to be an active disciple of Jesus? Seek his love and wisdom each time you receive the Eucharist.

Lord Jesus, increase my love for your Real Presence in the Eucharist.

August 7

Jesus summoned them and said to them, "You know that those who are recognized as rulers over the Gentiles lord it over them, and their great ones make their authority over them felt. But it shall not be so among you. Rather, whoever wishes to be great among you will be your servant." — Mark 10:42–43

We have all witnessed individuals who misuse their authority. These people believe because they are in charge, they have a right to criticize, tear down or belittle another human being simply because they are in a position of power. Jesus warns us about such actions, and tells us that if we desire to follow him, we must be servants to others. Jesus is not condemning the role of leadership; in fact, Jesus is telling us that servant leadership is the goal of all Christians. Our Lord is here to help us conduct ourselves virtuously as servant leaders.

When we receive the Body and Blood of Christ, we encounter the Real Presence of Jesus, who, in the Gospel, warned his disciples against pompous behavior, and instructed his followers to be servants to all. Our Eucharistic experience of Jesus gives us the grace to treat all people with respect and dignity, no matter what our positions in life are.

What is your leadership style? Pastoral or authoritarian? Seek the Lord's wisdom to help you be a servant leader.

Lord Jesus, help me to be of service to all those you send my way.

August 8

Tell the rich in the present age not to be proud and not to rely on so uncertain a thing as wealth but rather on God, who richly provides us with all things for our enjoyment. Tell them to do good, to be rich in good works, to be generous, ready to share, thus accumulating as treasure a good foundation for the future, so as to win the life that is true life. — 1 Timothy 6:17–19

We live in a country of great wealth; unfortunately, the distribution of riches is not equal. Those who have great financial means also have positions of power, prestige, and the admiration of others. For many individuals, fame, money, and power are their entire world. The Gospel invites us to turn away from the allure of wealth, and to refocus our attention on our relationship with God, who richly provides us with everything we need for true happiness. As faithful followers of Jesus, we need to empty ourselves of the entrapments of this world, that we may devote our attention to our lives with Jesus.

Spending time in quiet prayer before the Blessed Sacrament will help us center our busy hearts and refocus our priorities. Jesus is waiting for us. Seek his wisdom; receive his grace, and you will win the life that is true.

Does money or the Gospel rule your actions?

Lord Jesus, help me to love you above all else, that I may be rich in what has true value.

August 9

Whoever loses his life for my sake will find it. — *Matthew 10:39*

You have heard it said, "The road to heaven is not a straight path." From my experience, this statement is true, because life is a maze of difficulties, twisted pathways, and dark and scary roads. If we want to reach our heavenly goal, Jesus tells us to take up our cross and follow him no matter where the path may take us; for whoever loses his life for Jesus' sake will find it. Our call in life is to face each problem head on, and steadily work through it with the grace of God, for then we will be worthy of the Lord.

The Eucharist gives us the spiritual strength to persevere when life is difficult and we have lost our way. The bread of angels and the chalice of salvation we receive at the altar are divine food for our journey. We need the Real Presence of Jesus in the Eucharist to sustain us, as we carry our crosses from death to new life.

What is your most difficult cross to carry? Seek the Eucharistic Presence of Jesus to help you carry your burden.

Lord Jesus, help me to surrender all that keeps me from following you.

August 10

Everyone who has given up houses or brothers or sisters or father or mother or children or lands for the sake of my name will receive a hundred times more, and will inherit eternal life. — Matthew 19:29–30

In this Scripture passage, Jesus is not instructing us to turn our backs on our family; he is telling us not to put people or material goods before him. Nothing in our lives should take priority over our relationship with Jesus. If family members do not understand our Catholic Faith, then we must practice our Faith alone. Jesus assures us that anyone who gives up the people and things of this world for his sake will inherit eternal life. He will help us work through these difficult situations, and will even help bring our family members back to the Faith. Our role as faithful disciples of Christ is to stand firm in our faith in the Lord.

The Eucharist unites us to the heart of Christ, and showers us with the grace to persevere in our faith even in the midst of family obstacles. Place your needs before Jesus truly present in the Eucharist, seek his help, and he will reward you with abundant graces a hundred times over.

Are there people in your life who do not support you in your faith journey?

Lord Jesus, help me to place my relationship with you above everything else in this world.

August 11

Those who offer praise as a sacrifice honor me;
I will let him whose way is steadfast
look upon the salvation of God. — Psalm 50:23

The Eucharist is a sacred meal, a sacrament, and a sacrifice. A sacrifice always includes an offering. In the celebration of Mass, the gifts of bread and wine, placed upon the table of sacrifice, are transformed into the Body and Blood of Jesus through the power of the Holy Spirit. Following this mystical moment, the priest then offers to the Father the perfect sacrifice of Jesus, present in the consecrated bread and wine, as an offering of praise. Jesus invites us, too, to offer our lives at the Eucharistic table as a sacrifice of praise to God.

Within the celebration of Mass, the Eucharistic table becomes the altar of spiritual transformation, not only for the bread and wine, but for the People of God as well. The Holy Spirit is the agent of transformation, and the Spirit will transform our hearts if we are steadfast in our ways. Let us turn to the Lord in a spirit of praise and thanksgiving.

Are you willing to offer yourself to God as a sacrifice of praise?

Lord Jesus, help me, that I may offer everything in my life as a sacrifice of praise.

August 12

Instead, seek his kingdom, and these other things will be given you besides. Do not be afraid any longer, little flock, for your Father is pleased to give you the kingdom. Sell your belongings and give alms. Provide money bags for yourselves that do not wear out, an inexhaustible treasure in heaven that no thief can reach nor moth destroy, For where your treasure is, there also will your heart be. — Luke 12:31–34

What is your treasure? A family heirloom? A piece of valuable jewelry? Your house? Money? Cars? A luxury lifestyle? Jesus tells us that if we want to be his disciples, we must be willing to let go of excess material attachments, sell them, and share with those less fortunate. If we do all of this for the kingdom of God, we will receive an inexhaustible treasure in heaven, one that no thief can take from us. In essence, Jesus is telling us that the kingdom of heaven must be our heart's desire.

Jesus is present in the Eucharist, and he is here to help us change our attitudes about life; his Body and Blood that we share nourish us with his life-giving grace, giving our hearts a desire to be one with him in the glorious kingdom of heaven. Seek the Lord, for he is your greatest treasure.

What do you treasure most in life?

Lord Jesus, help me to place my relationship with you above the materialistic goods in my life.

August 13

Do you not know that your body is a temple of the holy Spirit within you, whom you have from God, and that you are not your own? For you have been purchased at a price. Therefore, glorify God in your body. — *1 Corinthians 6:19–20*

We spend a lot of time, energy, and money keeping our bodies healthy. We exercise, eat right, and consult our doctors as needed. Spiritually, our corporal bodies are important because we are made in God's image, and are called to be his Divine Presence in our physical world. When we cooperate with grace, the Lord works in us and through us to serve his people. The power of the Holy Spirit prompts us to do acts of charity, to serve those in need, and to love our neighbor as ourselves. Our bodies were purchased at a great price by the innocent Blood of Our Lord Jesus. Let us take great care that they may be vessels of God's grace and not temptations to sin.

Our encounter with Jesus in the Eucharist can strengthen us to be vessels of God's grace. Each time you receive Communion, open your heart and invite the power of the Spirit to dwell within you.

Are you aware that the indwelling of the Holy Spirit inspires you to do works of charity in the name of Jesus?

Lord Jesus, help me to be a vessel of grace, that I may accomplish good things in your name.

August 14

My son, give me your heart,
and let your eyes keep to my ways. — Proverbs 23:26

As parents and grandparents, as aunts and uncles, we have a responsibility to help pass on the Faith to our children. This is a daunting task, for the embers of faith have grown cold in many families, and our children are tempted in every way possible through social media platforms, livestreamed media, music videos, and more. The absence of God in our culture seriously jeopardizes the ability of families to practice their Faith. Yet the Lord knows the desires of our hearts, and is here to help us in our efforts to pass on the Faith to future generations.

The Eucharistic Body and Blood of Christ that we receive in Communion is spiritual food for doing the work of God. Each time we come to the table, the Lord invites us to offer our hearts to him; united with Christ, our actions can then reflect his love and compassion for all of God's children. Jesus is with us. Let us place ourselves before our Eucharistic Lord, trusting that Jesus will act in and through us so that our lives may accomplish his will.

How can you have a positive impact on the faith lives of the children in your family?

Lord Jesus, help me to be a role model of faith for future generations in my family.

August 15

For today the Virgin Mother of God
was assumed into heaven
as the beginning and image
of your Church's coming to perfection
and a sign of sure hope and comfort to your pilgrim people;
rightly you would not allow her
to see the corruption of the tomb
since from her own body she marvelously brought forth
your incarnate Son, the Author of all life. —
Preface of the feast of the Assumption

Today the Church celebrates the Assumption of Mary into heaven, body and soul. Mary's earthly body was saved from corruption because her immaculate womb carried our Savior to birth. Mary is in heaven with her Son, and her presence is a sign of hope and comfort to us. One day, by the grace of God, we too will join Mary and the saints in heaven.

The Body of Christ we receive in the Eucharist is the Real Presence of Jesus. Our Virgin Mother carried Jesus in her womb, blessing us with the Savior of our World, the Incarnate Son of God. The Eucharist is our spiritual nourishment for carrying on the work of our Savior. Let us come before our Eucharistic Lord, seeking to do his will.

Do you desire to live with a spirit of surrender and a willingness to do the work of the Lord?

Lord Jesus, help me to follow in the footsteps of Mary, my mother and yours.

August 16

If someone who has worldly means sees a brother in need and refuses him compassion, how can the love of God remain in him? Children, let us love not in word or speech but in deed and truth. — 1 John 3:17–18

We are all familiar with the saying "Talk is cheap." It is not enough to express our love and concern for the welfare of others; we are to act with charity toward all those in need. Especially in difficult economic times, it is tempting to think only of ourselves, and to save every penny we make; yet it is important to be aware that there are people suffering across the globe. We are incredibly blessed, and our lives with Christ challenge us to share our worldly means with those less fortunate.

When we partake of the Eucharistic Body and Blood of Christ, we encounter the Real Presence of Jesus, who gave his life on the cross for us. Sacrificial love sits at the heart of being a Christian. Each time we receive the Eucharist, let us be mindful that we are the Body of Christ, called to love our brothers and sisters in Christ, not in word or speech, but in deed and truth.

How do you show your love for others?

Lord Jesus, I recognize how blessed I am. Help me to lovingly share my blessings with those in need.

August 17

For on the night he was betrayed he himself took bread, and giving you thanks he said the blessing, broke the bread and gave it to his disciples, saying: "Take this, all of you, and eat of it: For this is my Body which will be given up for you." — Institution Narrative, Eucharistic Prayer III

People often mistakenly call Eucharist "blessed bread," because the prayer text makes mention that Jesus said the blessing. It is important to remember that Jesus was Jewish, and the blessing he prayed as he took bread into his holy hands is called the *berakha*. It is a Jewish blessing of praise and thanksgiving offered to our Father in heaven and prayed at every Passover Supper. Catholics do not eat bread that has only been blessed. During the consecration of the Mass, the Holy Spirit transforms the gifts of bread and wine into the Body and Blood of Jesus, the sacramental Real Presence of Christ.

When we partake of the Eucharistic bread and wine, we participate in Christ's sacrament of love, transforming us into the very mystery that we receive. Jesus gave of himself at the Last Supper, and he invites us to give of ourselves each time we dine at his Eucharistic table.

What are you willing to offer to the Lord, that you may experience spiritual transformation?

Lord Jesus, transform the darkened areas of my life into your radiant light.

August 18

"I delight to do your will, my God;
your law is in my inner being!"
When I sing of your righteousness
in a great assembly,
See, I do not restrain my lips,
as you, LORD, know. — Psalm 40:9–10

When you think about your Catholic Faith, does it make you feel joyful? Do you feel like singing the praises of God to your family and friends? If not, why not? Our faith in Jesus should be a source of great joy, and we should desire to share this joy with others. We are called to delight in doing the will of God and not hesitate in sharing our faith with all those we meet.

Each time you receive Communion, I invite you to visualize Jesus standing right in front of you. His Real Presence is in the Eucharist and this spiritual reality should fill you with awe and joy. Jesus is waiting for you; his Body and Blood is given to you for your spiritual nourishment, that you may have strength to live your faith each day. Come and receive, that you may sing of your encounter with Jesus in the Eucharist.

In what ways is your faith a source of joy to you?

Lord Jesus, may your Eucharistic Presence fill me with joy of the Spirit, that I may readily share my faith with those you send my way.

August 19

Conduct yourselves with reverence during the time of your sojourning, realizing that you were ransomed from your futile conduct, handed on by your ancestors, not with perishable things like silver or gold but with the precious blood of Christ as of a spotless unblemished lamb. — *1 Peter 1:17–19*

We are sojourners in this life, making a living day-to-day, traveling, working, and moving across the globe, always in search of our final destination: heaven. The world and all that is in it is transient; all of these material goods will pass away. Heaven is our home, and through the precious Blood of the spotless unblemished Lamb, the gates of paradise are open to us. The gift of salvation won for us by Jesus is more precious than gold or silver.

Encountering Jesus in the Eucharist helps us to refocus our attention toward our heavenly home, and not the things of this passing world. Jesus gave his life for us, that we may have eternal life with him. Let us conduct ourselves with reverence, aware that we have been ransomed at a precious price.

If you consider heaven your final destination, how does this affect the way you live each day?

Lord Jesus, help me to conduct myself with reverence, that I may be worthy of my heavenly home.

August 20

Like a sheep he was led to the slaughter,
and as a lamb before its shearer is silent,
so he opened not his mouth.
In (his) humiliation justice was denied him.
Who will tell of his posterity?
For his life is taken from the earth. — Acts 8:32–33

Scripture refers to Jesus as the Lamb of God because he willingly sacrificed himself for our sins. In the Old Testament, it was the Jewish custom to sacrifice an unblemished lamb to God for the atonement of sin; Jesus is the unblemished Lamb, who willingly sacrificed his life for the sins of all people. Through this act of salvation, Jesus opened the gates of paradise to all who believe in him.

Our encounter with Jesus in the Eucharist invites us to reflect upon this mystery of our Faith, and upon the ways that we can imitate the life of Jesus. We live in a society where groups of people act and react with violence; yet Jesus, the gentle Lamb of God, shows us a different way to live. When we partake of the Body and Blood of Jesus, we gain the strength to resist violence in any form and to walk away from all those who desire to lead us astray. Let us seek to pattern our lives after that of Jesus, the Lamb of God.

How do you react when you are unjustly accused?

Lord Jesus, help me to follow your humble and peaceful way of life.

August 21

Clear out the old yeast, so that you may become a fresh batch of dough, inasmuch as you are unleavened. For our paschal lamb, Christ, has been sacrificed. Therefore, let us celebrate the feast, not with the old yeast, the yeast of malice and wickedness, but with the unleavened bread of sincerity and truth. — *1 Corinthians 5:7–8*

When St. Paul speaks of the image of old yeast, he is referring to our sinful habits and behaviors. We must clear them out so that we may become new creations in Christ. The yeast of sin grows and multiplies, and if we desire to live with sincerity and truth, it is necessary to rid ourselves of any remnants of old yeast — old sins — for we are to be the image of unleavened bread, pure and undefiled, ready for the paschal feast. Jesus is our Paschal lamb. He sacrificed his life on the cross for us for the forgiveness of sin.

Each time we receive the Body and Blood of Jesus, we have an opportunity to clear out all that keeps us from Our Lord. His precious Blood, shed for us for the forgiveness of sins, can help cleanse our lives, that we may be a batch of fresh, unleavened dough in the hands of our risen Lord.

What remains of the old yeast that you need to remove from your life?

Lord Jesus, help me to clear out all that keeps me from living my life as a new creation in you.

August 22

May he remember your every offering,
graciously accept your burnt offering,
Grant what is in your heart,
fulfill your every plan. — Psalm 20:4–5

The Lord desires our goodness, for we are created in his image and likeness, and we have a purpose and plan in life. For us to find fulfillment, it is important that we be in relationship with the Lord, so that the actions of our hearts are in sync with what the Lord has created us to do. In this Scripture passage, when the psalmist speaks of the heart, he is not addressing a specific organ in our body; rather, the heart is the core of who we are. Our hearts express our deepest longings in life. If our heart is in alignment with God, then the Lord will fulfill our every plan, for our plans will be his.

When we encounter Jesus in the Eucharist, we have the opportunity to offer ourselves to the Lord in the hopes of aligning our hearts to that of Our Lord Jesus. Partaking of his Body and Blood fills us with the grace needed to reflect deeply on who we are and who God created us to be. Let us come before Our Lord in the Eucharist, asking that our deepest longings in life may be what God desires for us.

What core values drive your actions in life?

Lord Jesus, help my heart to seek only what is above, and not what is of this world.

August 23

You should put away the old self of your former way of life,
corrupted through deceitful desires, and be renewed in the spirit
of your minds, and put on the new self, created in God's way in
righteousness and holiness of truth. — *Ephesians 4:22–24*

Every New Year's Eve, it is customary to make a "New Year's Resolution" in an attempt to improve ourselves in the coming year. Whether our resolution is to lose weight, give up a bad habit, or begin a self-help program, making a New Year's resolution is a great way for us to seek to put on a new self, a new way of being in righteousness and holiness. Yet we cannot create ourselves anew without the help of the Holy Spirit, who is the agent of transformation. If we are serious about renewing ourselves in mind, body, and spirit, let us turn to the Lord for help in letting go of our former way of life, that we may embrace new lives in Christ.

Each time we receive the Eucharist, we have an opportunity to experience spiritual transformation. The Real Presence of Jesus in the Eucharist has the power to recreate us anew, that we may have the courage to put away our former way of life, renewed in the spirit of our minds, as we put on a new self in Christ.

What needs transforming in your life?

Lord Jesus, may I be renewed in God's way in righteousness and holiness of truth.

August 24

Cast your care upon the LORD,
who will give you support.
He will never allow
the righteous to stumble. — Psalm 55:23

Major decisions require the Lord's help; however, we often fail to understand this, and instead choose pathways in life without first giving the situation to God. Many of my friends and colleagues are at the age of retirement, and making the decision when, how, and where to retire is scary. For many, it is very difficult to take that next step in life. The Lord calls us to cast our cares upon him, for he will never allow his people to stumble. If you are struggling with a major decision in life, whether it is retirement, purchasing a home, or changing jobs, spend time in prayer first before making any decisions. Seek the Lord's wisdom to help you choose wisely, for the Lord is with us, and every detail of our life is important to him.

Taking our concerns before Our Lord in the Blessed Sacrament is an excellent way for us to seek the Lord's help in making a decision. Jesus is present to us, and in the quiet of the adoration chapel or church, we can cast our concerns before the Lord, and he will give us support in helping to make the right decision.

What major decision are you facing? Bring this situation to God.

Lord Jesus, help me to bring my concerns to you, that with your help, I may choose wisely.

August 25

So humble yourselves under the mighty hand of God, that he may exalt you in due time. Cast all your worries upon him because he cares for you. — 1 Peter 5:6–7

In high school, I had a crush on a boy who was an upperclassman. We would pass by each other in the hallway, and he never noticed me. One day, I bumped into him in the library, and he smiled at me. This encounter made my day! At one time or another, we have all sought the affection of someone, and we all remember how good it felt for that person to notice us. Do you realize that our Father in heaven, who loves and cares for you, is always seeking your attention? Even when we did not deserve it, God sent his only Son, Jesus, to restore our covenant relationship with him. God loves us unconditionally.

We experience the love of God when we encounter Jesus in the Eucharist. The Body and Blood of Christ we receive draw us into the heart of Our Lord, and invite us to enter into a relationship with God. Let us humble ourselves under the mighty hand of God, that he may exalt us.

Have you had an experience where you felt that God loves you infinitely?

Lord Jesus, thank you for your gift of salvation. May the Eucharist free me from the worries of life, that I may focus my attention on loving and serving you.

August 26

*If you then, who are wicked, know how to give good gifts to
your children, how much more will your heavenly Father give
good gifts to those who ask him. — Matthew 7:11*

Every Christmas, my family teases me because I go overboard with presents. I find such joy in giving gifts to my family. I listen all year long when they express their desire for something, and I mentally file their wishes away so that I have a list of things they really want by the time Christmas comes. I know my family is grateful for the effort I make, and my thank you comes in the form of their smiles on Christmas morning. If I, with all of my imperfections as a human being, know how to give good gifts to my children, how much more will our heavenly Father give to those who ask him?

The greatest gift we have from our heavenly Father is the gift of Jesus in the Eucharist. God sent his only Son to save us from our sins. On the night before Jesus died, he gave us the gift of the Eucharist, that he would be with us for all time. The Eucharist holds for us the gifts of eternal life, forgiveness, peace, mercy, and love.

What gifts has Our Lord given you?

Lord Jesus, help me to cherish the gift of your Presence in the Eucharistic elements of bread and wine.

August 27

Train the young in the way they should go;
even when old, they will not swerve from it. — Proverbs 22:6

Parenting is one of the most rewarding vocations we can experience. The joy of raising our children in the Faith, and of watching them grow into the people God created them to be, is truly a blessing. As parents of adult children, I understand that at some point in our lives, we have to let them go; we have to launch them into the world as adults, trusting that they will not swerve from the path we have given them. Letting go is difficult. It calls for a strong faith in the Lord. We cannot rely on our children to make us happy — our source of joy must be in Jesus.

Spending time in prayer before the presence of Jesus in the Blessed Sacrament can help us refocus our attention on our relationship with Jesus. In the silence of the adoration chapel, we can give our children to the Lord, asking him to lead and guide them, trusting that the Lord loves them even more than we do. Jesus is waiting for us to come to him. Let us seek his Presence in the Blessed Sacrament.

Do you struggle with letting your grown children stand on their own?

Lord Jesus, grant me the grace to trust in your providential love, that in your time, my child will become the person you created him or her to be.

August 28

Cleanse your people, Lord, we pray,
from every taint of wickedness,
that their gifts may be pleasing to you;
and do not let them cling to false joys,
for you promise them the rewards of your truth. — Prayer
over the Offerings, Thursday in the Third Week of Lent

Have you ever had a smudge on your eyeglasses? It is so annoying, because even one tiny smudge can blur your vision, or can cause undue glare on your eyes. Cleaning our eyeglass lenses calls for great care, for if we rub too hard, we will scratch the lenses, and that can really be harmful to our vision. Sin, much like a smudge on our lenses, can blur our vision of what is right and wrong, causing us to cling to false truths instead of the truth of the Gospel.

Our encounter with Jesus in the Eucharist can help cleanse us of our bad habits, and of our tendencies toward sin. Jesus, present in the Eucharist, invites us to rid ourselves of every taint of wickedness, that the gift of our lives may be a pleasing sacrifice to Our Lord. May we come before the Lord in the Eucharist with pure hearts, seeking the truth of salvation and the rewards of eternal life.

What is one bad habit you would like to offer to the Lord?

Lord Jesus, cleanse me of my sin and help me not to cling to false truths that lead me away from you.

August 29

Accept, we pray, O Lord,
the sacrifice of Reconciliation and praise,
and grant that, cleansed by its working,
we may offer minds well pleasing to you. — Prayer over
the Offerings, Saturday after Ash Wednesday

Call to mind your deepest longings and desires; the hopes and dreams that you have for the future. Are you willing to entrust these desires to the Lord so that together you may be one in mind and spirit? Or are you hesitant to do so, because the deepest desires of your heart might not be compatible with the pure love of Jesus experienced in the Eucharist?

Jesus sacrificed his life for us on the cross for our sins, and restored our covenant relationship with the Lord. Each time we partake of his Body and Blood at the Eucharistic table, we have the opportunity to experience cleansing from all that keeps us from loving and praising Our Lord. We need to be willing to offer up our lives as a pleasing sacrifice to God for his gift of salvation, to align the deepest longings and desires of our hearts with the Lord's plan of salvation. Let us open our hearts and minds to receiving the transforming grace that awaits us in the Eucharist.

Are there things you need to purge from your life in order to walk with Jesus?

Lord Jesus, help me to live my life in alignment with the pure love I receive in the Eucharist.

August 30

Do nothing out of selfishness or out of vainglory; rather, humbly regard others as more important than yourselves, each looking out not for his own interests, but [also] everyone for those of others. Have among yourselves the same attitude that is also yours in Christ Jesus. — Philippians 2:3–5

Recently, at the end of the workday, the doorbell rang to our office suite. I answered it, and a young woman was inquiring about the RCIA program. I introduced myself and proceeded to take her to the person who could assist her. As she sat down, she mentioned that she also wanted to speak with me once she was finished meeting with the RCIA director. I hesitated for a moment, since I was ready to leave, and then said, "Sure, I will wait for you." In that moment, I realized that her spiritual needs were more important, particularly since she was inquiring about the RCIA program, and I did not want to be selfish. I wanted to offer hospitality to this young woman, as I knew Jesus would do.

When we encounter Jesus in the Eucharist, we experience the humility of Jesus, who regarded all people as equal, and treated each person with respect. The grace we receive in the Eucharist can help us to turn away from acts of vainglory and selfishness, and to refocus our attention on helping the needs of others.

Do you struggle with helping others?

Lord Jesus, help me to live with a humble heart open to helping others.

August 31

May the power of this sacrifice, O Lord, we pray,
mercifully wipe away what is old in us,
and increase in us grace of salvation and newness of life. — Prayer
over the Offerings, Wednesday in the Fourth Week of Lent

During his life on earth, Jesus healed the sick, fed the poor, ate and drank with sinners, and proclaimed liberty and peace to captives. He taught us how to forgive, how to reconcile, how to love God and one another; in essence, Jesus taught us newness of life. At the Last Supper, Jesus shared himself in the bread and wine, instructing his disciples to "do this in memory of me." When we receive the Eucharist, we accept Christ's invitation to carry out his entire life's work leading up to and including the action of the Last Supper.

"Do this in memory of me" is a liturgical call to action; it is an invitation for all believers to turn away from sin and to love and serve the Lord and one another. The power of the Eucharistic sacrifice will increase in us the grace of salvation and newness of life. Let us come before the Lord with hearts open to transformation.

What is one bad habit that you desire to change? Offer this to the Lord, seeking transformation.

Lord Jesus, help me to wipe away what is old and sinful, that I may live with the newness of life received in the Eucharist.

~ DISCIPLESHIP ~

September 1

Can you drink the cup that I am going to drink? — Matthew 20:22

Jesus used cup imagery throughout the Gospels. In this particular Scripture passage, when the mother of James and John confronts Jesus about a privileged status for her sons, Jesus poses this question to the two brothers: "Can you drink the cup that I am going to drink?" James and John freely respond yes to the invitation of Jesus, even though they had no idea of what they are committing to. They did not grasp who Jesus was, nor that he was about to be crucified; yet they still said yes.

Each time we come to Communion, Jesus is metaphorically waiting at the altar to ask us the very same question, "Can you drink of the cup?" What are the implications of this question for us? How do we find the courage to drink deeply from the cup of Christ without knowing where the road may take us? Our encounter with Jesus in the Eucharist can help us to become courageous in our faith, that we may follow the Lord wherever he may lead. Let us come to the table of the Lord with hearts open to readily accepting the Lord's invitation.

What cup is the Lord placing in your hands? What is preventing you from freely drinking of the cup of Christ?

Lord, may the Eucharist give me the strength to be your faithful disciple in this world.

September 2

Remember your leaders who spoke the word of God to you. Consider the outcome of their way of life and imitate their faith. Jesus Christ is the same yesterday, today, and forever. — Hebrews 13:7–8

The Christmas holidays bring out the best in everyone, especially when it comes to food. Whether I am making my favorite Christmas cookies, or bringing a new appetizer to a party, the best compliment someone can give me about my dish is that they want my recipe. They desire to recreate this wonderful and delicious dish so that they, too, can enjoy it and share it with their friends and family. We should feel the same way about our Faith. We should be so alive in our Catholic Faith that people want to know more about Jesus because of us. If we imitate the life of Christ, we have the recipe for eternal life, and everyone should desire this too.

Our mystical encounter with Jesus in the Eucharist should fill us with the joy of salvation, and this joy should be present in our lives, so that our family and friends take notice and they ask about our faith. Jesus Christ is the same yesterday, today and forever, and we who know and love the Lord should joyfully lead others to know and love him too.

Do you speak joyfully of your faith in Jesus?

Lord Jesus, help me to imitate your life, that others may come to know and love you through my actions.

September 3

*Blessed are they who hunger and thirst for righteousness,
for they will be satisfied. — Matthew 5:6*

Who are the hungry of the world? We do not have to look far. Perhaps it is our children, who hunger and thirst for words of affirmation and unconditional love in a world that seeks only to reward the best and the brightest. Who are the hungry of this world? Perhaps it is our young people, who hunger for morals and truth in a society that has lost its way. Who are the hungry of this world? Could it be your coworkers, the neighbor next door, or the person sitting across from you at the dinner table? God's people are spiritually hungry, and through our reception of the Eucharistic bread and wine, we can become nourishment for all those who hunger and thirst for righteousness.

We can satisfy the hunger and thirst of others by simple acts of kindness and compassion. Perhaps it is shoveling show for an elderly neighbor, visiting a sick friend, or picking up some groceries for a friend. The Eucharist challenges us to turn away from being self-centered, that we may focus our love and attention on satisfying the needs of others.

Today, who is one person that you can offer an act of kindness to without expecting anything in return?

Jesus, through my reception of the Eucharist, may I feed all those who hunger and thirst for your Divine Presence in their lives.

September 4

*This is how all will know you are my disciples, if you
have love for one another. — John 13:35*

I never play the lottery; however, there was a huge mega jackpot recently, and my husband encouraged me to take a chance, so I agreed. As I drove up to the local gas station to buy my ticket, I noticed that there was a homeless man sitting on a bench outside the gas station. It was winter, and he was poorly dressed for the elements. Reaching for my wallet, I could feel Jesus nudging me. I came out of the store, not with a lottery ticket, but with a steaming hot cup of coffee and a donut for the homeless man. I also noticed he had no gloves, so I gave him my mittens. Getting back into the car, I felt like I had won the lottery, because I knew that Jesus had placed this man in my presence, and gave me the grace to respond with love.

Our reception of the Body and Blood of Jesus renews our baptismal call to discipleship by inflaming our hearts with a true desire to love and serve our brothers and sisters in Christ. Let us pray we can see the world through the eyes of Christ.

Who is your homeless man? Who in your life can you lovingly offer help and assistance to?

Lord Jesus, help me to love and care for the people you have placed in my life.

September 5

We are ambassadors for Christ, as if God were appealing through us. We implore you on behalf of Christ, be reconciled to God. — *2 Corinthians 5:20*

Every Ash Wednesday, we hear this Scripture passage from Saint Paul, telling us that we are ambassadors for Christ. An ambassador is a loyal and trusted friend who speaks and acts on behalf of another. This is what Christ is calling us to do: to speak and act on his behalf. Jesus is entrusting us to share the good news of the Gospel with all people, not just with those we know or those who look or act like us. Where do we find the courage to carry out our mission in life as ambassadors of Christ? It is at the Eucharistic banquet.

Through our encounter with Jesus in the Eucharist, we obtain the strength and grace needed to proclaim the Good News of salvation to all we meet. We share the joy of the Gospel not in words, but in deeds. Are we kind, are we compassionate, are we forgiving? Are we welcoming, are we nonjudgmental, are we loving? Our experience of Jesus in the Eucharist sends us into the world to be his Presence to all.

In what ways can you notice and respond with joy to the needs of those around you?

Lord Jesus, thank you for entrusting me with the mission of acting on your behalf. Help me to be a faithful ambassador.

September 6

Is it not sharing your bread with the hungry,
bringing the afflicted and homeless into your house;
Clothing the naked when you see them,
and not turning your back on your own flesh? — Isaiah 58:7

Our reception of the Eucharist is not only a moment of personal grace; it is our spiritual nourishment, sustenance, and strength for doing the work of God, which, as the Prophet Isaiah reminds us, includes caring for our neighbor. Isaiah's last line can be problematic for many people because so many families are in turmoil. Many of our loved ones have chosen lifestyles that are not in line with our Catholic Faith. As family members, what are we to do?

Scripture instructs us to minister to them. Our family members need to experience the mercy and love of Jesus through us. The lost sheep in our families need the Good Shepherd, not a judge. Our reception of the Eucharist can give us the grace we need to meet our loved ones wherever they are in life, and to offer them the unconditional love and mercy of Jesus. Let us trust that God is at work in us.

Who are the lost sheep in your family? Ask the Lord to help you bring his loving Presence into their lives.

Lord Jesus, Good Shepherd, help me to minister to the lost sheep of my family with a tenderness like yours.

September 7

Blessed are you when they insult you and persecute you and utter every kind of evil against you [falsely] because of me. Rejoice and be glad, for your reward will be great in heaven. — *Matthew 5:11–12*

There's a fable about two frogs that ran a race. The giant frog trained all year while the little frog rested. On the day of the race, the townspeople came out to cheer on the two frogs. Shortly after the race began, the townspeople started jeering at the frogs. Soon, the big frog dropped out of the race; while the little frog hopped on, eventually crossing the finish line to the astonishment of everyone. The reporter from the town rushed over to the little frog to ask him how he was able to accomplish such a task; but the little frog's mother intervened, saying, "I am sorry, he cannot hear you; he is deaf."

Discipleship is risky. Like the little frog, we have to turn "a deaf ear" to those who tell us that the bread and wine are merely symbols. We need to stay the course and keep our eyes focused on the finish line, which is Christ. Our reception of Jesus in the Eucharist gives us the courage to take a risk for the sake of the Kingdom. While not always easy, our reward in heaven will be great.

Have you experienced a time when you had to defend your faith?

Jesus, may your Eucharistic Presence help me stay the course.

September 8

*When Jesus raised his eyes and saw that a large crowd was coming to
him, he said to Philip, "Where can we buy enough food for them to eat?"
He said this to test him, because he himself knew what he was going to
do. Philip answered him, "Two hundred days' wages worth of food
would not be enough for each of them to have a little [bit]." One
of his disciples, Andrew, the brother of Simon Peter, said to him,
"There is a boy here who has five barley loaves and two fish; but
what good are these for so many?" Then Jesus took the loaves,
gave thanks, and distributed them to those who were reclining, and
also as much of the fish as they wanted. — John 6:5–9, 11*

It is important to note that there would have been no miracle story
of the fish and loaves without the meager gifts of this young boy. Much
like the Gospel story, Jesus needs our gifts and talents to help him spiritually nourish all those who hunger and thirst for God. When we come
to the Eucharistic banquet, we receive the grace to grow in our awareness of our call to discipleship. Let us come before the Lord with hearts
eager to share our gifts with others.

**How is God calling you to use your gifts and talents to nourish
his people?**

*Lord, help me to willingly share my gifts with all those who seek to know and
love you.*

September 9

Many of the Samaritans of that town began to believe in him because of the word of the woman who testified, "He told me everything I have done." When the Samaritans came to him, they invited him to stay with them; and he stayed there two days. Many more began to believe in him because of his word, and they said to the woman, "We no longer believe because of your word, for we have heard for ourselves, and we know that this is truly the savior of the world." — John 4:39–42

There is a bit of the Samaritan woman in all of us. She is a seeker, a sinner, and an evangelist. Her heart yearns for the truth, and when she finds it in Jesus, she cannot keep this good news to herself. The Samaritan woman leaves everything to go and share her experience with her townspeople, who come to know Jesus through her witness.

When we encounter the Real Presence of Jesus, we experience his truth in a most profound and life-changing way. May we desire to meet Jesus in the Eucharist, and share our experience with our family, friends, and those that God sends our way.

In what ways can your experience of Jesus in the Eucharist transform you into a Spirit-filled disciple of Christ?

Lord Jesus, may your Eucharistic Presence inspire me to boldly proclaim your truth to all I meet this day.

September 10

*"The Eucharist commits us to the poor. To receive in truth
the Body and Blood of Christ given up for us, we must recognize
Christ in the poorest, his brethren." — CCC 1397*

A friend of mine was late for Mass. As he drove to church in haste, he passed a homeless man who was struggling to get his wheelchair over a curb. My friend kept driving. While he made it to Mass on time, this experience had a profound effect on him. Throughout Mass, he felt great remorse for not stopping to lend a hand to the disabled man in a wheelchair. He realized that he had failed to recognize and respond to the presence of Christ in the poorest of souls. Have you had a similar experience? Perhaps you have passed by a person at an intersection holding a sign asking for money. How did you respond?

When we unite ourselves to Jesus in the Eucharist, we unite ourselves to the merciful heart of Jesus, who calls us to recognize and respond to his Presence in all people, especially the poor. This is not an easy task, but with the Lord's help, we can minister to those whom God sends our way.

Who is your homeless man? Whose number do you ignore when it shows up on your caller ID?

Lord Jesus, may the Eucharist open the eyes of my heart, that I may see and respond to your Divine Presence in the people I encounter each day.

September 11

The liturgy is the summit toward which the activity of the Church is directed; at the same time it is the font from which all her power flows. — *Sacrosanctum Concilium, par. 10*

This statement from the Second Vatican Council underscores the primacy of the celebration of Mass in our lives. The sacred liturgy should be the high point of our spiritual lives, for here we encounter Jesus in four ways: in the priest, in the congregation, in the Scripture, and most especially in the Eucharist. As the font of the Church's power, the celebration of the Eucharist carries with it a sense of mission. If our encounter with Jesus stops at the church door, then we have not experienced the Mass as the font of our spiritual lives.

At the end of every liturgy, we are sent into the world to advocate for peace and justice, to feed the poor, to evangelize souls, and to defend all human life. How can we achieve any of this on our own? We cannot; we need the Eucharist. It is our source of spiritual nourishment needed for doing mission. Christ gave us the gift of himself in the elements of bread and wine, that we may have divine food to sustain us for our mission in life. Let us go forth from the table of the Lord strengthened by our reception of Jesus in the Eucharist.

What does your mission field look like?

Lord Jesus, may your Presence in the Eucharist empower me to be a faithful disciple.

September 12

> *The Christian people [are] "a chosen race, a royal priesthood, a holy nation, a redeemed people"[; it is] their right and duty by reason of their baptism.* — Sacrosanctum Concilium, par. 14

I was born in the 1950s, before the Second Vatican Council, and was baptized a few weeks after I was born. My baptism was celebrated on a Wednesday evening in the church rectory. My mom, who was Lutheran, was not present to witness the priest sprinkle holy water on my forehead to wash away original sin. In the Second Vatican Council, the Church emphatically declared that the baptized Body of believers are a chosen race, a royal priesthood, a holy nation, and God's own people by right and duty of their baptism. As such, we gather at the Eucharist as a priestly people, a holy nation, anointed for mission at the Eucharistic table of Christ.

The waters of the baptism font incorporate us into the living Body of Christ, and give us the right and duty to carry on the mission work of Jesus. Through our communion with Jesus at the Eucharistic table, Christ grants us his Spirit, who summons us to Christian discipleship and mission: "As the Father has sent me, so I send you" (Jn 20:21).

What does your baptism mean to you?

Lord, through the waters of baptism we rise to a new life in you. May your Eucharist give me the strength to carry out your mission.

September 13

Sing to the LORD, all the earth,
announce his salvation, day after day.
Tell his glory among the nations;
among all peoples, his wondrous deeds. — *1 Chronicles 16:23–24*

I enjoy watching the reality singing shows on television, because the people in the competition share their God-given gifts and talents with joyful exuberance. As they perform, their musical talents draw us into the joy of song and fill us with wonder. Our Christian faith invites us to share the Good News of Jesus in a similar manner. We are people of the Resurrection, and as such, the faith we share with our family and friends should be one of joy, hope, and redemption.

At the Eucharistic banquet, Jesus invites us to drink deeply from the chalice of discipleship. This invitation from Our Lord should fill us with joy, for Christ died for our sins. Spiritual joy is contagious. Let us sing out the Good News of Jesus; let us tell all people about the wondrous deeds of the Lord. Let us drink deeply from the Eucharistic chalice of salvation.

In what ways does your faith fill you with joy? Share that joy with others today.

Lord Jesus, help me to sing your song of salvation to all I meet this day.

September 14

Be imitators of me, as I am of Christ. — *1 Corinthians 11:1*

There is an old saying: "Imitation is the most sincere form of flattery." I find great wisdom in this sentiment, for when we imitate someone, we are outwardly telling people that we admire this individual so much that we want to be just like him or her. Therefore, we strive to imitate the person's mannerisms and fashions, and even the code of conduct that that person lives by.

Saint Paul, in his letter to the Corinthians, writes that we must imitate Christ. In partaking of the Eucharist, we become the very mystery we receive. To imitate the life of Jesus means treating others with mercy, forgiving those who hurt us, and loving God above all else and our neighbor as ourselves. Are we up to the task? Jesus is here to help us. His Divine Presence in the Eucharist will fill us with the grace of transformation we need to imitate his Presence in our lives.

Do you have a role model? What are the desirable qualities in this person that you want to emulate?

Lord Jesus, may your Eucharistic Presence strengthen me, so that my actions may imitate your life in word and in deed.

September 15

Then I heard the voice of the Lord saying, "Whom shall I send? Who will go for us?" "Here I am," I said; "send me!" — Isaiah 6:8

I fly frequently, and sometimes airlines will overbook a flight, so they offer certificates to anyone willing to give up their seat and take a later flight. Without fail, there is always a flurry of people flocking to the reservation counter to get their free certificate, as if they are saying, "Here I am. I will go." It would be wonderful if we were that excited about answering the Lord's invitation to share our faith with others.

Each time we partake of the Eucharistic Body and Blood of Jesus, the Lord is posing the same question to us as he did to Isaiah: "Whom shall I send?" "Who will go for us?" How will you answer the Lord? Our participation in the Eucharistic banquet affirms our response to the Lord, "Here I am, send me." Our encounter with Jesus in the Eucharist transforms us into the very mystery we receive, and sends us into the world to be Jesus to others.

Are you willing to respond to the Lord's call to discipleship?

Lord Jesus, send me into the world, that I may joyfully proclaim your Gospel message to all people.

September 16

For so the Lord has commanded us, "I have made you a light to the Gentiles, that you may be an instrument of salvation to the ends of the earth." — Acts 13:47

Any of us who has experienced a blackout knows the important of light. A single ray of light in the darkness can calm our fears and anxieties, and gives us a sense of direction as we stumble about in the dark. Our world is broken, and people across the nations fumble around without light, and without any sense of direction. We live in the moment, and only for ourselves. But Jesus has commissioned us, his faithful followers, to be a light to those who stumble in darkness, and to bring his message of salvation to the corners of our globe.

When we partake of the Eucharistic Body and Blood of Jesus at the Eucharistic table, we immerse ourselves in the radiant light of the Risen Christ. We gain clarity of vision as to how we can accomplish our mission in life, which is to shine a light on all who walk in darkness. Through the Eucharist, Jesus unites his heart with ours, and gives us grace to bring his message of light and love to all those in need.

How might you be a light today to your family and friends?

Lord Jesus, help me illuminate the darkened corners of our globe with your message of salvation.

September 17

As you enter a house, wish it peace. If the house is worthy, let your peace come upon it; if not, let your peace return to you. Whoever will not receive you or listen to your words — go outside that house or town and shake the dust from your feet. — Matthew 10:12–14

Disappointment can be a bitter pill to swallow. When we are excited about something, whether it is a relationship, a job, or even a new idea, and it does not turn out as we hoped, we can feel defeated. We may even give up trying. Surely, the apostles experienced the same feelings when Jesus sent them to share the Good News of the Gospel. Disappointment is part of our human experience. As Christians, we have to dispel feelings of defeat and disappointment before they overcome us, and keep our eyes fixed on Christ. Jesus will provide us with everything we need.

Our encounter with Jesus in the Eucharist gives us the grace to stay grounded in our Faith, so that bitterness may not take root in our hearts. Jesus will never let us down. His Eucharistic Presence will lift us out of despair and help us to refocus our attention on living as disciples of Christ.

How do you deal with defeat and disappointment?

Lord Jesus, help me to turn away from feelings of defeat, that I may focus my attention on sharing my faith with others.

September 18

Go, therefore, and make disciples of all nations, baptizing them in the name of the Father, and of the Son, and of the Holy Spirit, teaching them to observe all that I have commanded you. And behold, I am with you always, until the end of the age. — Matthew 28:19–20

This commandment given by Jesus to his apostles as he ascended into heaven is given to us, too, for we are his disciples through baptism. Our Christian faith is not meant to be a private matter between us and God. It is our baptismal right and duty to make disciples. The notion of sharing our faith with others makes some people feel uncomfortable. Growing up, my mom taught us that it was impolite to talk about religion or politics, because they are private matters. This is understandable, for talk is irrelevant if our actions do not support our Christian faith.

Dining at the Eucharistic table of Jesus gives us the necessary grace to share our faith with others, in a joyful and loving way, to let others see Christ in us. The Eucharist is our spiritual nourishment for doing the work of God. May our encounter with Jesus in the Eucharist help us to observe all that the Lord has commanded us to do.

How can you share the Gospel message of Jesus today?

Lord God, may the Eucharist give me the courage to boldly proclaim your message of salvation to my family and friends.

September 19

Then he said to his disciples, "The harvest is abundant but the laborers are few; so ask the master of the harvest to send out laborers for his harvest." — Matthew 9:37–38

At one point or another, most of us have volunteered our time and talents in service to our parish community, or at a local food bank, or even working on a committee for a worthwhile cause. Volunteers are always welcome — the more people who are there to help, the greater the chance that the event or project will be successful.

Jesus was keenly aware of the task before him, and he called on his disciples to share in the laborious work of spreading the Gospel. Two thousand years later, the harvest is still abundant, and the laborers remain few. As disciples of Jesus, he is sending us into the world now to act on his behalf. To help us accomplish the work of discipleship, Jesus gives us his Body and Blood in the Eucharist as spiritual nourishment for our journey. Let us come before the Lord at the Eucharistic table, seeking the grace to answer God's call to discipleship.

In what ways do you feel called by God to share your faith with others?

Lord Jesus, send me into the world, that I may lovingly serve all those in need.

September 20

Therefore, as we celebrate the memorial of his Death and Resurrection, we offer you, Lord, the bread of life and the Chalice of salvation. — *Anamnesis, Eucharistic Prayer II*

At Mass, a divine exchange of love occurs between God and us. Let me explain. Our Creator God made wheat and grapes; through the work of human hands, we took wheat, grapes, and created bread and wine for all to enjoy. Jesus chose these table elements, the gifts of humanity, to impart his Divine Presence for all time. At Mass, the People of God bring forward gifts of bread and wine for consecration; the Spirit transforms these gifts into the Body and Blood of Jesus, changing human gifts into divine. The priest then offers up the consecrated gifts of bread and wine — the perfect sacrifice of Jesus — to the Father in heaven. We then receive the divine gift of the Eucharist, and at the end of Mass, the priest sends us into the world to be Eucharist for one another. We return each Sunday to repeat this divine gift exchange.

The Eucharist is the Real Presence of Jesus, both divine and human; it is the gift exchange of pure love between God and his people. Let us give thanks to the Father in heaven for the gift of Jesus' Body and Blood, present in the consecrated elements of bread and wine.

How do you spiritually nourish those in your life?

Lord Jesus, I am so grateful for your gift of the Eucharist.

September 21

Train yourself for devotion, for, while physical training is of limited value, devotion is valuable in every respect, since it holds a promise of life both for the present and for the future. This saying is trustworthy and deserves full acceptance. — *1 Timothy 4:7–9*

Our Catholic Faith offers us a treasury of spiritual disciplines to assist us on our journey in life. Training ourselves to read Scripture every day can help us come to know and love Our Lord through his written word. Personal prayer practices, like daily recitation of the Rosary, invite us into the heart of our Blessed Mother by meditating on the life of Jesus in the mysteries. Spiritual direction helps us recognize the movement of the Spirit in our lives. The most valuable devotion in training for our spiritual lives is the practice of Eucharistic adoration, for it holds a promise of life both for the present and for the future.

When we pray before the Blessed Sacrament, we are in the presence of Our Lord, who gave his life for us. Jesus is longing for us to be with him, that he may speak to us words of love, encouragement, and hope. In the words of Saint Timothy, train yourself for this devotion; it is trustworthy and deserves full acceptance.

Is adoration part of your spiritual practices?

Lord Jesus, help me to devote time to you in prayer before the Blessed Sacrament.

September 22

"Are these all the sons you have?" Jesse replied, "There is still the youngest, but he is tending the sheep." Samuel said to Jesse, "Send for him; we will not sit down to eat until he arrives here." Jesse had the young man brought to them. He was ruddy, a youth with beautiful eyes, and good looking. The LORD said: There — anoint him, for this is the one! Then Samuel, with the horn of oil in hand, anointed him in the midst of his brothers, and from that day on, the spirit of the LORD rushed upon David. — 1 Samuel 16:11–13

There is a saying: "God doesn't call the equipped; he equips the called." The story of young David illustrates this so well. Our Lord anoints each one of us, with our unique gifts, to be his disciples. He does not judge by appearance, but by the purity of our hearts.

Jesus desires us that we step aside from the busyness of daily activities to spend time with him before his Presence in the Blessed Sacrament, that we may quiet our hearts and listen as the Lord speaks to us. Let us come before the presence of Jesus in the Blessed Sacrament, and allow the Holy Spirit to help prepare us to be his disciples in the world.

What is preventing you from being a disciple of Jesus?

Lord Jesus, quiet my mind, that I may hear you speaking in the recesses of my heart.

September 23

It was not you who chose me, but I who chose you and appointed you to go and bear fruit that will remain, so that whatever you ask the Father in my name he may give you. — John 15:16

As human beings, we like to choose. We choose whom we will marry, the names we will give our children, the places we live, and the parishes where we worship. The list is endless. Choice is a benefit of our God-given free will. John's Gospel tells us that Jesus has chosen you and me to go out and bear fruit for his kingdom. If we accept our mission in life, whatever we ask the Father in his name, he will give us. This is a powerful promise, and invites us to reflect on if our choices in life align with our mission as disciples of Jesus.

When we spend time in prayer in the presence of the Blessed Sacrament, we have an opportunity to do some soul-searching with Jesus. He is present to us, and will help us realign our choices in life, that we may be one with him in purpose and plan. In his loving Presence, he will take us by the hand and lead us if we choose to follow.

What will you ask the Father to give you in Jesus' name?

Lord Jesus, thank you for choosing me. May my life bear abundant fruit for your kingdom.

September 24

Rather, let the greatest among you be as the youngest, and the leader as the servant. For who is greater: the one seated at table or the one who serves? Is it not the one seated at table? I am among you as the one who serves. — Luke 22:26–27

My husband and I have our favorite places to dine out. We return to these restaurants not simply because of the food, but also to see the wait staff who serve us. They are incredibly friendly and they make us feel welcome. Through the years, we have developed a wonderful relationship with each one of our servers. In a way, parish life should be a similar experience. Many of us shop around for a parish, seeking a faith community where we feel welcomed and nourished in mind, body, and spirit. Hospitality is essential to our worship experience, and service to others is at the heart of hospitality.

Jesus modeled Christian discipleship through service. Joyfully serving others in the name of Jesus will draw people closer to Christ. Our encounter with Jesus in the Eucharist should fill us with the joy of discipleship, and should inflame our hearts to serve others in the name of Christ.

How important is the service of hospitality to your parish experience?

Lord Jesus, you gave us a model to follow. Help me to serve all those I meet this day, that through my actions others may come to know and love you.

September 25

Tell his glory among the nations,
among all peoples, his marvelous deeds.
For great is the LORD and highly to be praised. — Psalm 96:3–4

Some of us are tempted to consider faith to be a private matter. In reality, nothing could be further from the truth. Jesus told his apostles to go and make disciples of all nations (see Mt 28:19), and he summons us to do the same. The Gospels tell the stories of individuals whose lives Jesus transformed, and how they eagerly shared their experience of Jesus with others. These people gave personal testimony to their encounter with Jesus. Once the Lord touches your heart, it is almost impossible not to proclaim his wonders among all the people.

Jesus, the only Son of God, is sacramentally present to us in the Eucharist. If we seek transformation through our Eucharistic experience, our lives will slowly begin to transform, and the good news of spiritual transformation will not be something we can keep to ourselves. Our Lord is waiting for us to come to him. When the Lord touches our heart, our lives will begin to change, and we will tell his wonders among all the people, for the Lord is great and is to be highly praised.

Are you comfortable sharing your faith with others?

Lord Jesus, pour out your spirit upon me, that I may boldly proclaim my faith to others in word and in deed.

September 26

As you strengthen me with the Bread of heaven,
and gladden me with the chalice of the new covenant,
bring me, holy Father, to serve you faithfully
and to spend my life boldly and zealously for the salvation of all
humanity. — Prayer after Communion, Mass for the Priest Himself

The Sacrament of Baptism claims us for Christ, and we are anointed as priest, prophet, and king with the oil of chrism. Hence, it is our priestly duty as members of the baptized Body of believers to spend our life boldly proclaiming God's message of salvation to all people. This is not an easy task, for as lay people, our paths take us in many directions including marriage, parenting, and careers. Yet no matter what our vocations are, we all share the same core Christian identity: priest, prophet, and king.

Our shared experience of Jesus in the Eucharist provides the spiritual nourishment for us to proclaim the message of Jesus in the vocations that the Lord has chosen for us. Strengthened with the bread of heaven and gladdened with the chalice of the New Covenant, our encounter with Jesus in the Eucharist gives us the strength to zealously share our lives in loving service to Our Lord.

How do you live out your baptismal identity as priest, prophet, and king?

Lord Jesus, help me to spend my life in faithful service to you.

September 27

Keep us attentive to the needs of all that, sharing their grief and pain, their joy and hope, we may faithfully bring them the good news of salvation and go forward with them along the way of your Kingdom. — Intercessions, Eucharistic Prayer III, Mass for Various Needs and Occasions

We naturally tend to concentrate solely on the tasks that need our immediate attention; but in doing so, we miss opportunities the Lord may send us to serve the needs of our neighbors. Life is busy, and it pulls our attention in so many directions. How do we widen our range of vision, that we may see and respond to the needs of God's people when they come to us?

Our encounter with Jesus in the Eucharist can help us open our eyes, that we may see the needs of others, while giving us the strength to accompany those who are in crisis, or to share genuinely in their joy and hope. The Real Presence of Jesus we experience in the Eucharist gives us the grace to minister to people in need, while helping these individuals draw closer to Christ through our actions of love and service. Let us come before the Lord with open hearts, seeking to serve others.

The Eucharist gives us spiritual sight to see and respond to others. Who in your life needs your help?

Lord Jesus, may your Eucharist help me to faithfully serve my brothers and sisters in Christ.

September 28

We have partaken of the gifts of this sacred mystery,
humbly imploring, O Lord,
that what your Son commanded us to do
in memory of him
may bring us growth in charity. — Prayer after
Communion, Friday in the Fifth Week of Easter

When we encounter Jesus in the Eucharist, we have the opportunity to become the very mystery we receive. Stop and consider this spiritual reality for a moment. Are you aware of the transformation that awaits you each time you partake of Eucharist? Many of us have become so comfortable with routinely receiving Communion that we fail to experience the sacred mystery of the gift of Jesus. The ritual of receiving Communion has, for some, diminished to a grab-and-go experience, leaving no room for the reverence and awe that this mystical encounter with Jesus calls for.

Jesus is present to us in the Eucharist, and he is waiting for us to come before him with humble hearts, that he may lift us up and transform our lives. Every Mass makes present the once-and-for-all perfect sacrifice of Jesus. As we eat and drink of his Body and Blood, we do this in memory of Jesus, who sacrificed his life for our sins.

How has your experience of the Eucharist enhanced your charity toward others?

Lord Jesus, may my participation in the Eucharistic banquet help me to grow in acts of charity toward my neighbor.

September 29

May our participation at your table sanctify us,
and grant that through the Sacrament of your Church
all nations may receive in rejoicing the salvation
accomplished on the Cross by your only begotten Son. — Prayer
after Communion, Mass for the Evangelization of Peoples

My granddaughter is in junior high, and she has decided to try out for the school play. Regardless of what part she might receive, her participation in this extracurricular after-school activity takes a major commitment. It takes a sacrifice on the part of my granddaughter, for the rehearsal schedule is weekly for six months, and she is expected to attend all of the rehearsals, because her individual participation and formation of her role is vital to the success of the entire production.

Jesus is looking for a similar commitment from us when we participate at the Lord's table. When we receive the Eucharist, we are making the commitment to be a faithful follower of Jesus. Week after week, as we participate at the Eucharistic banquet, Jesus seeks our hearts so that our faith may grow and prosper. Our participation as a disciple is vital for helping to share the good news of salvation accomplished on the cross by Jesus, the only begotten Son of God.

How committed are you to your Catholic Faith?

Lord Jesus, help me to live as a faithful disciple, committed to sharing your news of salvation with all those you send my way.

September 30

O God, be gracious and bless us,
and let your face shed its light upon us, and have mercy.
So will your ways be known upon earth
and all nations learn your salvation. — Entrance
Antiphon, Mass for the Evangelization of Peoples

There comes a point in all our lives where we find ourselves at a crossroad, and we have a decision to make which will affect our life and the lives of those we love. The best way for us to prepare to make a major life decision is to turn the situation over to Our Lord in prayer, asking God to be gracious, to bless us, and to let his light guide our steps. Without the Lord's help, we take a great risk of choosing the wrong path.

Jesus is present to us in the Blessed Sacrament. Spending quiet time in prayer before him is an excellent way for us to receive his wisdom and counsel to assist us in making a decision. Jesus desires that we turn to him. Let us draw near to Our Lord in the Blessed Sacrament; let us bring him all that troubles us, for Jesus will shine his guiding light to help us every step of the way.

What major decision are you facing in life? Bring this situation to the Lord in prayer.

Lord Jesus, may your Presence in the Eucharist fill me with your wisdom, that I may choose wisely at every crossroad in life.

~ UNITY ~

October 1

In a similar way, when supper was ended, he took the chalice and, once more giving thanks, he gave it to his disciples, saying: "Take this, all of you, and drink from it: For this is the chalice of my Blood, the Blood of the new and eternal covenant, which will be poured out for you and for many for the forgiveness of sins." — Institution Narrative, Eucharistic Prayer II

On the night of the Last Supper, Jesus took the familiar event of the Passover supper and gave it new meaning. Scripture scholars believe pottery to be very common in ancient times, and most likely the apostles each had their own cups; yet Jesus ritually invites them to drink from his cup to signify the unity of the Body of Christ. Jesus used table fellowship as a symbol of God's openness and invitation for all people to be one Body in union with Christ.

At the table of the Lord, we unite ourselves to the humanity and divinity of Jesus, as we join our hearts in union with the Church, the living Body of Christ. This Eucharistic action of eating and drinking the Body and Blood of Christ invites us to look beyond our own lives and to lovingly care for the needs of others, for we are all united as brothers and sisters in Christ.

How can you see Christ in all people?

Lord, help me to love and care for all those you send my way.

October 2

Every day they devoted themselves to meeting together in the temple area and to breaking bread in their homes. They ate their meals with exultation and sincerity of heart, praising God and enjoying favor with all the people. — Acts 2:46–47

For the first three hundred years of our Church, the sacred space for early Christian gatherings was within a house. In this intimate gathering around a table, Christians came together as one community to praise God and to enjoy favor with their fellow believers; and in the action of breaking bread together, the Lord was in their midst. It is easy to understand how these early Christian gatherings shared an experience of community, because worship took place in small, intimate house settings. Over time, we have lost our spiritual sense of connectedness, because our church buildings are enormous, and it is impossible to know everyone. Yet, our call to be in unity with our brothers and sisters in Christ remains.

When we join our brothers and sisters at the altar, sharing in the action of the Eucharist, we have a wonderful opportunity to renew our sense of belonging to one another. At this Eucharistic table, the Lord is in our midst. Let us seek his divine grace to help reawaken our sense of belonging to one another.

What are some ways you can increase your sense of connectedness with your parish community?

Lord Jesus, may the Eucharist help us to recognize and respond to the needs of our brothers and sisters in Christ.

October 3

The principal fruit of receiving the Eucharist in Holy Communion is an intimate union with Christ Jesus. — CCC 1391

We enter into a spiritual union with Christ when we receive him in the Eucharist. We are familiar with the word *union* as it applies to the Sacrament of Matrimony when we say that the "two shall become one." We also hear this word used to describe people standing together in solidarity for a just cause. While these are wonderful examples, I think the Eucharistic reality of union with Christ calls us to step back and to reflect upon this wondrous mystical experience that occurs each time we receive Communion.

What exactly does "union with Christ" mean? When we partake of the Eucharist, we become the very mystery we receive. In doing so, we take on the spiritual qualities of Jesus, who is loving, kind, merciful, and forgiving. Our spiritual union with the Real Presence of Jesus helps us to live in the world with the heart of Christ. It invites us to see the world through the eyes of Jesus, and to lovingly minister to others in his name. What a wonderful gift awaits us at the Eucharistic table!

Do you feel worthy to be in union with Christ? Make an examination of conscience and receive the Sacrament of Reconciliation.

Lord, help me to be your Presence to all I meet this day.

October 4

As this reception of your Holy Communion, O Lord,
foreshadows the union of the faithful in you,
so may it bring about unity in your Church. — Prayer after
Communion, Mass for the Unity of Christians

Jesus gave us the gift of himself in the Eucharistic bread and wine as a foretaste of the heavenly banquet. The Eucharist is spiritual food for our journey in life; it is our sustenance for doing the work of God. Jesus prayed that we would all be one, as he and the Father are one (see Jn 17:21). The Lord desires that there be unity in his Church, for he suffered and died for the sins of all people for all time.

Jesus did not suffer death just for good people, or for those we consider worthy of salvation. Jesus came into this world to save all of humanity for generations to come. The hope of salvation is that all people will come to know and love Jesus, that we may be redeemed by the Blood of the Lamb. The Eucharist we receive gives us the strength to share our faith with others, in the hopes that all will come to know and follow Jesus as they turn from their sinful ways and embrace a life with Christ.

How can you help lead others to know and love Jesus?

Lord Jesus, may the Eucharist I receive lead me to inspire others to follow you.

October 5

Yet I live, no longer I, but Christ lives in me; insofar as I now live in the flesh, I live by faith in the Son of God who has loved me and given himself up for me. — *Galatians 2:20*

In our Christian tradition, there are three stages of spiritual development: purgative, illuminative, and unitive. These are fluid stages and because we are human, we can move in and out of each stage.

As we begin to grow in an awareness of God, we enter the purgative stage, which is often filled with fear and strife because we want to control people and events. In the illuminative stage of development, there is a joyous awareness of the presence of God, and a deep certitude that God is in all things. The third and highest state of spiritual development is mystical union with God. It is a gift from God, and while we cannot will it into being, we should certainly desire it. Many great saints like Teresa of Ávila experienced mystical union with God.

There is no better way for us to progress in our spiritual lives than to receive Jesus in the Eucharist. When we partake of his Body and Blood we come into union with Christ; and it is no longer we, but Christ living within us.

Which spiritual stage of development do you find yourself in today?

Lord Jesus, draw me into your Sacred Heart, that you and I may be united as one.

October 6

I urge you, brothers, in the name of our Lord Jesus Christ, that all of you agree in what you say, and that there be no divisions among you, but that you be united in the same mind and in the same purpose. — *1 Corinthians 1:10*

This letter, penned by Saint Paul to the Corinthian people some two thousand years ago, applies to the Christian people of today. Practically speaking, the unity that Saint Paul speaks of seems to be out of our reach, because we are so passionate about our own opinions and beliefs. Often this personalized rhetoric comes up against the universal truth of our Church, creating division in families, in parish life, and in the workplace. Yet Saint Paul's message is clear and unchanging; he is calling us to unity in Christ Jesus. How will we accomplish this monumental task?

Our reception of the Eucharistic Body and Blood of Jesus brings us into spiritual union with Jesus and with our brothers and sisters in Christ. This singular encounter with Jesus in the Eucharist draws us into the heart of Christ, with the hope and promise that we may all be one in his name. May this mystical moment of spiritual communion transform us and lead us to be of one heart and mind in Christ Jesus.

How do you handle division and conflict?

Lord Jesus, may your Eucharistic Presence grant me the grace to be in union with my brothers and sisters in Christ.

October 7

*For all of you who were baptized into Christ have clothed
yourselves with Christ. There is neither Jew nor Greek, there is
neither slave nor free person, there is not male and female; for
you are all one in Christ Jesus. — Galatians 3:27–28*

I read a quote on social media that said, "It is not who you are, but *whose* you are that is important." At our very core, we belong to Christ. We are children of our heavenly Father and members of the human family of God. Unfortunately, our world is intent on making distinctions that separate us from one another, creating disharmony and discord. The Lord does not care what we do for a living, nor what prestigious neighborhood we may reside in. We have clothed ourselves with Christ, and the Lord is calling us to live this identity in the world.

When we partake of the one bread and one cup of the Eucharist, we receive the graces to help us to belong to Christ above any other category the world imposes on us. Jesus shed his Blood for all of humanity. Let us approach the table of the Lord with hearts seeking unity with our brothers and sisters in Christ.

Do you struggle with certain groups or classes of people? Ask the Lord to help you.

Lord Jesus, help me to see beyond the distinctions the world has set forth, that we may be one in Christ.

October 8

The community of believers was of one heart and mind,
and no one claimed that any of his possessions was his own,
but they had everything in common. — Acts 4:32

After forty-six years of marriage and raising two children, my husband and I are trying to downsize, and we have accumulated many things. Some are sentimental items inherited from our parents when they passed away; other items belong to our adult children who claim they have no space for them. Others are goods we have bought and never really used. I clean out my closets monthly and donate to organizations that care for those in need. Our society reveres abundance, and the concept of sharing everything in common with others is hard concept for many to grasp. Sharing our goods is a lofty and achievable goal, if we are willing to refocus our priorities into loving God and our neighbor above all else.

Partaking of the Eucharistic Body and Blood of Jesus can help us see the face of Christ in the poor and the underprivileged. Our Communion at the altar brings us into union with Jesus and gives us the grace to see the world through his eyes. Let us pray that we may be open to sharing our abundant blessings with those in need.

Do you find it difficult to share your goods with others?

Lord Jesus, help me to see and respond to all those in need.

October 9

If there is any encouragement in Christ, any solace in love, any participation in the Spirit, any compassion and mercy, complete my joy by being of the same mind, with the same love, united in heart, thinking one thing. Do nothing out of selfishness or out of vainglory; rather, humbly regard others as more important than yourselves. — Philippians 2:1–3

A colleague of mine volunteered with an organization that mentors inner city children. After working all day, he would travel into the city several times a week to teach children, less fortunate than himself, the skills necessary to succeed in life. He found joy in empowering the young people to believe in themselves and in the good that they could accomplish for their community. A humble man, he never took any credit for the work he did in helping these underprivileged children succeed. While not everyone can mentor, we can work together with people, uniting ourselves in heart and mind, seeking to do the will of God, for we are his God's children.

Taking time to pray before the presence of Jesus in the Blessed Sacrament can help us gain clarity of vision and give us the grace to see the world with the eyes of Christ. Ask Jesus to fill you with his mercy and love, that you may be his Presence in the world.

Do you consider yourself above others?

Lord Jesus, help me to live with a humble heart that sees your Presence in all people.

October 10

But grace was given to each of us according to the measure of Christ's gift. He gave some as apostles, others as prophets, others as evangelists, others as pastors and teachers, to equip the holy ones for the work of ministry, for building up the body of Christ, until we all attain to the unity of faith and knowledge of the Son of God, to mature manhood, to the extent of the full stature of Christ. — Ephesians 4:7, 11–13

When a natural disaster, such as a hurricane or tornado, ravages a town, neighbors come together to help those who have been affected by the storm. Strangers help strangers, bonded by a true sense of community. In that community of helpers are carpenters, electricians, plumbers, food service people, and outreach coordinators who work together as one family to help those in need. In these occasions we witness the Body of Christ ministering to the Body of Christ.

The Lord has graced each one of us with different gifts for doing the holy work of God, and no one is more important than another. When we partake of the Eucharistic banquet, we gather as one community bonded in our shared faith in Christ Jesus. Our reception of the Eucharist strengthens our bond of unity with the Lord and one another.

What is your experience of community?

Lord Jesus, may your Eucharistic Body and Blood equip us for doing the holy work of God.

October 11

For by the grace given to me I tell everyone among you not to think of himself more highly than one ought to think, but to think soberly, each according to the measure of faith that God has apportioned. — Romans 12:3

When I graduated with my doctor of ministry degree, I was certain that God had called me to teach, so I sent my resume out to numerous Catholic colleges and universities in my area — and I received more rejection letters than I could count. Bewildered, I prayed in earnest for the Lord to show me my path in life. Eighteen months later, God brought me to the ministry role I currently serve in, and it has been life-giving. Without a doubt, I am doing the work that God created me to do, with the grace and faith that God apportioned to me to fulfill my role in his plan. God created each one of us, and we each have a purpose and mission to fulfill, though discerning what this mission is can be difficult.

Taking time for prayer before the Blessed Sacrament helps us to discern our pathway in life. Jesus is present and he is waiting for us to bring our cares and concerns to him. Seek his wisdom, and listen for him to speak to you. Pray and persevere.

Do you feel that you are fulfilling the Lord's plan for you?

Lord Jesus, thank you for my gift of faith. May I use it to fulfill the mission you have given me.

October 12

*As you sent me into the world, so I sent them into the world. And
I consecrate myself for them, so that they also may be consecrated
in truth. I pray not only for them, but also for those who
will believe in me through their word, so that they may all be one,
as you, Father, are in me and I in you, that they also may be in us,
that the world may believe that you sent me. — John 17:18–21*

Intimate union with Jesus in the Eucharist cannot be understated.
Jesus gave us the gift of himself through the elements of ordinary food.
He could have made the sun spin every day at noon, as a reminder
that he is with us always. Instead, he chose to take ordinary bread and
wine to impart his life through food that we would consume. When
we receive Communion, we are in union with Jesus: he in us, and we
in him. Through this sacred encounter with Jesus, we are consecrated
and made holy.

May this divine experience at the altar fill us with the love of God
and send us into the world to proclaim the truth of the Gospel so that
others may come to believe.

**In what ways does the knowledge that you and Jesus are made one
in the Eucharist impact how you live your life?**

Lord Jesus, help me to proclaim your truth to all I meet this day.

October 13

I ... urge you to live in a manner worthy of the call you have received, with all humility and gentleness, with patience, bearing with one another through love, striving to preserve the unity of the spirit through the bond of peace: one body and one Spirit, as you were also called to the one hope of your call; one Lord, one faith, one baptism; one God and Father of all, who is over all and through all and in all. — Ephesians 4:1–6

Those baptized as babies might find it hard to imagine that God has called them to be Christian, since their parents made the decision for them. At some point in our lives, each one of us has to make the conscious decision to follow Christ and to dedicate our lives to living out the Gospel message of Jesus, which is peace, love, and forgiveness for all people. When we look at the world around us, we can easily get discouraged. Fortunately, we are not alone; Jesus is here to help us.

Each time we eat and drink of the Body and Blood of Christ, we encounter the Real Presence of Jesus. He gives us the grace we need to help preserve the vision of our Christian faith where all people are treated as children of God.

At what point in your life did you choose to follow Christ?

Lord Jesus, may the Eucharist help me to live in peace and harmony with all people.

October 14

*May the God of endurance and encouragement grant you to think
in harmony with one another, in keeping with Christ Jesus, that
with one accord you may with one voice glorify the God and
Father of our Lord Jesus Christ. — Romans 15:5–6*

There is nothing so beautiful as classical music played by an orchestra. A full orchestra employs forty-four different instruments; yet, as the music begins, we hear one harmonious melody. The conductor's responsibility is to unify all the unique instruments, controlling the tempo and the sound of each one in order to create a single, unified harmony. This metaphor of a symphony can be likened to our lives with Christ.

Our Lord, as the conductor of our lives, invites us to be in harmony with one another. Jesus is not suggesting that we lose our identity, but rather that the notes of our lives harmonize with others to create one voice glorifying the Lord. We have the opportunity to experience union with Our Lord and our neighbor when we receive Communion. Jesus, who is present in the consecrated elements of bread and wine, invites us to partake of his Real Presence, that all who dine at table may become one voice glorifying the God and Father of Our Lord Jesus Christ.

How can you work together with others to glorify Our Lord?

Lord Jesus, help me to think in harmony with my neighbor, that together we may offer a unified voice of praise to you.

October 15

*I give you a new commandment: love one another. As I have loved you,
so you also should love one another. This is how all will know that you
are my disciples, if you have love for one another.* — *John 13:34–35*

There is a story of a bank teller robbed at gunpoint, and held hostage. Sitting on the floor of the bank, with a gun pointed at her, the bank teller told the robber that God loved him, and that she did too. She asked him if they could pray together. The young man started to cry, and soon afterward surrendered to the police. We can never underestimate the power of love. God is love, and his divine force of creation is what binds human beings together.

When we partake of the Eucharist, we experience the divine love of Jesus, who gave his life for our sins. Jesus' love is pure, and he pours it into our hearts each time we receive his Body and Blood. Our Communion unites us to Christ and to all those who believe in him.

How well do you follow Jesus' commandment to love those who are different from you?

Lord Jesus, help me to follow your example, that I may love my brothers and sisters in Christ.

October 16

I say to you, if two of you agree on earth about anything for which they are to pray, it shall be granted to them by my heavenly Father. For where two or three are gathered together in my name, there am I in the midst of them. — *Matthew 18:19–20*

There is power in prayer. When we pray together in groups of two, three, or more, Jesus is in our midst. His divine love draws our hearts together as one Body, unifying us in our common prayers of praise, petition, and thanksgiving.

Our encounter with Jesus in the Eucharist invites us to break through the barriers of indifference and tear down the walls of division, so that we may recognize that we are brothers and sisters in Christ. Jesus died for the sins of all. He made no distinctions. The Body and Blood we share at the altar feeds our souls and strengthens us with the grace to gather as one living Body of Christ, united in our love for Jesus.

What is your experience of praying together in a small group for a common cause?

Lord Jesus, hear my prayers and help me to walk in unity with my brothers and sisters in Christ.

October 17

And he gave some as apostles, others as prophets, others as evangelists, others as pastors and teachers, to equip the holy ones for the work of ministry, for building up the body of Christ, until we all attain to the unity of faith and knowledge of the Son of God, to mature manhood, to the extent of the full stature of Christ. — Ephesians 4:11–13

We begin our lives with Christ in the waters of baptism. With the oil of chrism, we are anointed priest, prophet, and king, and we all have a share in the glorious kingdom of God. From the unified Body of believers, the Lord calls forth some as apostles, others as prophets, and others as pastors, teachers, and healers. While we may have different vocations, we all begin our lives in the same way, as baptized members of the Body of Christ. It is our faith in Jesus that unites us as one Body, while we celebrate our diversity of spiritual gifts.

When we receive the Body and Blood of Christ, we attain the unity of faith and knowledge of the Son of God that we desire in spiritual maturity. Jesus is waiting for us to come to him, that he may enrich our lives and equip us for the work of our ministry in building up the Body of Christ.

What gifts has the Lord given to you? How will you use them for the betterment of others?

Lord Jesus, may I be equipped for the work that you have created me to do.

October 18

Put on then, as God's chosen ones, holy and beloved, heartfelt compassion, kindness, humility, gentleness, and patience, bearing with one another and forgiving one another, if one has a grievance against another; as the Lord has forgiven you, so must you also do. And over all these put on love, that is, the bond of perfection. — Colossians 3:12–14

There is an old saying: "Don't criticize someone until you've walked a mile in their shoes." There is truth to this, for often our first inclination is to condemn an action when we do not know the story or reasons behind it. The Lord calls us to bear with one another, and to forgive others, because the Lord has done this for us. We are God's chosen ones, called to walk in the shoes of Jesus, and to imitate his qualities of kindness, humility, gentleness, and patience. Over all things, we are to put on love, for this binds us together with our brothers and sisters in Christ in a bond of perfection.

When we partake of his Body and Blood we are renewed in the sacrificial love of Jesus, and we are given the grace to live our lives as holy and beloved children of the Lord, God's chosen ones.

Do you find yourself criticizing others? How can you develop habits of patience and kindness instead?

Lord Jesus, help me to imitate your life, for you are pure and perfect love.

October 19

And be thankful. Let the word of Christ dwell in you richly. … And whatever you do, in word or in deed, do everything in the name of the Lord Jesus, giving thanks to God the Father through him. — Colossians 3:15–17

There is a quote attributed to Meister Eckhart: "If the only prayer you ever say in your life is thank you, it will be enough." Gratitude is not pervasive in our consumer-driven society. Promotional ads on television and social media tell us that our lives will be better if we buy more, want more, and achieve more. There is no gratitude in this kind of messaging. Gratitude helps us to focus on the blessings that we have, not on what we want. When we cultivate an attitude of gratitude, we live as peaceful people, for we are satisfied with the gifts Our Lord has given us. Gratitude is a choice we must make each day.

The word *Eucharist* derives from a Greek word that means thanksgiving. Our reception of Jesus in the Eucharist fills us with a profound spirit of gratitude to God for the gift of his Son, who is the greatest gift of all. In him, we have everything we need. May we do all things in the name of Our Lord Jesus, giving thanks to God through him.

What can you thank God for today?

Lord Jesus, help me to be grateful for the abundant blessings you have given me.

October 20

I have given them the glory you gave me, so that they be one, as we are one,
I in them and you in me, that they may be brought to perfection as one,
that the world may know that you sent me, and that you loved them even
as you loved me. Father, they are your gift to me. — *John 17:22–24*

This poignant prayer from Jesus to the Father on the night before he died expresses his heartfelt desire for our unity. Jesus earnestly prays that his sacrifice on the cross may bring us to perfection as one, so that the world may know that the Father sent him. By imitating the life of Jesus, we will draw others to believe in him because of the love we share with our brothers and sisters in Christ.

When we partake of the Eucharist, we receive the Real Presence of Jesus, who desired that we may be brought to perfection as one. Bonded by his divine love, we are the Body of Christ, united to Jesus. May the Eucharist help us to live in peaceful harmony with all of God's people.

How can others come to know and love Jesus through your actions?

Lord Jesus, may your Eucharist perfect in me your sacrificial gift of love.

October 21

How good and how pleasant it is,
when brothers dwell together as one! — Psalm 133:1

Our world is polarized. We are at odds on hot-button issues including politics, religion, climate change, and morals; the list of these passion-evoking causes is endless, and we are hard pressed to find any goodness or pleasantry in any of this. Yet, Jesus gave his life on the cross for everyone. He prayed that we would all be one, as he is one with the Father. Our goal as followers of Jesus is not to despair, not to give in to angry discourse, but to seek to dwell in peace with others. We cannot do this alone; we need the help of Jesus.

Our encounter with the Lord in the Eucharist unites us to the Sacred Heart of Jesus, where we experience his fountain of mercy and forgiveness. This spiritual experience can help refocus our attention on being Christlike, rather than joining in with the turmoil of this passing world. Touched by the mercy of God, we can see goodness in all people, so that we may dwell together as one. Let us seek to live in unity with our brothers and sisters in Christ, and trust in the Lord to help us in our endeavor.

How do you react when confronted with polarizing issues?

Lord Jesus, may your Eucharistic Presence fill me with the grace to look beyond the chaos of our world and see the goodness in all people.

October 22

Finally, all of you, be of one mind, sympathetic, loving toward one another, compassionate, humble. Do not return evil for evil, or insult for insult; but, on the contrary, a blessing, because to this you were called, that you might inherit a blessing. — 1 Peter 3:8–9

"Don't get mad, get even" is a phrase quite popular in our modern culture, and it goes against everything that Jesus stands for. Throughout his public ministry, Jesus preached a Gospel message of love and compassion for our neighbor. If someone hurts us, we are to "turn the other cheek," "go the extra mile," and "forgive seventy times seventy times." There is no place for revenge in the life of a follower of Jesus, for it is an intentional act of evil on our part.

When we draw near to Jesus in the Eucharist, the human barriers that we put up against others can come crashing down. The Eucharist unifies us in heart and mind to Jesus and to our brothers and sisters in Christ. This grace of unity we receive helps us to be of one mind, sympathetic, compassionate, and loving toward one another.

Have you ever sought revenge on someone? How did it make you feel?

Lord Jesus, help me to live in unity with my brothers and sisters in Christ, that I may inherit a blessing.

October 23

*In this is love: not that we have loved God, but that he loved us
and sent his Son as expiation for our sins. — 1 John 4:10*

Jesus gave his life on the cross for sinners. He did not choose to die just for the wealthiest and most powerful people; no, Jesus poured out his innocent Blood for the poor, the destitute, the abused, the disbelieving, the marginalized, the illegal immigrants, the widows and orphans, and those who have no voice in society. Jesus, the only Son of God, suffered and died out of love for all mankind. We can show our gratitude to Jesus for his gift of salvation by loving all those Jesus loved. God is love, and if the Lord lives in us, then we must love one another.

The consecrated gifts of bread and wine that we receive at the altar are the Real Presence of Jesus. When we partake of this heavenly food, Jesus makes his home in our hearts, and his love is brought to perfection in us, when we love one another as he loves us.

Do you only love those who are like you? How difficult is it for you to love the underprivileged of society?

Lord Jesus, help me love those who are unlovable, that your divine love may be brought to perfection in me.

October 24

Have the same regard for one another; do not be haughty but associate with the lowly; do not be wise in your own estimation. Do not repay anyone evil for evil; be concerned for what is noble in the sight of all. If possible, on your part, live at peace with all. — Romans 12:16–18

When we watch the news at night, it is tempting to side with one group or another based on how the news reports on people's actions and motives. Our lives as Christians, however, bid us to regard one another equally, refusing to give in to the temptation to revenge and aggression toward those who hurt us. This is not easy for us to do; nor was it easy for the early Christian community to accomplish. Jesus is calling his people, from all ages, and all times, to live in peace with one another, to lean on the wisdom of God, and not our own, that we may be concerned for what is noble in the sight of all.

When we partake of the Eucharist, Jesus nourishes us with the spiritual wisdom to follow his ways, and not our earthly desires; to live in peace and harmony with one another. Let us come before the Lord seeking his divine help.

Do you struggle with relating to groups of people who are different than you?

Lord Jesus, help me see others as you see them, that I may love as you love.

October 25

*Let us then pursue what leads to peace and to building
up one another. — Romans 14:19*

My husband and I enjoy traveling for many reasons, one of which is the opportunity to experience the cuisine of different cultures. We especially like visiting neighborhood bakeries and sampling their local breads. There is something so comforting about the aroma of freshly baked bread. Food is transformational, because it has the ability to bring individuals of different backgrounds together. There is great peace in breaking bread with others.

When we come to the Eucharistic table, Jesus is inviting us to break bread with him. His Real Presence in the Eucharistic bread and wine is food for our spiritual journey, a journey that is shared with friends and family, strangers and acquaintances. The bread of angels that we receive at the table of the Lord nourishes us with the peace of the Risen Christ, and gives us the grace to share this peace with all those at table with us.

How have you experienced the Eucharist as an invitation to unity and peace in your life?

Lord Jesus, may your Eucharist fill me with the peace of the Risen Christ.

October 26

Rather, living the truth in love, we should grow in every way into him who is the head, Christ, from whom the whole body, joined and held together by every supporting ligament, with the proper functioning of each part, brings about the body's growth and builds itself up in love. — Ephesians 4:15–16

Our lives with Christ are journeys of many steps and stages. The Lord has equipped us with the necessary gifts to do what is expected of us; we need to open our hearts and minds to living in Christ and with the Body of Christ. We progress in our faith the more we become aware of God's purpose and plan for us, and of the important role we play in building up the Body of Christ in love.

Our spiritual journey leads us from the waters of the font to the table of the Lord, where we encounter the Real Presence of Jesus, our head. Our reception of Eucharist helps us to deepen our faith as we grow in the spiritual awareness that we are one Body of believers, held together by Christ's love. May we approach the table of the Lord seeking unity with our brothers and sisters in the Body of Christ.

In what way can you help others grow in their faith in and love for Jesus?

Lord Jesus, help me to do my part in building up the Body of Christ, that we may be one in you.

October 27

For if we have grown into union with him through a death like his, we shall also be united with him in the resurrection. We know that our old self was crucified with him, so that our sinful body might be done away with, that we might no longer be in slavery to sin. — Romans 6:5–6

Years ago, my friend Cathy wrote a beautiful reflection on the hands of the Body of Christ for an Extraordinary Minister of Holy Communion Night of Renewal. She noted the difference in the makeup of hands that comprise the Body of Christ as they come forward to receive Our Lord in the Eucharist. Some are small and tiny, others calloused from hard labor, still others crippled from arthritis. There are well-manicured hands, others aged and weathered, and even little hands still dirty from the playground; all are the hands that comprise the Body of Christ.

Jesus gave his life for each one of us, that sin may no longer rule our lives. When we come forward to receive the Eucharist, we are the living Body of Christ, people from all walks of life, redeemed by the innocent Blood of the Lamb. Let us receive the Eucharist with hands that are grateful for the gift of eternal life won for us by Jesus.

What do your hands say about you?

Lord Jesus, may your Eucharist cleanse me of my sinful ways, that I may live in the light of your resurrection.

October 28

*I am the good shepherd, and I know mine and mine know me,
just as the Father knows me and I know the Father; and I will lay
down my life for the sheep. I have other sheep that do not belong
to this fold. These also I must lead, and they will hear my voice,
and there will be one flock, one shepherd. — John 10:14–16*

A shepherd knows and loves his sheep, and he tenderly cares for each one that belongs to him. Sheep will only follow the voice of their shepherd, creating a bond of love between a shepherd and his sheep. Jesus is the Good Shepherd; he knows his flock and they know him. As our Good Shepherd, Jesus warns us against listening to other voices that might lead us astray: voices of hatred, power, prestige, discrimination, self-righteousness, and self-centeredness. If we mistakenly follow these voices, we will find ourselves lost and in need of rescue. Jesus desires that all sheep hear his voice, for he will lay down his life for them.

Our reception of the Eucharist opens our ears, that we may hear our Good Shepherd call to us. His gentle voice is calling all people to follow him, for there must be one flock and one shepherd. Let us bring ourselves to Jesus, the Good Shepherd, in the Blessed Sacrament.

Have you ever been a lost sheep? How did Jesus rescue you?

Lord Jesus, help me to hear your voice leading and guiding my steps each day.

October 29

The cup of blessing that we bless, is it not a participation in the blood of Christ? The bread that we break, is it not a participation in the body of Christ? Because the loaf of bread is one, we, though many, are one body, for we all partake of the one loaf. — 1 Corinthians 10:16–17

Jesus gave his life on the cross for everyone. He made no distinctions, no exclusions. Our Lord came into this world to save all people. However, our gift of free will often prevents us from participating in the Body of Christ when we choose to turn our backs on Jesus and follow the ways of this fallen world. Jesus is waiting for us to repent and come back to him, that we may participate in the Body of Christ as we are reunited to the Lord and one another.

On the night before he died, Jesus took bread, broke it, said the blessing, and gave it to his disciples; likewise with the cup. The Eucharist is the Real Presence of Jesus, and when we partake of the Eucharistic bread and wine, we share in the death and resurrection of Our Lord. Jesus, who gave his life for us, is inviting us to come home, to return to him, that we may join as one in the Body of Christ.

What is preventing you from participation in the Body of Christ?

Lord Jesus, help me to overcome the temptations of this world.

October 30

For in one Spirit we were all baptized into one body, whether Jews or Greeks, slaves or free persons, and we were all given to drink of one Spirit. Now the body is not a single part, but many. — *1 Corinthians 12:13–14*

The People of God are diverse and beautiful, made in the image and likeness of our Creator God, and we carry the Spirit of Christ within us. Unfortunately, through our fallen nature, our human sight often fails to see what unifies us, and sees only what divides us. The wide diversity of skin colors, cultures, and languages that comprise the People of God is a point of division, instead of unity. Jesus gave his life for all; he invites us today to return to him, that we may be one with him.

When we partake of the Body and Blood of Christ, we experience union with Jesus. This mystical encounter with our risen Lord offers us an opportunity to renew our vision, that we may be able to see that all are given to drink of one Spirit, for we are all baptized into one Body. Let us approach the Eucharistic table with hearts seeking unity, for the body is not a single part, but many.

Do you struggle with groups of people or with particular cultures?

Lord Jesus, help me to drink deeply from the cup of unity, for we are all one Body united with you.

October 31

We have received, O Lord, the Sacrament of unity; Grant us, we pray, that, living in your house in holy accord, we may possess the peace we hand on and preserve the peace we have received.
— *Prayer after Communion, Mass for Promoting Harmony*

I heard a story about an unbaptized college student who sought the help of the campus chaplain to explore the possibility of becoming Catholic. When the chaplain asked the young student what attracted her to Catholicism, she gave an astonishing answer. She pointed to the tabernacle located in the chapel and said she felt tremendous peace every time she was in the presence of the "gold box." She wanted to preserve this unexplained sense of peace she experienced in her life, so she sought to become Catholic.

Each time we receive the Eucharist, we encounter the sacramental presence of Jesus, the Prince of Peace, whose Divine Presence summons us to live in harmony with one other. In partaking of his Body and Blood, we receive the grace to live in peace with our brothers and sisters in Christ. Let us come before the Eucharistic table, that we may possess the peace we receive, and hand this peace onto others.

How can your reception of the Eucharist help you live in holy accord with others?

Lord Jesus, may your gift of peace fill my heart and help me to live in harmony with all those I meet this day.

~ Intimacy with God ~

November 1

As they continued their journey he entered a village where a woman whose name was Martha welcomed him. She had a sister named Mary [who] sat beside the Lord at his feet listening to him speak. — Luke 10:38–39

Mary, Martha, and Lazarus were ordinary people just like us; yet these siblings enjoyed something very special and unique, namely, intimate friendship with Jesus of Nazareth. He was their good and trusted friend who enjoyed their hospitality by sharing wonderful meals together in their family home.

Jesus desires to be in relationship with us, too. He seeks an intimate friendship with you and me, and he does not ask us to earn that friendship. Jesus just wants to love us for who we are.

The thought of intimacy with Jesus makes some of us uncomfortable; for we prefer to keep the Lord at a distance, turning to God only when we are in need of help. Jesus demonstrated his great love for us at the Last Supper when he took bread and wine, said the blessing, and broke it, saying, "Take and eat. ... Take and drink, all of you." When we receive the Eucharist, we are welcoming Jesus into our hearts, our homes, and our families.

In what ways will friendship with Jesus enhance the dynamics of your family, work, and personal life?

Lord Jesus, may my reception of Communion deepen my relationship with you and draw me closer to your most Sacred Heart.

November 2

The souls of the righteous are in the hand of God,
and no torment shall touch them.
They seemed, in the view of the foolish, to be dead;
and their passing away was thought an affliction
and their going forth from us, utter destruction.
But they are at peace. — Wisdom 3:1–3

We have all lost a loved one at some point in our lives. Whether a spouse, a child, our parents, or a dear friend, the loss is real, and the grief we experience is a tangible expression of our love for this person. This Scripture passage reminds us that the souls of our loved ones are in the hand of God. They are home, and no pain or suffering can ever torment them again. While we grieve their absence, we should rejoice that they are in heaven with Our Lord; they have achieved what we hope to do.

The Eucharistic Presence of Jesus spans the great divide between this world and heaven, between where we are now and where we hope to be. As we eat and drink of the Body and Blood of Christ, we unite ourselves to Jesus, and we receive a foretaste of heaven. Let us rejoice that someday we will be united with Jesus and our loved ones in heaven.

Which loved ones would you like to pray for this day?

Lord Jesus, may the Eucharist guide me to my heavenly home.

November 3

The seed sown on rocky ground is the one who hears the word and receives it at once with joy; But he has no root and lasts only for a time. ... The seed sown among thorns is the one who hears the word, but then worldly anxiety and the lure of riches choke the word and it bears no fruit. But the seed sown on rich soil is the one who hears the word and understands it, who indeed bears fruit. — Matthew 13:20–23

What kind of friend will you be to the Lord? How is the soil of your soul? Is it dry and rocky? Are you and Jesus mere acquaintances? Perhaps the soil of your soul has thorns, and you are a fair-weather friend, until the riches and allurements of this world tempt you. Perhaps the soil of your soul is rich and fertile, and you are blessed to enjoy a loving relationship with Jesus, one that bears abundant fruit.

Intimacy with God begins with seeds sown in soil that is rich in spiritual nutrients. The act of receiving Jesus regularly in the Eucharist enriches the soil of our souls and strengthens the bonds of friendship we share with Jesus. Our reception of the Eucharist helps us to bear an abundant harvest for the kingdom of God.

What is the condition of the soil of your soul?

Lord Jesus, may the Eucharist enrich my life, that I may bear good fruit.

November 4

Remain in me, as I remain in you. Just as a branch cannot bear fruit on its own unless it remains on the vine, so neither can you unless you remain in me. — John 15:4

As a branch cannot bear fruit on its own, we cannot exist apart from Jesus, or we will spiritually wither and die. We need the Real Presence of Jesus in the Eucharist to sustain us on our journey in life.

When we participate in the Eucharistic banquet, we receive the necessary graces to remain in a close and loving relationship with the Lord. The Eucharist is our spiritual food; it is a healing balm for our injured souls. Let us feast on the Body and Blood of Christ, that we may strengthen the bonds of our relationship with Jesus and remain in him, as he remains in us.

How can you turn the dry branches of your parched spirit into a healthy vine that is rich with abundant spiritual fruit?

Lord, may I never stray from you. Help me to find spiritual rest and refreshment at your Eucharistic banquet.

November 5

I am with you always, until the end of the age. — Matthew 28:20

We have all experienced loneliness at some point in our lives. Maybe it was a time after the loss of a loved one or the breakup of a relationship, or maybe we chose to be alone because we were fearful to place our trust in another. With Jesus, there is nothing to fear, for he is with us always, and we can experience his loving Presence in the Eucharist.

Jesus desired to remain with us for all time, so at the Last Supper he gave us the gift of himself in the elements of bread and wine. Each time we receive Communion, we encounter the Real Presence of Jesus, who promised to be with us always, until the end of the age. Jesus wants to heal us of our loneliness and draw us into his Eucharistic heart; he will never leave us to face our trials alone. With confidence, let us bring ourselves before the Eucharistic Presence of Jesus, seeking spiritual restoration for our wounded souls.

Have you ever experienced the Lord's loving embrace?

Lord Jesus, knowing you are with me always brings me comfort and peace. Help me to draw nearer to your Divine Presence in the Blessed Sacrament.

November 6

Jesus answered him, "Foxes have dens and birds of the sky have nests, but the Son of Man has nowhere to rest his head." — Matthew 8:20

This Scripture passage has always troubled me, because it seems that Jesus is telling us that he had no place to call home, no place to rest when he was tired. This thought makes me sad. We know that Our Lord had a home in Nazareth; yet, as an itinerant preacher, his ministry of proclaiming the Gospel kept him from his mother, Mary, for months at a time. So where did Jesus make his home?

While we may never know the answer to this question, what we do know is that when we receive the Eucharist, we are inviting Jesus to make his home in our hearts. Our reception of Communion draws us into union with our risen Lord, and offers us an opportunity to welcome him into our lives in a most intimate fashion. Let us be mindful of this spiritual reality each time we come to the Lord's table.

Is there anything preventing you from inviting the Lord to make his dwelling in your heart?

Lord Jesus, help me to have a pure heart, that I may lovingly welcome your Eucharistic Presence into my life.

November 7

Now you are Christ's body, and individually
parts of it. — 1 Corinthians 12:27

For over twenty years, I have facilitated formation classes for those who desire to become an extraordinary minister of the Eucharist at their parish. I love working with people who feel called to serve at the table of the Lord. In my training sessions, one of the spiritual realities that I bring to everyone's attention is the fact that when we offer or receive Communion, there is a triple presence of Christ at work. The extraordinary minister, who is a member of the Body of Christ, offers the Eucharistic Body of Christ, to the living Body of Christ. In that extraordinary, graced moment of offering and receiving, there is a triple presence of Christ at work, and I can think of no holier, more intimate moment with Jesus than this.

When we partake at the Eucharistic table, this triple presence of Christ — visible in the minister, in the Eucharist, and in the person receiving — draws us into the depths of the heart of Jesus. May we live each day fully aware that we are the living Body of Christ, bringing hope and healing to our broken world.

In what ways can your reception of Eucharist enhance the ways you love and care for others?

Lord, help me to live out my baptismal identity as a member of the Body of Christ, that my life may lead others closer to you.

November 8

All your works give you thanks, LORD,
and your faithful bless you.
They speak of the glory of your reign
and tell of your mighty works,
Making known to the sons of men your mighty acts,
The majestic glory of your rule. — Psalm 145:10–12

In this Scripture, the psalmist proclaims that the friends of the Lord make his Presence known throughout the land. Friendship with God is something we should desire; yet, for many of us, the thought of being in a relationship with God might be a bit intimidating. After all, we choose our friends, and they know everything about us. A good friend shares our same values, and over time, we build a connection of deep trust. When life gets difficult, our friends are there to support us.

Whether we realize it or not, we have a trusted friend in Jesus. He suffered and died for our sins out of love for you and me. Jesus is waiting for us at the Eucharistic table. He is inviting us to trust in him, for he will always be there for us, no matter how difficult life may get. Let us accept his Eucharistic invitation, and as his friends, may we make known his Presence and the glorious splendor of his kingdom throughout the land.

What is preventing you from being in a relationship with the Lord?

Lord Jesus, help me to realize the gift of divine friendship that awaits me at the Eucharistic table.

November 9

There was a strong and violent wind rending the mountains and crushing rocks before the LORD — but the LORD was not in the wind; after the wind, an earthquake — but the LORD was not in the earthquake; after the earthquake, fire — but the LORD was not in the fire; after the fire, a light silent sound. When he heard this, Elijah hid his face in his cloak and went out and stood at the entrance of the cave. A voice said to him, Why are you here, Elijah? — 1 Kings 19:11–13

As he did in this story of Elijah, the Lord does not communicate with us in grandiose ways, but rather in the most ordinary manner: perhaps a new thought, an inspiration, a sudden idea, a feeling of peace and tranquility. Be open and listen, for God will speak to your heart.

Under the appearance of consecrated bread, the Eucharistic Presence of Jesus in the Blessed Sacrament is waiting to speak to us. Only with the eyes of faith will we be able to hear his light, silent sound. Being in the presence of Jesus in the Blessed Sacrament is like sitting in the presence of a loving and trusted friend, who knows you and loves you. Talk to him; Jesus is there to listen and to help you.

Have you heard God speaking to you?

Lord Jesus, open my senses, that I may hear you speak to me.

November 10

*And that Christ may dwell in your hearts through faith; that you,
rooted and grounded in love, May have strength to comprehend with
all the holy ones what is the breadth and length and height and depth,
and to know the love of Christ that surpasses knowledge, so that you
may be filled with all the fullness of God. — Ephesians 3:17–19*

When my children were little, as they were practicing to receive
their first holy Communion, I taught them to make a throne with their
hands so that they could receive Jesus with reverence; in turn, I told
them that Jesus would make a home in their hearts. As adults, we also
need to invite Jesus to make a home in our hearts, so that we may have
the grace to comprehend, with all the holy ones, the fullness of God
in Christ Jesus. In doing so, we are creating an intimate and personal
relationship with the Lord.

Each time we receive the Eucharist, Jesus makes his home in our
hearts and desires to be in communion with us, that we may be rooted
and grounded in his love, which surpasses all knowledge. Let us welcome our Eucharistic Lord into our hearts each and every day.

Today, how can you invite Jesus to make a home in your heart?

*Lord Jesus, thank you for making your home in my heart. Help me to bring your
loving Presence to the people I meet this day.*

November 11

[The Lord] said to me, "My grace is sufficient for you, for power is made perfect in weakness." I will rather boast most gladly of my weaknesses, in order that the power of Christ may dwell with me. Therefore, I am content with weaknesses, insults, hardships, persecutions, and constraints, for the sake of Christ; for when I am weak, then I am strong. — 2 Corinthians 12:9–10

If asked, a great number of people might confess that speaking in public is somewhat daunting. Their hands sweat, their minds go blank, and some even feel weak in the knees. I used to react in the same way when I first began giving presentations, until I realized that I was not alone in my ministry efforts. Jesus was with me, so I called upon his Spirit to use me as his vessel. I asked the Lord to give me the courage to speak well and the wisdom to offer words that would touch the hearts of all in attendance. In my weakness, I am made strong.

I draw my strength and courage from the Eucharist. In receiving the Body and Blood of Christ, I am in union with Our Lord, and his grace is sufficient for me. In my weakness, the power of Christ lives in me, and works through me.

Are you nervous or anxious about a situation? Seek the wisdom of the Spirit to help you.

Lord Jesus, fill me with your life-giving Spirit, that I may accomplish all that you desire for me.

November 12

No one has greater love than this, to lay down one's life for one's friends. You are my friends if you do what I command you. — *John 15:13–14*

There is a time-honored phrase: "To have a friend, you must be a friend." In other words, if we want to be friends with someone, we should have an understanding of what comprises a good relationship. One key element in friendship is generosity: the capacity to give of oneself without looking for anything in return. In a healthy relationship, the emphasis is always on the other, and not on ourselves. Good friends generously give of their time, talent, and treasure to benefit the other.

In this Scripture passage, Jesus lovingly calls us his friends, if we do what he commands us. At the Last Supper, Jesus generously shared his life by giving us the gift of his Body and Blood. He asked nothing of us in return for the Eucharist: only that we "do this in memory of" him. Each time Mass is celebrated, we carry on what Jesus commanded us to do; and we do it in loving memory of the one who laid down his life for his friends.

Reflect on some other key elements present in a healthy friendship. Are any of these present in your relationship with Jesus?

Lord Jesus, may our encounter with you in the Eucharist strengthen our bonds of friendship.

November 13

Jesus answered and said to him, "Whoever loves me will keep my word, and my Father will love him, and we will come to him and make our dwelling with him. Whoever does not love me does not keep my words; yet the word you hear is not mine but that of the Father who sent me." — John 14:23–24

Have you ever given much thought to the spiritual truth that Jesus lives within you? If you were consciously aware of this, how would it change your behavior? Most of us go about our daily lives oblivious that Jesus is with us, every moment of every day. He has made his dwelling in our hearts. All he asks of us is that we love him and keep his word.

Our encounter with Jesus in the Eucharist reinforces our spiritual realization of his indwelling Presence. Each time we receive Communion, the bonds of love we share with our risen Lord are fortified and made stronger. Our union with Jesus in the Eucharist helps us to keep his word and deepen our love for him.

Jesus has made his dwelling in you. How does this impact your actions?

Lord Jesus, you are most welcome in my heart. Help me to never stray from your side.

November 14

There was a scholar of the law who stood up to test him and said, "Teacher, what must I do to inherit eternal life?" Jesus said to him, "What is written in the law? How do you read it?" He said in reply, "You shall love the Lord, your God, with all your heart, with all your being, with all your strength, and with all your mind, and your neighbor as yourself." He replied to him, "You have answered correctly; do this and you will live." — Luke 10:25–28

Everyone should memorize this Scripture passage, for it distinctly clarifies how we are to live our Christian faith: Love God with our entire being, and love our neighbor as ourselves. This is the Golden Rule that governs all of our actions. It is incredibly simple; yet why do we have so much trouble following it?

Our encounter with Jesus in the Eucharist offers us the grace to follow the law of God. If we approach the altar with hearts seeking to love God and our neighbor, the Lord will help direct our steps. Our union with the Lord in the Eucharist gives us a new clarity of vision, and grace to follow the way of life set before us by Jesus.

Which is easier to do: to love God or your neighbor? Prayerfully reflect on your answer.

Lord Jesus, may our encounter with you in the Eucharist give us strength to follow your commandment of love.

November 15

We drew courage through our God to speak to you the gospel of God with much struggle. Our exhortation was not from delusion or impure motives, nor did it work through deception. But as we were judged worthy by God to be entrusted with the gospel, that is how we speak, not as trying to please human beings, but rather God, who judges our hearts. — 1 Thessalonians 2:2–4

Have you ever been criticized by others for doing something nice? Perhaps people thought you had ulterior motives, when in fact your intentions were honorable. The Lord searches our hearts, and he knows if the reasons behind our actions are pure. Saint Paul encourages us to please God, and not human beings, for the Lord will judge us not as the world sees, but as he sees. It takes courage and confidence to proclaim the Gospel. We draw our spiritual strength for discipleship from our relationship with Jesus in the Eucharist.

When we partake of the Eucharist, Jesus fills us with spiritual courage and equips us with the necessary graces to overcome the criticism of others as we strive to live our lives in intimate union with the Lord. Let us seek the Lord's help each time that we come to the table.

Has anyone ever questioned your motives when you acted in kindness?

Lord Jesus, help me to be pure of heart, that my intentions and actions will reflect my love for you.

November 16

For I am convinced that neither death, nor life, nor angels, nor principalities, nor present things, nor future things, nor powers, nor height, nor depth, nor any other creature will be able to separate us from the love of God in Christ Jesus our Lord. — *Romans 8:38–39*

As human beings, we tend to use our emotions as a barometer of how close God is to us. When situations in our lives are going as we planned, or if we are feeling healthy and vibrant, life is good and we feel blessed. But where is the Lord when our lives are in shambles, we are in pain, and we don't know how we will even get through the day? The Lord is still with us, for nothing can separate us from the love of God in Christ Jesus Our Lord. Our closeness with God does not depend upon our human feelings, but rather upon the unbreakable bond of love we share with Jesus.

The pure love of Our Lord is waiting for us in the Eucharist. As we partake of this sacred banquet, we are filled with the loving presence of Our Lord who makes his dwelling in our hearts. No matter how we feel, nothing can separate us from the love of Jesus.

Do you feel closer to the Lord in good times or in difficult moments?

Lord Jesus, you are with me always. Help me not to rely on my feelings but on the bond of love we share, which is eternal.

November 17

Trust in the LORD with all your heart,
on your own intelligence do not rely;
In all your ways be mindful of him,
and he will make straight your paths. — *Proverbs 3:5–6*

We live in an age where we have everything we need at our fingertips. If we are hungry, we order online and have it delivered. If we seek knowledge, we look it up on the web. If we want to connect with someone, we call, message, or have a virtual session. All of this gives us a false sense of reliance on technology and on our own intelligence. Our Lord is calling us to trust in him with all our hearts, and not on our own intelligence. He promises to make straight our paths if we rely on him.

Our encounter with Jesus at the Eucharistic table supplies us with the grace to rely on God and not our own wills. His Body and Blood nourishes our souls and gives us strength to refocus our dependence upon God. We grow in grace as we rely on his Presence to lead and guide us. Come to the table of the Lord, with hearts seeking to receive the Eucharist, that Jesus may fulfill all your needs.

Whose wisdom do you rely on? God's or yours?

Lord Jesus, may your Eucharist help me to grow in my dependence upon you.

November 18

Our Father in heaven,
hallowed be your name,
your kingdom come,
your will be done,
on earth as in heaven.
Give us today our daily bread. — *Matthew 6:9–11*

Years ago, we purchased a new home for our growing family, but my husband had buyer's remorse days into the contract. The purchase agreement was binding. Two days before closing, the seller asked to change the date, and at last, we had our opportunity to break the contract. That day, our realtor took us to see multiple houses. The last one we viewed we bought on sight. I believe the Lord directed us to this home, for our life in Christ flourished there. God's will was done.

The Eucharist is our daily bread. When we partake of the Body and Blood of Jesus, we become one with the Lord, and this mystical moment can help us clarify our purpose in life in light of God's plan for us. Scripture tells us, "Seek and you shall find." Come to the Eucharistic table with hearts seeking to do God's will, and you will receive.

In what ways do you feel like you are following God's will for you?

Lord Jesus, help me to discover and follow your plan for me, that I may become who I was created to be.

November 19

Blessed those whose way is blameless,
who walk by the law of the LORD.
Blessed those who keep his testimonies,
who seek him with all their heart. — Psalm 119:1–2

Years ago, one of my ministries was that of a parish wedding coordinator. My responsibilities included conducting the rehearsal the night before, and assisting the bridal party on the day of the wedding. On rehearsal nights, after everyone left, I would clean up, turn off the lights, and just sit in the darkened church alone. The tiny flame flickering from the tabernacle candle reminded me that I was not alone, Jesus was with me; and I was at peace. I savored every moment of my special time with Jesus, talking to him as if I were having a conversation with a friend. I expressed what was on my heart, and I would then sit in silence to receive as the Lord spoke to me.

Spending time before Jesus in the Blessed Sacrament is a powerful way to deepen your relationship with Our Lord. He is there, waiting to bless you with his Presence. It is a moment of spiritual intimacy, when the Lord invites us to receive him into our hearts.

Are you able to make a commitment to spend time before the Blessed Sacrament at least once a week, even for five to ten minutes? Ask the Lord for his help.

Lord Jesus, help me to experience your peaceful Presence each time I pray before your Blessed Sacrament.

November 20

Looking around at those seated in the circle he said, "Here are my mother and my brothers. [For] whoever does the will of God is my brother and sister and mother." — Mark 3:34–35

When we consider our family trees and all of our ancestors from generation to generation, how many of us include Jesus and Mary? Clearly, Our Lord considers us family, if we do the will of his Father. The intimate relationship we share with our brother, Jesus, is the most precious gift of all, and we should never take it for granted.

When we encounter Jesus in the Eucharist, we have a graced opportunity to deepen the familial bonds that we share with our brother and Savior, Jesus. His love for us is so great that Jesus willingly gave his life on the cross that we may be with him for all eternity in heaven. Let us give thanks to God this day for the gift of our brother, Jesus. May we show our love for Jesus by doing the will of God.

Is it difficult for you to imagine that Jesus is part of your family?

Lord Jesus, take me by the hand and guide me on my path in life.

November 21

Faithful friends are a sturdy shelter;
whoever finds one finds a treasure. — *Sirach 6:14*

A good and trusted friend is a gift from God and someone we should never take for granted. These individuals are people we confide in, and we enjoy spending time together and share common values. Unfortunately, social media has distorted the real meaning of friendship, encouraging us to be "friends" with people who are complete strangers. In addition, young people use the term BFF (best friends forever) to describe their newest acquaintance on their social media page, only to discover that a day later, the same BFF is now out of their inner circle; so much for the term "forever." It seems like our culture has lost the true meaning of friendship.

Jesus is the most faithful friend we will ever have. Our relationship with Our Lord cannot draw from doctrine alone; it also must be a mutual relationship of love. Why? Jesus died for us. Who in our circle of friends would do that for us? Each time we receive Communion, we have an opportunity to tell Jesus how much we love him, as we seek to deepen our relationship with him. He is our best friend, a sturdy shelter in the storm. Jesus is our true treasure.

In what ways can you develop a friendship with Jesus?

Lord Jesus, thank you for being my constant companion, a sturdy shelter in the storm. I love you.

November 22

Draw near to God, and he will draw near to you. Cleanse your hands, you sinners, and purify your hearts. — *James 4:8*

Have you ever had the unsettling experience of someone following you without your permission? You somehow sense the presence of another walking behind you, and you are nervous because you do not know who it is or what they want. Jesus follows us, but he will never intrude on our personal space. Rather, he wants us to turn around and draw near to him. Jesus desires a personal relationship with each one of us so that he can be part of our everyday lives. He desires that we turn from our sinful ways and walk toward him, and Jesus will lead and guide us every moment of every day.

When we encounter Our Lord in the Eucharist, we have an opportunity to draw near to him, to give him our hearts, and to receive his abundant graces in return. Jesus loves us, and he has given us his Eucharistic Body and Blood as food for our spiritual journey, for he will satisfy our every need. Let us cleanse our hearts and return to the Lord, for he is waiting for us in the Eucharist.

Are you willing to draw near to Jesus, or do you prefer to keep him at a distance? Why?

Lord Jesus, help me to draw nearer to you with each passing day.

November 23

See what love the Father has bestowed on us that we may be called the children of God. Yet so we are. The reason the world does not know us is that it did not know him. Beloved, we are God's children now; what we shall be has not yet been revealed. We do know that when it is revealed we shall be like him, for we shall see him as he is. — 1 John 3:1–2

We are God's beloved children, brothers and sisters in Christ. Unfortunately, our society seeks to diminish the presence of God, and sinful results are evident in the complete lack of respect for life. Violence fills our streets each day, because people do not feel connected as members of the family of God; nor do they know God. Yet his love for us is beyond human understanding.

When we encounter Jesus in the Eucharist, we experience the pure love of Our Lord. His Body and Blood, given for us, can help strengthen us to live in this world as faithful children of God, united to Christ and to one another. Let us seek to become the very mystery we receive at this Eucharistic table.

Do you struggle with seeing other people as members of the family of God?

Lord Jesus, as a member of the family of God, may I treat others as my brothers and sisters in Christ.

November 24

Jesus said to him, "I am the way and the truth and the life. No one comes to the Father except through me." — John 14:6

It is bewildering that as human beings, we place so much emphasis on technology. Smartphones put the world at our fingertips, connecting us to people, the internet, and everything in between; and innovative technology allows us to drive and park our cars without using our hands. Technology has become essential to life, but to what end? One could make the analogy that Jesus is our spiritual GPS, for without him, we will get lost; we will not find our way back home to the Father in heaven, for Jesus is the Way, the Truth, and the Life.

Strictly adhering to a set of rules will not assure us salvation; only through relationship with a person will we be saved. God sent his only Son that humanity might gain eternal life. On the night before he died, Jesus gave us the gift of his life, mediated in the consecrated elements of bread and wine, as spiritual nourishment for our long journey home to heaven. May we approach the Eucharistic table with hearts seeking to follow Jesus, for he is the Way, the Truth, and the Life.

When was a time in your life that you felt lost because you strayed from Jesus?

Lord Jesus, help me to follow you every day on my pathway in life.

November 25

Wherever you go, I will go,
wherever you lodge I will lodge.
Your people shall be my people
and your God, my God. — Ruth 1:16

The beloved story of Naomi and Ruth reminds us of God's unconditional love for us. The pivotal moment in this Old Testament story comes when Ruth defies all logic by remaining with her mother-in-law, making a declaration of faith that she will go wherever Naomi goes, and that Naomi's God will be her God. This Scripture story reminds us that even when things seem hopeless, God is ever faithful and always at work in our lives. God never gave up on us, and at the proper time, God sent his only Son, Jesus, into the world to redeem humankind. What great love God has for his people.

The Eucharist is the Real Presence of Jesus, the only Son of God and our Redeemer. When we receive Communion at the Eucharistic table, Jesus fills our hearts with the grace of redemption. May our encounter with Jesus in the Eucharist give us the strength to proclaim to our family and friends that we are Jesus' people, and that he is our God.

How can the story of Naomi and Ruth inspire you with the courage and strength to follow Jesus?

Lord Jesus, make your home in my heart, that I may follow you all the days of my life.

November 26

So be imitators of God, as beloved children, and live in love, as Christ loved us and handed himself over for us as a sacrificial offering to God for a fragrant aroma. — Ephesians 5:1–2

Any parent will tell you that they would willingly sacrifice their own comfort, their own happiness for that of their children. Many parents work long hours, sometimes juggling two jobs, just to make ends meet so that their families have a safe place to live and food on their table. God our Father is no different. We are his beloved children, and out of love for us, God sent his only Son, Jesus, who willingly sacrificed his life to restore our covenant relationship with God, a relationship that had been severed through sin.

Each time we partake of the Eucharistic Body and Blood of Christ, we participate in the sacrificial offering of Jesus. In holy Communion, we receive his Real Presence and are filled with his pure sacrificial love, and he invites us to be his gift of love in our world. As Jesus offered himself as a ransom for sin, let us offer our lives in loving service to the Lord and one another. Let us be imitators of Christ.

In what ways does your life imitate the love and sacrifice of Jesus?

Lord Jesus, help me to imitate you, that I may willing to offer up the comforts of my life in order to help others.

November 27

For we are his handiwork, created in Christ Jesus for the good works that God has prepared in advance, that we should live in them. — Ephesians 2:10

We often see images of the news of wealthy celebrities who are doing wonderful philanthropic work. Before we praise them for their efforts, it is prudent for us to consider their motives — many perform works of charity not to give glory to God, but in the hope of impressing their fans with their benevolence. This is not what God intended. We are the handiwork of God, redeemed by the Blood of the innocent Lamb, who suffered, died, and rose from the dead, that we may become a new creation in him. We should do good works because we have faith in Jesus, not because we are trying to earn God's grace or to impress others.

Each time we partake of the Eucharist, we receive the grace to live as new creations in Christ. The Body and Blood of Jesus has the power to turn us away from the allurements of this passing world and create us anew, that we may be in intimate union with Our Lord. Let us come to the Lord's table ready to receive the spiritual nourishment needed to do the good works that God has prepared in advance.

What motivates you to do good works?

Lord Jesus, renew me in mind, body, and spirit, that I may become a new creation in you.

November 28

But I say to you, love your enemies, and pray for those who persecute you, that you may be children of your heavenly Father, for he makes his sun rise on the bad and the good, and causes rain to fall on the just and the unjust. — Matthew 5:44–45

Growing up, I was not part of the popular crowd of girls at my grammar school, and was often the recipient of their nasty comments and rude behavior. I would complain to my mom about how I was treated; and her advice was always the same: "Just be kind; God loves them too." Looking back on my mom's wisdom, I believe she was putting into practice what Jesus spoke about in Matthew's Gospel. That said, it is not easy to love your enemies and pray for those who persecute you. In fact, it is almost impossible; however, with God, all things are possible.

Our encounter with Jesus in the Eucharist can wash away our need for revenge, and restore us to our identity as children of our heavenly Father. With the help of Jesus, we can gain the strength to love our enemies, and to lift up in prayer all those who hurt us. Let us come before our Eucharistic Lord with hearts seeking to do the will of Jesus.

Who do you consider your enemy? How do you treat them?

Lord Jesus, may the Eucharist give me the courage to love and pray for my adversaries.

November 29

But now you have had yourselves washed, you were sanctified,
you were justified in the name of the Lord Jesus Christ and
in the Spirit of our God. — 1 Corinthians 6:11

The good news of the Gospel is that in Christ Jesus, we are sanctified, and we are no longer defined by our past sins and transgressions. Washed clean in the Blood of the innocent Lamb of God, we now share in the life of Our Lord Jesus Christ. The Lord does not remember the sins of our past; he loves us and desires that we live our life in holiness, not regret.

The Eucharist unites us in faith to the heart of Jesus, who showers us with the grace and courage to let go of our past. Redeemed and sanctified, we receive new life in the name of the Lord Jesus Christ and in the Holy Spirit. Let us come before Jesus with hearts grateful for his gift of holiness.

Do memories of your past sins impact your life with Christ?

Lord Jesus, may the grace I receive in the Eucharist help me to live each day in holiness.

November 30

*Until now you have not asked anything in my name; ask and you
will receive, so that your joy may be complete.* — John 16:24

In one of my first jobs out of college, it was time for my performance review. I shared with a trusted friend my desire for a raise, and
that I was nervous to discuss this topic with my boss. My friend told me,
"He's not a mind reader; if you don't ask, how will he know what you
want?" Fortunately for us, the Lord already knows what is in our hearts.
He is aware of what we seek before we ask. Jesus is simply telling us to
come to God with our desires, to seek his help, to depend on him, and
he will give us everything we need.

One of the most fruitful ways to bring our prayer intentions to the
Lord is in the presence of the Blessed Sacrament. The sacramental Real
Presence of Jesus is waiting for us to come to him with our needs and
desires. Spending time in adoration affords us the graced opportunity
to deepen our faith and love in Jesus, so that whatever we ask, we will
receive, and our joy may be complete.

What is a need that you can bring to Jesus in prayer today?

*Lord Jesus, you promise that anything we ask in your name we will receive. With
hope and trust in you, I ask for the following prayer intention: _____. May
your will be done.*

~ TRANSFORMATION ~

December 1

What difference does it make if the bread and wine turn into the Body and Blood of Christ, and we don't? — Godfrey Diekmann, OSB

This quote, attributed to the late Fr. Godfrey Diekmann, hangs on my office wall. It is a constant reminder to me of what Eucharist calls us to be. Fr. Diekmann's words challenge us to do some authentic soul-searching about our experience of receiving Jesus in the Eucharist, for the divine transformation that occurs during the Eucharistic celebration should not end with the elements of bread and wine. Through the power of the Holy Spirit, we, the living Body of Christ, must also experience spiritual transformation at the altar, or what difference does it make?

Think for a moment. If we pray reverently before the Real Presence in the Blessed Sacrament, yet fail to experience the risen Lord in those we meet each day, what difference does it make? If we eat and drink at the table of the Lord, yet turn a deaf ear to the cries of the poor, what difference does it make? The Eucharist calls us to become the very mystery we receive, and in doing so, we become spiritual nourishment for all those who hunger for God.

How can you bring the presence of Christ to your family, friends, and all who God sends your way this day?

Jesus, help me to be open to spiritual transformation each time I receive you in the Eucharist.

December 2

*Stop judging and you will not be judged. Stop condemning and
you will not be condemned. Forgive and you will be forgiven. ...
For the measure with which you measure will in return be
measured out to you. — Luke 6:37–38*

We judge people every day, maybe without realizing it, randomly commenting on the way people dress, their behavior and viewpoints, even their political and religious views. We are quick to judge those who are not like us. Jesus calls us to stop judging and stop condemning. He challenges us to forgive those who have hurt us. Why? Because God will judge us at the end of time, based on how we have treated others. This should make us pause and reflect on ways we can transform our lives. Fortunately, the presence of Jesus in the Eucharist is here to help us.

Each time we come to the altar, we have an opportunity to experience transformation as we unite our hearts to Jesus. Partaking of the Eucharistic bread and wine invites us to conform our human hearts to that of the compassionate heart of Jesus, who is kind, merciful, and forgiving. Let us seek the gift of spiritual transformation each time we receive the Eucharist.

In what ways can you stop judging others?

Lord, help me to see your Divine Presence in all people, so that I may love and care for them.

December 3

Whoever is in Christ is a new creation: the old things have passed away; behold, new things have come. — 2 Corinthians 5:17

It is customary at the end of every year for us to make new year's resolutions in the hopes of becoming better people. Some of us resolve to lose weight, others to save money, still others to seek new employment. While all of these efforts are good, there is no better way for us to become new creations than to encounter Jesus in the Eucharist.

When we receive the Body and Blood of Jesus, our hearts are united to Christ, and we become the very mystery that we receive. Most of us never realize the mystical opportunity for spiritual transformation that awaits us at the table of the Lord. Jesus is inviting us to surrender our old selves, that we may embrace our new lives with him. Entrusting ourselves into the hands of the Lord is not an act of passivity, but is rather a courageous act of faith in the Lord. Each time we approach the altar, let us willingly join ourselves to the Lord, that we may embrace the new lives that await us in him.

What are you willing to surrender to Jesus, that you may fully experience the grace of spiritual transformation?

Lord Jesus, touch my heart and help me to become a new creation in Christ.

December 4

While he was with them at table, he took bread, said the blessing, broke it, and gave it to them. With that their eyes were opened and they recognized him, but he vanished from their sight. Then they said to each other, "Were not our hearts burning [within us] while he spoke to us on the way and opened the scriptures to us?" So they set out at once and returned to … the eleven and those with them. — Luke 24:30–33

We live in a self-absorbed society that places emphasis on personal happiness rather than the well-being of our neighbor. Like the two disciples on the road to Emmaus, we often miss the presence of Christ in other people, because they are strangers or because we simply do not want to be involved.

The Real Presence of Jesus in the Eucharist can remove the scales from our eyes and invite us to recognize and respond to the Divine Presence of God in all people. Let us pray to recognize Jesus in the breaking of the bread, that we may experience transformation and set out at once to share the Good News with all we meet.

In what way can your Eucharistic experience with Jesus transform you into a Spirit-filled disciple?

Lord Jesus, may my encounter with you in the Eucharist transform my sight, that I may readily see your Divine Presence in all those I meet.

December 5

*The sacrifice of Christ and the sacrifice of the Eucharist
are* one single sacrifice. — *CCC 1367*

Jesus' story did not end on Good Friday, but rather with his glorious resurrection from the dead on Easter Sunday. The death and resurrection of Jesus comprise the paschal mystery, and this forms one single act of salvation. The Church celebrates this mystery of our faith at every Mass. Each time we come to the Eucharistic table, our Catholic Faith invites us to unite our crosses to the perfect sacrifice of Jesus, with the paschal hope and assurance that newness of life is possible. This takes great trust and perseverance on our part, for spiritual transformation is a process. Jesus is here to help us on our journey.

His Eucharistic Presence fills us with hope and gives us the grace to carry our crosses, believing that they will lead us to the new life of transformation. The Eucharist draws us into the heart of Risen Christ and offers us the grace to live our lives in the radiant light of his redemption.

What crosses are you carrying right now? Spiritually offer up your crosses with the perfect sacrifice of Christ celebrated at the altar.

Lord Jesus, may the paschal mystery we celebrate at Mass transform my heart and fill me with the renewed hope and promise for transformation.

December 6

There is an appointed time for everything,
and a time for every affair under the heavens.
A time to give birth, and a time to die;
a time to plant, and a time to uproot the plant.
A time to kill, and a time to heal;
a time to tear down, and a time to build.
A time to weep, and a time to laugh. — Ecclesiastes 3:1–4

There is a saying: "We plan, and God laughs." While most people might chuckle at this statement, it has a deeper theological meaning. God has a master plan for each one of us, and there is an appointed time for everything to unfold as the Lord desires—not as we desire. We are to be in tune with the will of God and to be all that the Lord calls us to be. Doing this will transform our life; we will begin to see the Lord's hand at work in all the seasons of our life, and in all the events and people we hold so dear.

Spending time in adoration is a wonderful spiritual practice. The Real Presence of Christ in the Blessed Sacrament is waiting for you. Talk to him in the silence of your heart and listen as the Lord speaks to you.

How difficult is it to give up control over others?

Lord Jesus, help me to listen to the promptings of the Holy Spirit, that he may lead and guide me in life.

December 7

Do not conform yourselves to this age but be transformed by the renewal of your mind, that you may discern what is the will of God, what is good and pleasing and perfect. — *Romans 12:2*

I met a woman at a party last year who had been on carb-free diet for over two years and had lost over eighty pounds. She showed me the before and after photos, and her transformation was remarkable. In the course of our conversation, she disclosed that in losing all that weight, she also lost the negative feelings that she carried from poor self-esteem. Smiling, she told me that now she feels good, looks good, and has great energy. She is a new person.

While physical transformation is rewarding, spiritual transformation is our goal as Christians. At every Mass, we are invited to unite ourselves to the perfect sacrifice of Jesus with the hope of experiencing a transformation of mind, body, and spirit. May our reception of the Eucharistic Body and Blood of Jesus help us to turn away from the trappings of this world in order to discern the will of God each day.

What area of your life most needs transformation?

Lord Jesus, may my reception of the Eucharist help me to discern what is good and pleasing to you.

December 8

May the Sacrament we have received,
O Lord our God,
heal in us the wounds of that fault
from which in a singular way
you preserved Blessed Mary in her Immaculate Conception. — *Prayer*
after Communion, Solemnity of the Immaculate Conception

The Solemnity of the Immaculate Conception celebrates the doctrine that Mary, from the moment of her conception in the womb of her mother Saint Anne, was conceived without the fault of original sin. In a singular way, God preserved the womb of Mary to receive the miracle of the Incarnation, when Jesus, the Son of God, was conceived by the power of the Holy Spirit in the womb of his mother, Mary, taking on human flesh. Jesus is true God and true man and shares the flesh and blood of his mother, Mary.

In the Holy Sacrifice of the Mass, Jesus gives us his Body and Blood under the appearance of the consecrated bread and wine. It is true food for our spiritual journey. As we receive the Body and Blood of Christ in the Eucharist, we, like Mary, have an opportunity to welcome Jesus into our hearts as the Lord makes his home with us.

How do you keep your heart pure, that you may be worthy to receive Jesus into your soul at Communion?

Lord Jesus, help me to keep my heart pure and undefiled, that I may receive you in the Eucharist.

December 9

"Joseph, son of David, do not be afraid to take Mary your wife into your home. For it is through the holy Spirit that this child has been conceived in her. She will bear a son and you are to name him Jesus, because he will save his people from their sins." All this took place to fulfill what the Lord had said through the prophet: "Behold, the virgin shall be with child and bear a son, and they shall name him Emmanuel," which means "God is with us." — Matthew 1:20–23

From the moment of his miraculous conception, by the power of the Holy Spirit in the womb of the Blessed Virgin Mary, Jesus' mission in life has been to save us. He is the fulfillment of the promise God made to his people long ago. His birth heralded a new era of grace for humanity. Throughout his ministry, Jesus proclaimed a Gospel of repentance and salvation for his people. At the Last Supper, Our Lord imparted his Divine Presence to us for all time in the gifts of bread and wine.

We celebrate the fulfillment of God's promise each time we partake of the Eucharist. God is with us, and through our reception of the Eucharist we become one with Our Lord, Emmanuel, who came into this world to save us from our sins.

How will you experience the presence of Emmanuel this Christmas?

Lord Jesus, help us to see your Divine Presence at work in our family and friends.

December 10

While they were there, the time came for her to have her child, and she gave birth to her firstborn son. She wrapped him in swaddling clothes and laid him in a manger, because there was no room for them in the inn. — Luke 2:6–7

There is a painting by the medieval artist Lorenzo Lotto entitled *The Nativity*, which depicts the birth of Jesus with his parents, Mary and Joseph, adoring him in the manger; in the background on the wall hangs a cross. While the image is a bit jarring for the viewer, the artist sought to intimately connect the birth of the Christ Child with the death of Jesus. The manger that Jesus was placed in was a wooden box used to feed barn animals. The cross, constructed of wood, was the tool of torture used to sacrifice the innocent Lamb of God.

The mystery of the Incarnation that we celebrate at Christmas is a foretaste of the sacrifice that Our Lord offered for us. For on the night before he died, Jesus took bread and wine, said the blessing, and gave us the gift of his very self as spiritual food for our journey. May the presence of the Christ Child draw us ever deeper in the life of our Savior, who suffered and died that we may have eternal life.

How do you celebrate the Nativity of Our Lord?

Lord Jesus, you are the Savior, the Incarnate Son of God. Nourish me with your Body and Blood, that I may have life eternal.

December 11

When the time for Pentecost was fulfilled, they were all in one place together. And suddenly there came from the sky a noise like a strong driving wind, and it filled the entire house in which they were. Then there appeared to them tongues as of fire, which parted and came to rest on each one of them. And they were all filled with the holy Spirit and began to speak in different tongues, the Spirit enabled them to proclaim. — Acts 2:1–4

On that first Pentecost, the Holy Spirit rushed upon the apostles in the Upper Room, birthing our Church into being and transforming the apostles from frightened individuals into spirit-filled evangelists. Filled with the fire of the Spirit, they courageously took the Gospel message to the ends of the earth.

At every Mass, the bread and wine are transformed by the power of the Spirit into the Real Presence of Jesus. The power of the Spirit that birthed the Church into being at Pentecost, and transforms bread and wine into the Real Presence, is the same Spirit that seeks to transform our lives. Let us come before the Eucharistic table with open hearts, asking the Holy Spirit to transform our lives, that we may become the very mystery we receive.

What needs transformation in your life? Ask the Spirit to transform your fears into courage, and your distrust into belief.

Lord Jesus, may the Spirit transform my life, that I may boldly proclaim the Gospel to family and friends.

December 12

But when he comes, the Spirit of truth, he will guide you to all truth. He will not speak on his own, but he will speak what he hears, and will declare to you the things that are coming. He will glorify me, because he will take from what is mine and declare it to you. — *John 16:13–14*

Transformation is difficult; it calls us to take a long look at ourselves, and to admit that we need help with our faults, our shortcomings, and our bad habits. Once we face the truth, it takes even greater courage to resolve to change our lives. Transformation is soul work that involves the Spirit of truth, who is here to guide us to rediscover our identities in Christ.

Spending time in personal prayer before the Blessed Sacrament offers us a wonderful opportunity to reassess our lives, and to ask the Spirit for help to grow in grace. Jesus is present to us in the Blessed Sacrament. He is inviting us to turn away from our former ways of life and embrace new lives in Christ. Let us ask the Lord to send the Spirit of truth, that he may guide us along the path of righteousness.

What issues in your life are you willing to give over to the Lord in the hope of experiencing transformation?

Lord Jesus, send your Holy Spirit upon me, that I may speak the truth that I have received from you.

December 13

Amen, amen, I say to you, whoever believes in me will do the works that I do, and will do greater ones than these, because I am going to the Father. And whatever you ask in my name, I will do, so that the Father may be glorified in the Son. — John 14:12–14

Have you ever experienced a situation where you were speaking with someone, and your words were so profound that you had no idea where they came from, yet it was exactly what this person needed to hear? The Lord often uses our voices, so that he can speak a word of encouragement or consolation to someone in need. Jesus uses our hands and feet to accomplish his work, if we are open to being vessels of grace. Alone, we can do nothing extraordinary; with Jesus, we can accomplish the work of God. There is no limit to what God can accomplish in us, if we are open to the transforming power of the Spirit working within.

Each time we partake of the Eucharist, the Real Presence of Jesus pours out his grace of spiritual transformation upon us, that we may glorify the Father through the works we do in the name of the Son. Let us ask the Lord for the grace to do his work each day.

Do you desire the Lord to work through you?

Lord Jesus, may my life be of service to all who call upon your name.

December 14

Christ wanted to entrust us with his body and blood which
he shed for the forgiveness of sin. If you receive this well,
you are what you receive. — *St. Augustine, Homily*

I invite you to reflect upon these words of St. Augustine. He is explaining that when we receive the Eucharist, there is a triple presence of Jesus in our midst. We are the Body of Christ, receiving the Body of Christ, from the priest, who is acting in the person of Christ. The single act of Eucharistic reception is a profoundly sacred and holy moment that unites us to Our Lord.

This mystical moment within the celebration of Mass commissions us to live as people of forgiveness, because the Lord shed his Blood on the cross so that we could be forgiven. Becoming the very mystery we receive transforms our life. We become Christlike, and this brings with it a responsibility to model our life after Jesus in the Gospels: to forgive seventy times seventy times, to heal those who come to us, and to offer mercy and compassion to all we meet.

Do you view yourself as the Body of Christ? How does this spiritual awareness affect your behavior?

Lord Jesus, transform my heart, that I may recognize your Presence in the faces of my family and friends, my coworkers, and the strangers I meet each day.

December 15

For if we have grown into union with him through a death like his, we shall also be united with him in the resurrection. We know that our old self was crucified with him, so that our sinful body might be done away with, that we might no longer be in slavery to sin. — Romans 6:5–6

Anyone who has undergone surgery understands the experience of being "put under" by general anesthesia. As the patients, we feel no pain while we are under, and when we awaken, we are only aware of our present surroundings. We have no experience of what we might describe as dying to our consciousness, and rising out of a state of unconsciousness. We are only in union with the present moment. Our Christian lives are a similar experience, for we come into union with Jesus by dying to our sinful selves, in the hope of reawakening and sharing in his resurrection.

Every Mass celebrates the death and resurrection of Jesus. When we partake of his life saving Body and Blood, we spiritually participate with Jesus in a death like his, and we unite ourselves with him in the Resurrection. Our new lives in Christ free us from the bondage of sin and death.

Have you had an experience where you felt reborn, as if you were renewed in your faith with Christ?

Lord Jesus, help me to cast off the shadow of sin, that I may live in the light of your glorious resurrection.

December 16

You are the salt of the earth. But if salt loses its taste,
with what can it be seasoned? — Matthew 5:13

By saying that we are the "salt of the earth," Jesus was paying us a compliment. In ancient times, salt was a precious commodity. Since there was no means of refrigeration, people used salt to preserve their food, which, in turn, enabled them to feed their families. Salt is pure; and its taste is undeniable. Once food is salted, you cannot undo the taste of salt; it is that potent. However, if salt mixes with other spices and seasonings, it can lose its taste, its potency. Jesus is telling us that, as salt of the earth, we must remain pure, undefiled from the toxins of this world, or we risk losing our relationship with Christ.

Our Eucharistic experience of eating and drinking at the table of Our Lord can help strengthen our resolve to remain pure of heart and not to give in to the temptations of this passing world. The Real Presence of Jesus offers us the grace to turn away from sin and to be faithful to the Gospel.

In what ways can your experience of the Eucharist help you to remain pure and undefiled?

Lord Jesus, help me to remain pure, that my life may bear witness to the truth of the Gospel.

December 17

For it is loyalty that I desire, not sacrifice,
and knowledge of God rather than burnt offerings. — Hosea 6:6

Our Lord is not looking for rituals and sacrificial offerings; he is looking for our hearts. Jesus desires that we know and love God, that we may follow his statutes. He seeks loyalty that arises from a faithful and obedient spirit, fueled with a genuine desire to love and serve the Lord. Jesus seeks intimacy with us.

The time we spend in prayer before the Blessed Sacrament offers us a wonderful opportunity to deepen the bonds of love between Jesus and us. He is present in the Eucharist, and desires only that we make our relationship with him a priority in our lives. Jesus is ever faithful, ever loving, and ever present. Let us enter into this divine relationship with hearts desiring to love and serve Jesus all the days of our lives.

Are you ready to offer your heart to the Lord?

Lord Jesus, may I offer my life in love and loyalty to you.

December 18

It is truly right and just, our duty and our salvation, always and everywhere to give you thanks, Lord, holy Father, almighty and eternal God. — Preface, Eucharistic Prayer I

This preface of Eucharistic Prayer I is prayed over the gifts of bread and wine before the consecration. The words of this prayer remind us that it is our baptismal duty *always and everywhere* to give God thanks. I would think that most people thank God for the blessings of life they receive; but how many of us thank God for the difficulties that we experience? Our encounter with Jesus in the Eucharist can give us the spiritual courage to be grateful both in good times and in difficult moments.

As we partake of the Body and Blood of Jesus, we are filled with every grace and blessing. The Lord himself helps us to envision all of life as blessing, and to be grateful for every gift given to us by God. Renewed in grace, we can begin to see problems not as obstacles, but as opportunities for spiritual growth. We learn to give thanks to God always and everywhere for all of his blessings.

How often do you thank God for the blessings in your life?

Lord Jesus, help me to live with a grateful heart, that I may always and everywhere give you thanks.

December 19

If we are afflicted, it is for your encouragement and salvation; if we are encouraged, it is for your encouragement, which enables you to endure the same sufferings that we suffer. Our hope for you is firm. — 2 Corinthians 1:6–7

The call to holiness is universal among believers who have faith in Jesus. Mother Teresa of Calcutta's life offers us a modern-day example of the holiness of Christ living within the flesh. In her life as a religious sister, Mother Teresa ministered day and night to the sick, the poor, and the dying of India. This humble servant of God credits her relationship with Jesus in the Eucharist with transforming her life into one of heroic and humble service. In a speech she gave to the Eucharistic Congress in 1976, Mother Teresa stated, "We need our life to be woven with the Eucharist; that's why we begin our day with Jesus in the Eucharist." This extraordinary woman of faith dedicated one hour daily in prayer before Jesus in the Blessed Sacrament.

If we desire spiritual transformation, let us follow Mother Teresa's example and dedicate a holy hour of prayer before Jesus in adoration. Faith in the Son of God, present in the Eucharist, will transform our hearts and minds into that of Jesus.

Do you awaken each day giving yourself over to the Lord?

Lord Jesus, transform my heart, that I may be your loving Presence in the world.

December 20

For I received from the Lord what I also handed on to you, that the Lord Jesus, on the night he was handed over, took bread, and, after he had given thanks, broke it and said, "This is my body that is for you. Do this in remembrance of me." — 1 Corinthians 11:23–24

I remember my first Communion vividly, even though it was a very long time ago. What I remember most, however, is my Communion veil, which my mother packed away for safekeeping. Decades later, when my daughter made her first Communion, she wore my Communion veil; and most recently, my two granddaughters wore my veil for their respective first Communions. My Communion veil has become the precious heirloom in our family, handed down from generation to generation to mark this most special occasion in the faith lives of my family members.

On the night that Jesus instituted the Eucharist at the Last Supper, He instructed his disciples to do this action in remembrance of him. For over two thousand years, the Church has faithfully celebrated the Eucharist as Jesus commanded. One could say the Eucharist is the precious heirloom of the family of believers, for it is the Real Presence of Jesus, handed down from generation to generation. Let us never take the presence of Jesus in the Eucharist for granted.

What do you remember about your first Communion?

Lord Jesus, help me to faithfully celebrate your Presence in the Eucharist each time I come to Mass.

December 21

So be perfect, just as your heavenly Father is perfect. — Matthew 5:48

To be perfect is to be as good as we can be. Every person is unique, endowed with various skills, talents, and gifts given to us by our Creator God. To be humanly perfect is to use these God-given attributes and talents to the best of our ability, for the glory of God. If we do this, we will excel in seeking perfection. While this is commendable, Jesus calls us to an even higher degree of perfection. He desires us not only to be perfect in our actions, but also to be perfect in our thoughts and desires, so that we can attain true holiness.

Jesus, present to us in the Eucharistic bread and wine, is here to help us transform our lives that we may be holy, as our Father in heaven is holy. The grace we receive in the Eucharist has the power to help us eradicate unholy thoughts and desires. We cannot do this alone; we need the help of Jesus. Let us come before Our Lord in the Eucharist, seeking his transforming grace and wisdom as we journey toward our goal of perfection.

Do you desire to be perfect in the eyes of the Lord?

Lord Jesus, remain with me each day to help me achieve holiness, that I may be perfect as my heavenly Father is perfect.

December 22

*And do not grieve the holy Spirit of God, with which you were
sealed for the day of redemption. — Ephesians 4:30*

The Holy Spirit is the third Person of the Trinity, and is the very
breath of God that lives within us. As Christians, we are people redeemed by the cross of Jesus, yet we are still capable of committing
sin, and our sinful actions grieve the Holy Spirit of God with which
we have been sealed. The Holy Spirit prompts us to do actions that are
beneficial to our relationship with God; it is essential for us to be aware
of his Presence at work in our lives. Often, we experience the presence
of the Spirit at an emotional level when we are making a decision. Are
we at peace, or does our decision stir up feelings of anxiety? The Holy
Spirit gently leads us, nudging us to choose wisely. The Spirit will never
be demanding or aggressive; if this happens, those negative emotions
are not of God.

Spending time in prayer before the Blessed Sacrament will help
us to become aware of the movement of the Spirit in our lives. Jesus
is present to us in the Eucharist, and his gentle Spirit will speak to us,
filling our souls with the peace and joy needed to recognize his work
in our lives.

How do you discern the Spirit at work in your life?

Lord Jesus, open my heart, that I may sense the Spirit guiding me.

December 23

If then you were raised with Christ, seek what is above, where Christ is seated at the right hand of God. Think of what is above, not of what is on earth. — Colossians 3:1–2

We spend much of our days engaged in mindless activities, routines that we enact daily out of habit instead of intent. Functioning at this robotic level can be productive, for we accomplish many tasks: cleaning our homes, cooking meals, carpooling kids, commuting to work, even routinely saying memorized prayers. Nevertheless, we need to engage our hearts and minds intentionally with Jesus, rather than with what is only on earth. Scripture reminds us that if we have risen with Christ, we should seek what is above.

Our encounter with Jesus in the Eucharist has the power to awaken our hearts and minds to the glory of life that awaits us in Christ Jesus. As we partake of the Eucharistic Body and Blood of Jesus, let us ask the Lord to increase our awareness of his Presence in our lives, that our priorities may focus on what is above, not on what is on earth. Our home is in heaven, and all of our actions on earth should reflect this spiritual reality to come.

How do you make time for prayer each day in your busy schedule?

Lord Jesus, help me to engage my heart and mind on you this day, that my actions may give glory to God.

December 24

*"Joseph, son of David, do not be afraid to take Mary your wife
into your home. For it is through the holy Spirit that this child
has been conceived in her. She will bear a son and you are to name
him Jesus, because he will save his people from their sins." All this
tookbplace to fulfill what the Lord had said through the prophet:
"Behold, the virgin shall be with child and bear a son,
and they shall name him Emmanuel,"
which means "God is with us." — Matthew 1:20–23*

From the moment of his miraculous conception, by the power of
the Holy Spirit, in the womb of the Blessed Virgin Mary, Jesus' mission
in life has been to save us. He is the fulfillment of the promise God
made to his people long ago. His birth heralded a new era of grace
for humanity. Throughout his ministry, Jesus proclaimed a Gospel of
repentance and salvation for his people. At the Last Supper, Our Lord
imparted his Divine Presence to us for all time in the gifts of bread and
wine.

We celebrate the fulfillment of God's promise each time we partake
of the Eucharist. God is with us and through our reception of Eucharist;
we become one with Our Lord, Emmanuel, who came into this world
to save us from our sins.

How will you experience the presence of Emmanuel this Christmas?

Lord Jesus, help us to see your Divine Presence at work in our family and friends.

December 25

He was in the beginning with God.
All things came to be through him,
and without him nothing came to be.
And the Word became flesh
and made his dwelling among us,
and we saw his glory,
the glory as of the Father's only Son,
full of grace and truth.
— John 1:2–3, 14

In this Scripture passage, John is testifying to the truth that Jesus is the Incarnate Word of God, who became flesh and made his dwelling among us. Existing before all time, Jesus took on human form and humbled himself to save humanity. As the beloved apostle, John walked with Jesus for three years, and he saw the glory of the Father through the saving actions of Jesus. The graciousness of God our Father is visible in his only Son, whose life and ministry invites us to live each day with the knowledge that God is with us. We are not alone; we are people redeemed by the only Son of God. Our encounter with Jesus in the Eucharist strengthens us in faith, inviting us to repent and transform our lives. Without Jesus, we walk in darkness. He is our light; let us come to the Eucharist inviting the Lord to make his dwelling in our hearts.

What is your experience of Jesus as the Word-made-Flesh?

Lord Jesus, help me to walk in the radiant light of your salvation.

December 26

*So, as you received Christ Jesus the Lord, walk in
him, rooted in him and built upon him and
established in the faith as you were taught, abounding
in thanksgiving.* — Colossians 2:6–7

As my children grew up into adulthood, someone told me the saying attributed to Dr. Jonas Salk, "Give children roots and wings. Roots to know where home is, wings to fly away and exercise what's been taught to them." I hoped and prayed that, as parents, we had given them the roots to stand firm in their faith, no matter how bad the windstorm, and wings to soar, that they would use their God-given talents for the betterment of others. The same is true about our relationships with Jesus. We need strong roots to form a firm foundation in Christ Jesus that will not crumble under the pressures of this world, and the freedom to go out into the world and share the joy of our faith with all those we meet. We should build our lives solidly on Jesus Christ.

The Eucharist provides us with the spiritual nutrients needed for the root system of our Catholic Faith to grow deep and strong. Nourished by the Body and Blood of Jesus, we have the courage to boldly proclaim his goodness to the world.

In what ways does the idea of roots and wings apply to your faith life?

Lord Jesus, help me to grow strong in my relationship with you, that I may freely share my faith with all I meet.

December 27

Live by the Spirit and you will certainly not gratify the desire of the flesh. For the flesh has desires against the Spirit, and the Spirit against the flesh; these are opposed to each other, so that you may not do what you want. But if you are guided by the Spirit, you are not under the law. — *Galatians 5:16–18*

Our human nature has a propensity to sin. Through his death and resurrection, Jesus broke the bonds of sin and redeemed humanity, giving us his Spirit on Pentecost. It is the Spirit that leads and guides us each day, protecting us from falling back into our former ways of life. Sin is always tempting us, and the Spirit is always leading us; only we have the power to choose which path we will follow in life.

When we receive Jesus in the Eucharist, we gain the grace needed to turn away from sin and to walk each day in the light of the Spirit. Our desire for the sins of our past diminish greatly as the Spirit leads us to newness of life in Christ Jesus. Our Eucharistic encounter with Jesus can be life-changing. Let us come before Our Lord with hearts open to conversion.

How can you seek the Lord's help when you are tempted to sin?

Lord Jesus, may the Spirit lead me today, that I may not gratify the sins of my past.

December 28

Everyone who listens to these words of mine and acts on them will be like a wise man who built his house on rock. — Matthew 7:24

Followers of Jesus have the distinct advantage of standing on the rock of righteousness, for our ethical and moral foundations draw upon the teachings of Christ, the only Son of God. Unfortunately, our modern-day culture is doing its best to sidestep the teachings of Jesus, watering down or even eliminating Scripture passages to suit their own needs. Metaphorically, they are building their houses on sand; and in time, their houses will collapse. With Jesus, we build on solid rock.

Encountering the presence of Christ in the Eucharist offers us the courage and strength to stand up for our Faith and for the teachings of Jesus. Filled with spiritual fortitude, we receive the grace needed to walk away from immoral behavior and attitudes so prevalent in our society. Jesus is present in the Eucharist and his guiding hand will redirect our steps, that we may stand firm on the rock of righteousness, and not on the shifting sands of time.

How do you react when confronted with unethical situations?

Lord Jesus, help me to stand firm in my faith and to lovingly lead others back to you.

December 29

When [the shepherds] saw this, they made known the message
that had been told them about this child. Then the shepherds
returned, glorifying and praising God for all they had heard and
seen, just as it had been told to them. — Luke 2:17, 20

The night that Jesus was born, the shepherds were keeping watch in the fields over their flock. It was an ordinary evening — that is, until the angel of the Lord appeared and told them, "Do not be afraid. ... For today in the city of David a savior has been born for you who is Messiah and Lord" (Lk 2:10–11). Scripture tells they went in haste and found Mary and Joseph, and the infant lying in the manger. This encounter changed their lives forever, for they shared the message of his miraculous birth with everyone they met, glorifying and praising God for all they had heard and seen.

Our experience of Jesus in the Eucharist can be life-changing for us if we understand who we are encountering. It is Jesus, the Incarnate Son of God, born of the Virgin Mary, who suffered, died, and rose from the dead; he is sacramentally present to us in the Eucharist. Let us approach the table of the Lord with profound awe and gratitude, glorifying God.

How can the Eucharist transform your life this Christmas season?

Lord Jesus, thank you for coming into this world to save us. May my life give you praise and glory.

December 30

Now, Master, you may let your servant go
in peace, according to your word,
for my eyes have seen your salvation,
which you prepared in sight of all the peoples,
a light for revelation to the Gentiles,
and glory for your people Israel. — Luke 2:29–32

These prophetic words of Simeon in the Temple, as he held the Christ Child in his arms, are a beautiful reminder to all that God sent his only Son Jesus into this world to redeem all of humanity — no exceptions, no exclusions. Our role in the plan of salvation is to repent of our sins and to follow the way of Christ. During his three years of public ministry, Jesus showed us how we are to live in this world. The Gospels offer us examples from his life that we should follow.

When we spend quiet time before the Blessed Sacrament, Our Lord can speak to us, offering us wisdom and encouragement to transform our lives. He is present to us in the Blessed Sacrament, and we need to seek him, for he is a light to all people. When we sit in his Divine Presence, Our Lord can implant a new thought onto our hearts, or fill us with feelings of peace that will prompt us to follow a certain pathway in life.

In what way has Jesus transformed your life?

Lord Jesus, help me to live each day in the light of your salvation.

December 31

Watch carefully then how you live, not as foolish persons but as wise, making the most of the opportunity, because the days are evil. Therefore, do not continue in ignorance, but try to understand what is the will of the Lord. — Ephesians 5:15–17

A few years ago, I binge-watched some new series on television that I would not normally have the time or inclination to do. While these programs might have captivated my interest, the lack of morality in each of the episodes was astonishing. For the most part, these shows offer us a snapshot into the world of greed, deceit, and immorality. It is disturbing to think that our young people grow up watching this. Is it any wonder that society lacks the wisdom of the Lord when the media feeds us this kind of programming on a daily basis?

Our spiritual nourishment and sustenance for living in this world is in the Eucharist. Jesus is present to us in his Eucharistic Body and Blood, and he gives us the strength to live not as foolish persons but as wise individuals, who seek to do the will of the Lord. Let us come to the Eucharistic table of Jesus seeking to live in the transforming light of his redeeming grace.

Where do you look to for examples of morality and ethics?

Lord Jesus, strengthen me with your life-giving bread, that I may do the will of the Lord.

~ HOLY WEEK ~

Palm Sunday

[Christ Jesus,] though he was in the form of God,
did not regard equality with God something to be grasped.
Rather, he emptied himself,
taking the form of a slave,
coming in human likeness;
and found human in appearance,
he humbled himself,
becoming obedient to death,
even death on a cross.
Because of this, God greatly exalted him
and bestowed on him the name
that is above every name,
that at the name of Jesus
every knee should bend,
of those in heaven and on earth and under the earth,
and every tongue confess that
Jesus Christ is Lord,
to the glory of God the Father. — Philippians 2:6–11

As we commemorate Palm Sunday, Scripture reminds us that Jesus, though he was in the form of God, took on human likeness and humbled himself, becoming obedient to the point of death, even death on a cross. By Good Friday, the cheers and acclamations that Jesus received from the crowds, as he proceeded on his journey into Jerusalem, take on a dramatic shift.

On the night before he died, Jesus gave us the gift of the Eucharist, so that his Presence would be with us for all time. This is why, when we receive Our Lord in Communion, every tongue should confess that Jesus Christ is Lord, to the glory of God the Father.

How can the passion of Jesus lead you to deeper communion with the Lord?

Lord Jesus, help me to glorify you in word and in deed.

Monday

The LORD is my light and my salvation. ...
When evildoers come at me
to devour my flesh,
These my enemies and foes
themselves stumble and fall. — Psalm 27:1–2

At times, we have all felt like the world was closing in on us, as if we did not have a friend in the world. At moments like this, we need to stay focused on Our Lord, for he is our light and our salvation. Jesus, as he journeyed to Jerusalem, knew his enemies were looking to devour his flesh; yet, he continued on his mission, which ultimately led him to the cross. Jesus never wavered in his mission to do the work of the Father.

The Eucharistic Presence of Jesus gives us strength to withstand the emotional attacks we suffer at the hands of others. Jesus is with us, and his Eucharistic Presence fills us with the grace to overcome evil and hardships, because the Lord is our light and salvation.

Call to mind a time when you felt all alone. How did you handle this situation? Did you turn to Jesus in prayer?

Lord Jesus, hold my hand, that I may not fall under the pressures of this world, for you are my light and my salvation.

Tuesday

When he had said this, Jesus was deeply troubled and testified, "Amen, amen, I say to you, one of you will betray me." — John 13:21

Betrayal is one of the most painful experiences that can happen to us, for it means that someone we loved and trusted has turned their back on us. We have all had this kind of experience, and it is incredibly painful to endure. Jesus was no different. He knew that Judas has betrayed him, and his heart was surely broken. In spite of the act of betrayal, Jesus proceeded to share the Passover supper with his apostles. At this Last Supper, Jesus gave us the gift of himself in the elements of bread and wine, that he might be with us for all time.

Partaking of the Eucharist, especially during Holy Week, invites us to renew our love and commitment to Jesus for his act of salvation. Eating and drinking of his Body and Blood offers us an opportunity to deepen the bonds of friendship and love we share with Jesus. He gave his life for us; let us resolve to live for him.

Have you ever betrayed Jesus?

Lord Jesus, may I never stray from your love and friendship.

Wednesday

One of the Twelve, who was called Judas Iscariot, went to the chief priests and said, "What are you willing to give me if I hand him over to you?" They paid him thirty pieces of silver, and from that time on he looked for an opportunity to hand him over. — Matthew 26:14–16

How could Judas sell out his beloved friend and teacher for thirty pieces of silver? Did Judas understand the ramifications of his actions? What did he think was going to happen to Jesus after this blatant act of betrayal? While the actions of Judas are reprehensible, one can only imagine how Jesus felt knowing that one of his trusted apostles sold him out for money. The devil is cunning, and will attack us at any given moment. Unless our relationship with Jesus is strong, we, too, can sell out Our Lord for the allurements of this passing world.

Our encounter with Jesus in the Eucharist gives us the grace to stand firm in our faith, and to walk away from the temptations of this world. Jesus is our rock and our salvation. Without him, we will fall into temptation and sin. Let us seek to draw nearer to Our Lord each time we receive his Body and Blood, that we may never stray from his side.

Reflect on a time you strayed from your faith. What brought you back?

Lord Jesus, may the Eucharist fill me with the courage to turn away from sin and temptations.

Holy Thursday

So when he had washed their feet [and] put his garments back on and reclined at table again, he said to them, "Do you realize what I have done for you? You call me 'teacher' and 'master,' and rightly so, for indeed I am. If I, therefore, the master and teacher, have washed your feet, you ought to wash one another's feet. I have given you a model to follow, as I have done for you, you should also do." — John 13:12–15

In John's Gospel, Jesus first washes the feet of the apostles at the Last Supper; for the Eucharist is born in loving service to God and our neighbor. I think it is worth noting that in this Gospel, Jesus washed the feet of *all* the apostles, including Judas. What did Jesus experience when he knelt down at the feet of his betrayer? Service to our neighbor does not exclude anyone. We cannot choose whom we will serve; we are called to "wash the feet" of saints and sinners alike.

Our encounter of Jesus in the Eucharist gives us renewed sight to see the world with the eyes of Christ, that we may readily respond to all those in need. Jesus gave us a model to follow, and we must do the same.

We model Christ by our actions. Whom can you lovingly serve this day?

Jesus, help me to see your Divine Presence in all those who are in need of help.

Good Friday

When they came to the place called the Skull, they crucified him and the criminals there, one on his right, the other on his left. [Then Jesus said, "Father, forgive them, they know not what they do."] They divided his garments by casting lots. — Luke 23:33–34

Crucifixion is an execution method that strips a person of all human dignity. At his crucifixion, as Jesus endured excruciating pain, suffering, and the jeers of bystanders, he reacted by asking, "Father, forgive them, they know not what they do." The crucifixion of Jesus invites us to do some soul-searching. Who would you be in this story? Would you be one of those who condemn Jesus? Or are you a bystander jeering at Our Lord? Or are you the good thief asking Jesus to remember you when he gets into his kingdom? Is it easy for us to respond that we would stand by Jesus; but do our actions today reflect ridicule or forgiveness?

Our encounter with Jesus in the Eucharist fills us with the courage and conviction to stand with Jesus in a world that tries to deny God. The Eucharist unites us to the merciful heart of Jesus and invites us to forgive others as Jesus has forgiven us. May the Eucharist nourish us with Christ's love for humanity.

Who do you relate to in this crucifixion scene?

Lord Jesus, help me to live as a person of forgiveness, that I may imitate your love for us.

Holy Saturday

We know that Christ, raised from the dead, dies no more; death no longer has power over him. As to his death, he died to sin once and for all; as to his life, he lives for God. — Romans 6:9–10

We have all lost someone, and those immediate hours after the death of a loved one are often the hardest, for we are still trying to process what has just transpired. A myriad of emotions can sometime paralyze us from making decisions. The same can probably be said for the friends and family of Jesus the day after his crucifixion. Scripture tells us that his apostles were hiding in fear, for their faith was shaken. Without Jesus, their master and teacher, what would they do next? They waited. The Gospel tells us that on the third day, Christ was raised from the dead. Death no longer has power over us, for we have been saved by the death and resurrection of Jesus.

It is good for us to spend time in meditative prayer on this sacred day. Jesus died to sin, and now he reigns in glory with God. His Real Presence in the Eucharist helps us to rise from the depths of our sinful ways and to live our lives for God.

What do the death and resurrection of Jesus mean for your life?

Lord Jesus, help me to be a faithful disciple, that I may live each day for God.

Easter Sunday

When she had said this, she turned around and saw
Jesus there, but did not know it was Jesus.
Jesus said to her, "Woman, why are you weeping? Whom are you
looking for?" She thought it was the gardener and said to him, "Sir,
if you carried him away, tell me where you laid him, and I will take
him." Jesus said to her, "Mary!" She turned and said to him in
Hebrew, "Rabbouni," which means Teacher. — John 20:14–16

Mary Magdalene was heartbroken at the death of Jesus. Early, on the morning of the third day, she and two other women brought spices to anoint the body of their beloved friend and teacher. When they arrived at the tomb, it was empty. Moments later, Mary, in profound grief, encounters Jesus in the garden, but she fails to recognize him. It is only when Jesus says her name, "Mary," that she turns and sees him, and cries out, "Rabbouni," which means Teacher.

Each time we receive Jesus in the Eucharist, he calls us by name. Do we hear him? Are we aware of this intimate encounter with our risen Lord in the Eucharist? As we celebrate the great feast of Easter, let us come to the table with hearts open to hearing the Lord call us, for we are Easter people, redeemed by his Blood. Alleluia.

What does the Resurrection mean to you?

Lord Jesus, by your death and resurrection, you have given the world hope. May my life bear witness to your act of salvation.

Acknowledgments

To my family: my husband, Joe, my daughter, Lauren Nelson, and my son, Joey, for your love and encouragement in helping me bring this manuscript to fruition. Thank you for believing in me, and for creating a sacred space at home where I could find inspiration for writing. May the Eucharistic Presence of Jesus fill you with peace and joy every day of your life.

To the staff and affiliates of Mayslake Ministries, who inspire me each day: It is an honor to complete the trilogy of our daily devotionals: *Every Day with Mary*, *Every Day with Joseph*, and now *Every Day with Jesus*. May these books be a daily spiritual accompaniment to all those who seek a deeper relationship with Jesus.

I would like to thank my former professor at Catholic Theological Union, Fr. Edward Foley, a Capuchin Franciscan, esteemed preacher, and author. When I was a graduate student, you transformed my life with your love and passion for the Eucharistic Presence of Jesus. I am forever grateful.

I am so grateful to the editorial staff at Our Sunday Visitor, especially Rebecca Martin and Mary Beth Giltner. This book would not be possible without your vision, friendship, and support. Thank you for walking the journey with me and for helping me to create a daily devotional that will draw readers closer to the Eucharistic Presence of Jesus.

About the Author

Dr. Mary Amore holds a doctor of ministry degree in liturgy and master of arts in pastoral studies from Catholic Theological Union. Dr. Amore is the author of four books: *Primary Symbols of Worship and the Call to Participation*, *Every Day with Mary*, *Every Day with Joseph*, and *Every Day with Jesus*, as well as the creator of two DVD series: *Eucharist: Pathway of Transformation, Healing, and Discipleship*, and *From Mary's Heart to Yours*, published by Pauline Media. A Cardinal Bernardin Scholar and a distinguished member of the North American Academy of Liturgy, Mary has been a presenter at the LA Congress, University of Dallas Ministry Conference, Fresno Diocesan Congress, and Diocese of New Hampshire Ministry Conference, as well as conducted parish missions, retreats, and adult faith formation programs. Dr. Amore is also the creator and host of two cable television shows, *Soul Snackin* with Dr. Mary Amore and *A Willing Spirit*, and has hosted a radio show on Radio Maria. Married, the mother of two young adults, and proud grandmother of two girls, Dr. Amore serves as the full-time executive director of Mayslake Ministries.